Outward bound

Outward bound

Relocation and community care for people with learning difficulties

Tim Booth
Ken Simons
Wendy Booth

Open University Press
Milton Keynes · Philadelphia

Open University Press
Celtic Court
22 Ballmoor
Buckingham
MK18 1XW

and
1900 Frost Road, Suite 101
Bristol, PA 19007, USA

First Published 1990

British Library Cataloguing in Publication Data

Booth, Tim, 1947–
    Outward bound: relocation and community care for people with learning
    difficulties.
    1. Great Britain. Mentally handicapped persons. Community care
    I. Title   II. Simons, Ken   III. Booth, Wendy
    362.30941

    ISBN 0-335-15431-X
    ISBN 0-335-15430-1 (pbk)

Library of Congress Cataloging-in-Publication Data

Booth, Timothy A.
    Outward bound: relocation and community care for people with learning
    difficulties / Tim Booth, Ken Simons, Wendy Booth.
        p.   cm.
    Includes bibliographical references.
    ISBN 0-335-15431-X—ISBN 0-335-15430-1 (pbk.)
    1. Mentally handicapped—Care—Great Britain—Case studies.
    2. Mentally handicapped—Institutional care—Great Britain—Case
    studies.   3. Mentally handicapped—Deinstitutionalization—Great Britain—Case
    studies.   I. Simons, Ken, 1953–   .   II. Booth, Wendy, 1946–   .   III. Title.
    HV3008.G7B66   1990
    362.3'85'0941—dc20
    90-32165 CIP

Typeset by Rowland Phototypesetting Ltd
Bury St Edmunds, Suffolk
Printed in Great Britain by St Edmundsbury Press Ltd
Bury St Edmunds, Suffolk

To the Fourth Musketeer
Chris Melotte

Contents

Acknowledgements

We have accumulated many debts in the course of this study. Chris Melotte of Kirklees Social Services Department helped to conceive the study in the first place, was a party to our original application to the Trust, played an instrumental role in getting the research off the ground and has since been closely involved in every stage of our progress. His contribution has been immeasurable in both a personal and a professional capacity, and we are pleased to record our appreciation of his unstinting work for the project.

The project was funded by the Joseph Rowntree Memorial Trust. We have been well served by the Trust's advisers on mental handicap – initially Jan Porterfield and latterly Linda Ward – who were always available when they were needed. Janet Lewis, too, the Trust's Research Director, has been an unfailing source of support, as has Derek Thomas who, as Chairman of our Advisory Group, generously allowed us to lean on his wide experience.

We are deeply grateful to the participating authorities (Kirklees Social Services Department and Huddersfield, Dewsbury and Wakefield District Health Authorities) who so willingly gave their backing to the study, granted us the access we required, and put up with our probing and questioning for almost three years. Among the managers who paved our way into the agencies and took the brunt of our curiosity, we should like particularly to thank the local representatives on our Advisory Group – Liam Hughes, Tony Keighley, Beryl Johnson and Harvey Richardson – as well as Nick Frizelle and the other members of the Fieldhead Hospital Management Team.

We were fortunate in having the support of a number of committed and experienced senior practitioners in both field and clinical settings within the participating authorities. Our thanks go to Dr Rao Punukollu and Dr Sanderson, David Parkin and Brian Mettrick.

The circle of people drawn into the study steadily widened as the research progressed. It is impossible to name individually all those to whom we have reason to be grateful. Certainly our task has been lightened enormously by the readiness of nursing and residential staff to give us their time and to juggle their work to accommodate us. Follow-up studies inevitably ask a lot of respondents and ours has been no exception. Moreover, the nature of our research has required us to spend a good deal of time in some units. Yet we have never met with anything other than a smile and a welcome.

Jill Kerkhoff was our research secretary for the duration of the project. She managed the office with unassuming efficiency, taking every new challenge in her stride, while somehow even discreetly compensating for our own manifest shortcomings. Her capacity for absorbing an enormous amount of work seemed limited only by our capacity to produce it. It is inconceivable that the project would have fulfilled its aims (and on time) without her.

We should also like to thank the editors of the following journals for permission to draw on material from articles originally published by them: *British Journal of Mental Subnormality*; *British Journal of Social Work*; *International Journal of Rehabilitation Research*; *Practice*; *Research, Policy and Planning*; and *Social Policy and Administration*.

Finally, we owe a special debt of gratitude to the movers and their families. Their story is at the heart of our research. They let us into their lives during what was for many a challenging and sometimes stressful period of change. They shared their thoughts and feelings with an openness and candour we hardly seemed to deserve. We came to know our group of families and movers as people rather than just as respondents. In some cases the interviews marked the beginning of a relationship that has continued outside the study. Our earnest hope is that the work we have done remains faithful to the trust they have shown in us.

Tim Booth
Ken Simons
Wendy Booth

1

The policy context

Current mental handicap policies aim to bring about a shift in responsibility and resources for residential care from health to local authorities and from large institutions to small homely units (House of Commons 1985). They are being pursued in two broad ways: partly by building up those services necessary to reduce the need for long-term admission, but crucially, so far as this book is concerned, by closing long-stay wards or complete hospitals and moving the patients with the cash out into the community.

The number of people living in hospital has fallen steadily in the past 20 years from 59,000 in 1969 to fewer than 32,000 by 1986. During the decade from 1976 the resident population of NHS mental handicap hospitals and hospital units contracted each year and declined by about 30 per cent over the period as a whole. The drop in the numbers of children was particularly marked at more than 80 per cent. This general trend masks two underlying processes or what may be seen as two stages in a process of deinstitutionalization.

Initially the contraction in the hospital census was brought about by a steady and continuing decline in the rate of permanent admissions, especially among children. For example, first admissions fell by over 37 per cent in the ten years from 1972. The result was that the resident population started losing more people by deaths than it was gaining by new entrants to the system (Wertheimer 1986). More recently, especially since the official beginnings of the care in the community policy in 1983, this trend has been maintained and possibly accelerated by moving people out of hospitals. The number of patients discharged after spending five years or more in hospital increased by over a half (52 per cent) during the period 1982–6. Since 1982 there has been a drop of 6,890 (20 per cent) in the number of long-stay (5 years+) patients in mental handicap hospitals. Let us briefly set these important changes in their policy context.

The policy background

The White Paper, *Better Services for the Mentally Handicapped*, was published in 1971. It set the course which policy on services for mentally handicapped people should follow into the early 1990s, and specified planning targets for local and hospital authorities which it was hoped could be achieved over the following 15–20 years (DHSS 1971). The pattern of services outlined in the White Paper involved a shift in the balance from hospital to community care with an expansion in local authority services and a relative reduction in the numbers cared for in hospitals. The White Paper figures suggested that a six-fold increase in local authority residential places was required, alongside a drop of nearly 50 per cent in hospital places.

These recommendations were grounded on a set of general principles bearing on the needs and rights of mentally handicapped people and their families, and a thoroughgoing appraisal and critique of the hospital services. The White Paper acknowledged that serious problems of isolation and size, unsuitable buildings, overcrowding, poor living standards, inadequate treatment and understaffing were common, and concluded that hospitals too often provided only 'a life of minimal satisfaction for patients and staff alike'.

The White Paper drew back from the full implications of this analysis. Action was needed to improve services, but the approach was cautious and the pace was slow. Most of the planned increases in revenue and capital expenditure were allocated to the hospitals (Jaehnig 1979). No new large hospitals were to be built nor any hospitals of 500 beds or more enlarged, but new hospitals providing up to 200 in-patient beds were planned. The rate of development was seen to hinge on the capacity and willingness of local authorities to expand their provision of residential homes and adult training centres 'taking into account the many other calls on resources'. Nationally, the White Paper envisaged capital investment in these services rising by about 2 per cent a year for the next ten years.

Even this modest target proved too ambitious, and the upheavals caused by the 1974 reorganization of local government and the NHS further hindered the joint planning on which the strategy depended. When Barbara Castle, then Secretary of State for Social Services, reviewed the progress that had been made since the White Paper in a speech to the National Society for Mentally Handicapped Children in 1975, she acknowledged that financial constraints had meant a much slower rate of growth than expected and that a great deal remained to be done. As a sign of the Government's continuing commitment to the improvement of services in this field, she announced the establishment of a National Development Group for the Mentally Handicapped (NDG) to advise ministers on the development and implementation of policy.

This commitment was reaffirmed the following year in the Government's consultative document on priorities (DHSS 1976). Again this stressed the importance of shifting resources out of hospital care into community care, and proposed that mental handicap services should receive a greater share of planned expenditure in the lean years ahead following the oil price hike. Professor Peter Mittler, the first chairman of the NDG, greeted this promise enthusiastically. 'After decades of neglect,' he said, 'mentally handicapped people are now beginning to get nearer to the priorities they deserve.' At the same time, joint finance was introduced as a source of new money for growth, to cushion the social services against the more severe consequences of budgetary restraint and to oil the wheels of collaboration between the health and social services (Booth 1981b, 1983a). In the first two years of the scheme over 30 per cent of the allocation was used for mental handicap projects. But in the face of mounting public expenditure cuts following the 1976 sterling crisis, a growing squeeze on local government spending and the rapid spread of standstill budgeting, these extra resources were, at best, no more than enough to hold the line. The task of making the plans a reality began to look horribly like pushing string.

In 1978 the NDG frankly reviewed the position in a report to the Secretary of State. 'We are', they declared, 'not satisfied that enough people are being discharged to local authority services' (NDG 1978). With the approach of the end of the first decade of the 20-year plan set out in the 1971 White Paper, 'more attention needs to be given to people in hospital who could make use of community services, and who deserve a greater share of community resources than they have so far received.' In their view no one should be in a mental handicap hospital unless it could be shown that their needs could be met only by the specialist service the hospital provides. Yet, they observed, the number of people in hospital had been reducing only very slowly, at a rate of under 2 per cent a year. Moreover, about 1,300 people were still being admitted to hospital for the first time every year, and about 7,000 children and young people under 18 were spending much of their childhood in hospital.

Contrary to the strategy outlined in *Better Services*, the NDG deemed it 'unlikely that local services will develop at the rate that is necessary to enable people who should not be in hospital to live and work in the community'. Progress would have to be forced. A new initiative was required. Joint finance had helped, but it was only a modest step towards tackling the fundamental problem of the transfer of resources:

we think that the time has now come for a specific commitment by each RHA, AHA and hospital to reduce the number of hospital residents and for local authorities to enter into a planned commitment to provide services for those who no longer require hospital services.

In order to facilitate this bold approach, the NDG felt some system of earmarking funds for mental handicap services would be essential.

The 1978 NDG report is one of the first official statements to sound a note of impatience about the lack of progress in shifting the balance of care towards the community services, and to contemplate a more directive and interventionist approach by government in the face of the obstacles to change hampering health and local authorities. It called on the Government to do more to provide the resources to implement White Paper policy and to bring about the necessary action.

Stirred by these criticisms, the Secretary of State decided the time had come to take stock of the achievements since 1971 and 'to consider whether any changes to the guidance set out in the White Paper might be needed'. He invited Professor Peter Mittler as chairman of the NDG to assist a team of departmental officials in conducting the review. Their report was published in 1980 (DHSS 1980). The review team reaffirmed the view that 'services for people living at home are central to a successful policy of community-orientated care', but concluded that these services 'are still in their infancy'. The growth in the number of places in residential homes for children had been 'disappointingly small', and though there had been a considerable expansion of local authority day and residential places for adults, and a corresponding increase in expenditure, the numbers still fell short of what was required to meet assessed need. Consequently, while the number of people in mental handicap hospitals had been decreasing gradually, it was still 'far in excess of what the White Paper suggested would be right'. Moreover, the review team calculated that the White Paper target for hospital places for children was excessive and the number of hospital places eventually required for adults had probably also been overestimated. By this reckoning, what progress had been made since 1971 amounted to running on the spot a bit faster.

One of the principal reasons, the report states, for the 'disappointingly slow' development of local services, aside from the planning problems that beset health and local authorities, was the change in economic fortunes. The public expenditure assumptions in the White Paper proved to be 'unrealistic' and 'over-optimistic'. It had been 'written at a time of expansion. Since then restraints in public spending have meant that authorities could not progress as rapidly as was originally hoped'. Furthermore, at least in the short to medium term, 'the resource position is unlikely to improve significantly'.

This pessimistic scenario led the review team to ask whether the policy of building up local services should be deferred or abandoned, with the implication that existing levels of hospital provision and use would remain substantially unchanged until well into the next century. They concluded that any such suggestions would be a counsel of despair. The next step should be to look at ways of facilitating the change to a pattern of local services within existing resource constraints, and this, they made clear, entailed tackling the problems of joint planning and cross-financing at the local level.

These issues were already creeping up the policy agenda. In 1981 the DHSS published the report of an internal study of community care set up partly to examine the 'patterns of service and interactions between the NHS and the Personal Social Services'. One of the general messages to emerge was that 'if Departmental policies are to continue to seek a move away from long-term hospital care wherever this is appropriate to people's needs and wishes, ways must be found to ensure that the balance of resources between the NHS and PSS reflects the desired rate of change in responsibilities' (DHSS 1981a). Following close on the heels of the study, the Department issued a consultative document on transferring patients and resources from the NHS to the PSS which examined ways of meeting this challenge. It stated the problem bluntly:

> There are many people in hospital who would not need to be there if appropriate community services were available. But the legal, administrative and financial framework within which health and local authorities operate presents obstacles to their transfer.
>
> (DHSS 1981b)

The consultative document was generally well received, and its broad aims attracted widespread support. A circular followed setting out the main decisions on the suggestions that had been mooted and giving guidance on follow-up action (DHSS 1983). The tapering arrangements for joint finance were adjusted to make the scheme more flexible and to sustain care in the community projects until savings accrue on the hospital side. The scheme was also extended to cover housing and education. Health authorities were empowered to offer lump-sum payments or continuing grants from their normal budget allocations for as long as necessary in order to enable long-stay hospital patients to move into the community. It was intended that eventually these payments would be put on a permanent footing by a central transfer of funds. Finally, a programme of pilot projects was set up with central funding of some £15 million over four years to demonstrate how these new opportunities for partnership might be used.

By comparison with the scale of the task, this response was modest and cautious. Bolder solutions were shelved or rejected as undesirable or impracticable. As an essentially temporary financial expedient, the joint finance scheme is not up to the job of correcting long-term structural problems. Indeed, as the Social Services Select Committee noted in 1985, 'as a means of means of transferring further responsibilities from the NHS to local authorities it is now virtually played out' (House of Commons 1985). The proposed arrangements for transfer (or dowry) payments between the health and social services have themselves been grafted on to a system in which relationships between the two sides are more often characterized by conflict than cooperation. They will not work without good collaboration based on mutual commitment and a common purpose, but experience has shown that such a spirit of partnership is a rare thing. And the loss of conterminosity in administrative boundaries following the 1982 NHS reorganization rendered it even more difficult to achieve.

If these measures alone hardly seemed enough to remove the checks holding up progress, other developments were helping to change the pattern of incentives and facilitate the transfer of people from hospital. The Minister of Health began pressing authorities to close hospitals within specified time limits. The effects of cuts in health service budgets made the possibility of finding savings by closing hospitals a tempting one for health administrators. At the same time, the introduction of general management into the NHS following the Griffiths review (DHSS 1984) was also having an impact on thinking. The appointment of new district general managers on fixed-term contracts tied to a system of performance review that often specified target reductions in long-stay mental handicap beds brought about a new alignment between managerial self-interest and national priorities.

Another significant development was the raft of changes in the benefit system during the early 1980s. These resulted in both a hugely increased public subsidy via supplementary benefit for private residential care and a new source of funding from board and lodging payments for group homes and similar independent living schemes (Firth Report 1987). Their impact was swift in each of these sectors of provision. Local authority statistical returns to the DHSS show that the number of places for people with mental handicaps in private homes more than doubled from 1,617 to 3,908 between 1980 and 1986. Over the same period there was an almost four-fold increase (from 93 to 347) in the number of units within the private sector. Even these figures probably underestimate the true extent of the growth in provision, as DHSS statisticians acknowledge, because of the under-recording of these types of homes in recent years (DHSS 1987). In 1986 alone the number of places in private homes and hostels increased by about a quarter.

Equally, there has been a substantial growth of independent living schemes. A recent study of such accommodation in four local authority areas showed that over three-quarters (79.5 per cent) of the 149 schemes surveyed had been opened since 1983, and over half (55.4 per cent) had started up since 1985 (Booth *et. al.* 1988). Over a quarter (28.9 per cent) of their occupants had previously been living in mental handicap hospitals, and almost two in every five (38.1 per cent) had moved from hostels, frequently in order to make way for people being transferred from hospitals.

The upshot of all these initiatives and developments has been to give a new momentum to the longstanding goal of shifting the balance from hospital to community services. People are now being relocated from hospital (and from larger hostel units into ordinary-type housing) in greater numbers than ever before. This much at least is well documented. What is less well understood are the implications of relocation for those whose lives are being so dramatically changed. This study set out to throw some light on this important issue.

Transatlantic reflections

Britain is not alone in pursuing a policy of running down or closing mental handicap hospitals. The United States in particular has proceeded further and faster down the same road. Many times more people have moved out of big state hospitals over a longer number of years, and a great deal more research on outcomes has been done. We shall have occasion to draw on this literature later in this book. In the meantime, a brief account of the deinstitutionalization movement in the USA will help to set the scene and to show up the similarities and differences with British experience.

1967 was the watershed year when the first drop was recorded in the annual average daily population of American public institutions for the retarded. It marked the beginning of a progressive decline that is still continuing today. Initially this decline was gradual with the institutional population falling by just 8 per cent between 1967 and 1971 (Gollay *et al.* 1978). Thereafter it accelerated rapidly. In November 1971 President Nixon pledged the nation 'to enable one-third of the more than 200,000 retarded persons in public institutions to return to useful lives in the community'. By 1974 the number of people in state institutions had plummeted by a quarter.

This can hardly be credited as an achievement of the Nixon Administration. For the President never followed up his 1971 policy declaration with any legislative package or initiative to Congress (Hammer and Howse 1977). Even within the Department of Health, Education and Welfare (HEW), deinstitutionalization did not become a Secretarial objective in the Department's operational planning system until 1976 (US Comptroller General 1977). It was much more a matter of happenstance.

Nixon's pledge coincided with wider social forces pulling in the same direction. Thus, for instance, there was a natural decline in new admissions simply because of a fall in the US birthrate. The introduction of federal Medicaid funding for residents in public institutions, under Title XIX of the Social Security Act 1971, was also indirectly responsible for a decline in their numbers. The standards imposed by the programme – for example, no more than four beds per room and not less than 60 square feet per bed – required many states to reduce their institutional population in order to remodel and upgrade their facilities (Lakin *et al.* 1985).

Civil rights issues, too, gave impetus to the deinstitutionalization movement. Following the landmark decision in the case of *Wyatt* v. *Stickney*
(1972) that no person should be admitted to an institution unless it was
first shown to be 'the least restrictive habilitation setting', there followed a
stream of litigation. Federal courts upheld the right of mentally retarded
people to treatment, to education, to liberty, and to care and residence in
the least restrictive environment. A succession of court-ordered closures of
state institutions and successful out-of-court settlements followed. By
June 1975 over 100 court cases affecting the rights of mentally disabled
people had been completed or were pending in 39 states. As the US
Comptroller General (1977) reported to Congress, it was the federal
courts – rather than the executive or legislative branches – that
were 'instrumental in both requiring the return of institutionalized
persons to the community and preventing the placement of others into
institutions'.

Between 1977 and 1982 every state reduced the number of residents in
its public institutions and decreased the proportion in units of 16 or more
people (Lakin *et al.* 1985). Over this five-year period the size of the
residential population in large state hospitals fell by just over a fifth. Most of
the 33,000 residents were relocated in small group homes whose numbers
nearly doubled between 1977 and 1982. The percentage of residents in
facilities with 15 or fewer places increased by almost a half during this time
– from 16.3 per cent in 1977 to 26.1 per cent in 1982 (Hill and Lakin 1984).
Compared with a decade earlier, the average size of large state institutions
had fallen from 700 beds to 475 beds by 1981 (US Department of Health
and Human Services 1986).

These trends gained additional momentum in the 1980s. Spurred on by
such evidence of success, professional and user groups pressed on with
their aggressive advocacy of the rights of people with a mental handicap. In
some instances closure provided the only feasible alternative to continuing
litigation. In most states they found themselves pushing at an open door.
Other economic and political forces were lining up behind a policy of
closures.

The 'New Federalism' of the Reagan Administration, combined with the
supply-side nostrums of Reaganomics, led to cuts in federal funding of
social programmes and a substantial shift in the domestic fiscal burden
from the federal level to state governments. In addition the 1981 recession
brought low corporate profits and high unemployment which, in turn,
further squeezed state tax revenues while pushing up welfare spending
(Braddock and Heller 1985). In this context the attention of state gov-
ernors' budget officials began to focus ever more fixedly on the rising unit
costs of state institutions. Between 1977 and 1984 the average nationwide
per diem rose 36 per cent in real terms as the institutional population
declined faster than institutional overheads (Braddock *et al.* 1986). The

possibilities for economies in this field were also pointed out by prison department officials. They coveted the space in underused institutions as a solution to the growing problem of prison overcrowding. Large hospitals could be converted to prisons for half the cost of new construction (Braddock and Heller 1985).

The upshot of these currents in public policy was a spate of closures and a further run-down in the institutional population. By 1985, 18 state mental handicap hospitals had been closed and six were in the process of closing: 17 of these had been either completed or scheduled since 1982. Institutional spending declined each year between 1982 and 1986. The average daily population of state institutions in 1985 was estimated at only 54 per cent of the 1967 average (Lakin *et al.* 1985). Fifteen years on, President Nixon's goal had, in terms of sheer numbers, been achieved.

The Kirklees Partnership in Community Care

Our study should be seen as part of this wider canvas. Ultimately all these national and international trends and developments emerge out of the actions of people in localities. Ultimately too their significance must be assessed in terms of the lives of the people behind the statistics. This study seeks to convey something of the human meaning of these trends by exploring the impact of a community care programme in one local area on the individuals and families involved. The programme was known as the Kirklees Partnership in Community Care.

The Kirklees Partnership in Community Care (KPCC) is a joint planning initiative involving a local authority (Kirklees Metropolitan Council), two district health authorities (Dewsbury and Huddersfield) and representatives from local voluntary organizations. The purpose of the KPCC is to develop and implement plans for community care in Kirklees. These plans involve people with mental health problems as well as people with learning difficulties, although this study deals only with the latter.

The first phase of services developed under the KPCC had a number of distinctive characteristics: the move to (supposedly) less institutional settings, a shift from hospital to social services provision, the initial steps towards utilizing ordinary housing, and the adoption of a very pragmatic, gradualist approach rather than a comprehensive overall strategy. Unlike the specially funded 'Care in the Community' programme (PSSRU 1987), there were no additional resources or demonstration projects. This was a set of ordinary local agencies pursuing national policies within normal financial, political and administrative constraints.

Most of this book is an evaluation of the outcomes of these policies as seen by the people who moved, their families, and the staff who worked with them. Before moving on to this task, however, the remainder of this

chapter sets the local context and describes in more detail the features of
the Partnership.

Background and origins of the KPCC

Prior to the Partnership the services in Kirklees were based largely on
conventional patterns. The Social Services Department was in the process
of opening one house for five people, but most of its residential places were
in large hostels and day activities were based in Social Education Centres.
Most of the local NHS provision was in long-stay hospitals. Of the
two District Health Authorities (DHAs), Huddersfield had gone furthest
down the road towards some form of community care. There was
a well-established multidisciplinary Resource Team (the equivalent of
a Community Mental Handicap Team) which operated a large hostel
and two small houses (one specifically for children) outside of the
hospital framework. In contrast, Dewsbury had no staff working specifically in this field until 1978. The DHA relied on hospital beds in other
Districts. Between 1978 and 1986 a small resource team was gradually
established, but there was still no direct provision of residential places in
the community.

People had moved out of hospital and into social services provision prior
to the KPCC, but these had been one-off and small-scale occurrences, the
exception rather than the rule. Two important stimuli – one local and one
national – led to the formation of the KPCC. First, in 1984 the Yorkshire
Regional Health Authority produced a draft regional plan that included a
proposal to close Fieldhead Hospital. Although Fieldhead is managed by
Wakefield Health Authority, both Dewsbury and Huddersfield relied on it
to provide the majority of long-term hospital places for people with
learning difficulties from Kirklees. The closure proposal was vigorously
resisted by Wakefield Health Authority and has never been confirmed; the
current plans for the hospital involve shrinkage and some change of
function but not closure. Nevertheless, both Dewsbury and Huddersfield
decided that it would be in their own long-term interests to develop their
resources and to cease relying on Fieldhead as a major residential facility.
Rather than being about a hospital attempting to off-load its patients back
to their originating authorities, this was a situation where the two DHAs
elected to withdraw people for whom they were responsible. Without the
pressure of imminent hospital closure, the relevant authorities were able to
determine their own timetable and control the scale of operation, avoiding
the extremely unsatisfactory *ad hoc* arrangements (including fairly large-
scale movement between hospitals) that have been a feature of some
relocation programmes (see Korman and Glennerster 1985; Phillips and
Radford 1985).

The second stimulus was the issuing by the central department of the

Care in the Community circular (DHSS 1983) with its announcement of revised mechanisms for the joint planning of community care projects. Of particular interest was the loosening of restrictions on the use of joint funding. In 1984 the local authority organized a conference to review the implications of the circular, and the subsequent discussions resulted in the formation of the KPCC.

It would be wrong to suggest that financial considerations were the only spring to drive the clockwork; ideas about the quality and appropriateness of particular kinds of services undoubtedly played their part. However, the easing of financial restrictions on joint funding provided powerful motives for all the agencies involved. For the Social Services Department, in an age of ratecapping and retrenchment, the transfer of earmarked funds from the NHS presented an unequalled chance to expand and improve services. For the health service planners, although they were notionally losing resources, shifting funding from hospitals and placing it in the joint planning arena actually increased their control over its use.

The first plans for the Partnership (KSSD 1985), drafted within the Social Services Department, were radical in their outlook. The aim was to develop a 'comprehensive' service for all people with learning difficulties from Kirklees, using the existing pattern of service delivery merely as 'a point of departure'. Great stress was placed on the importance of basing the developments on the needs of individuals rather than organizational considerations: 'Individual Programme Planning is essential. There should be no pre-judgement of whether a person with a mental handicap is a "health patient" or a "social services client"'.

There was support for joint management of services with a central role for what were styled as multidisciplinary Resource Teams. Above all there was a commitment to the principle of normalization and a heavy emphasis on the use of ordinary housing, including challenging new developments such as life-sharing schemes.

Relatively few of these ideas found their way into the finally agreed version of the KPCC developments, although the principles on which they were based continued to be quoted in subsequent policy documents. As the next section shows, the proposals eventually endorsed were very different in both tone and detail.

Aims and objectives of the KPCC

The final plans adopted by the KPCC, outlined in a position statement (KPCC 1985) at the end of 1985, represented a much more cautious, pragmatic approach. The aim of developing a 'comprehensive' service had disappeared, and the emphasis was now much more sharply focused on the priority of moving people out of hospital, although there were still references to the needs of people already in the community:

Although these services are designed for those leaving hospital they have been designed within the context of the need to improve and provide a network of services for all people with mental handicaps.

The earlier commitment to joint management had been watered down. The initiative was now mainly concerned with the transfer of people between NHS and social services facilities. However, the multidisciplinary Resource Teams were to be centrally involved in the moves, and there was a proposal for the formation of special Project Teams comprising full-time seconded social services staff supported by NHS staff on part-time secondments.

The plans contained detailed proposals for the first year of the partnership. Twenty-seven hospital patients would move into social services hostels. Some of these places would be provided by the opening of a new hostel, but the majority (then reckoned to be about 15) would be made available by the 'transfer of current residents, who are both able and willing to live more independently, into satellite units'. These satellites (implicitly based on a core and cluster model, with the hostel as the core) were to make use of ordinary housing, as were the developments envisaged for the second year (33 places in small units). Already there was an expectation that some of this later provision might be run by the voluntary sector. Throughout this first two years it was anticipated that the appointment of a family placement officer would generate ten additional places.

These proposals represent a retreat from the more radical approach of the original outline, with its espousal of plans tailored to individual users and based primarily on new developments in ordinary housing. Nevertheless, there was still a commitment to improving, wherever possible, the services being delivered. The aim, the position statement declared, was to develop 'a high quality service providing accommodation and the necessary support'.

Rather than pursue the particular vision of community care originally conceived – one based on the principles outlined in *An Ordinary Life* (Kings Fund 1980) – the aims of the initiative had narrowed down to the less demanding objective of establishing a range of services to 'provide real alternatives to hospital care . . . both in the present and in the future'. In practice it had proved too difficult to gain agreement within the KPCC on the development of a more radical scheme, as a Social Services Department report (KSSD 1986a) later acknowledged:

> While there has been a welcome effort to move away from the large hospitals and campuses, there are divergent views about the alternatives . . . for the time being Kirklees should adopt a pluralist approach.

The approach in Kirklees was essentially opportunist. While the development of community care was seen as desirable, there was little shared understanding within or between the agencies involved about what this might mean in practice. Rather than begin by thrashing out a coherent, comprehensive strategy – and risk the possibility that the whole process might be bogged down by disagreements – the philosophical issues were side-stepped, and the focus was on building a consensus around the limited practical steps that could be achieved in the short run. No long-term goals were specified (except the vague notion that all hospital patients might 'possibly' move out into some unspecified provision in the community): all future developments were to be designed in the light of experience gained in the early stages.

Principles

The position statement also laid out a set of 'service principles' (see Figure 1). These principles are expressed at the level of heart-warming but vague generalizations. They were not accompanied by any attempt to operationalize them: to define what they meant in practical terms that could be implemented the following Monday morning.

Figure 1 Statement of principles for planning community care

a) Community Care must offer a person a quality of life at least as good and preferably better than that which he or she enjoyed in hospital.

b) A broad range of services will be required to enable such a person to enjoy a life as near normal as possible. Nine to five, weekday only services will not be sufficient on their own.

c) Community Care is not about moving groups of patients about en-block. It must be about individual plans and appropriate packages of services for individual people, and, where appropriate, their families.

d) The needs of a person with a mental illness or mental handicap will change over time and the services developed must have the flexibility to respond appropriately.

e) Also, over time, services will need to change in order to adapt to the changing needs and demands of people with mental illnesses and mental handicaps.

f) A range of services will be provided by a range of different agencies. It is vital that these services be jointly planned and that the routes of access to them be recognised and observed by all agencies.

g) Each person or family should have one individual worker to whom they can relate and that worker should ensure the coordination and appropriateness of the services provided.

h) Each individual and his or her family should be centrally involved in decisions affecting their lives.

i) If the needs of a person indicate that they require permanent care in an establishment or group home that establishment should be regarded as their home. If their needs change they should not be forced to move to a different establishment, rather the professional input should be varied to meet their changed need.

Nor is it difficult to demonstrate that the reality did not correspond with these principles. For example, the developments were not based on individual plans as required by principle (c). On the contrary, at their heart was a set of existing facilities (the hostels), and it was clear that much of the early activity was going to focus on finding suitable people who would fit into these facilities. Clearly what we have here are not design principles, but symbolic statements of ideals.

The contradiction between the 'philosophy' and the practice was acknowledged in Kirklees. As a later report (KPCC 1987) notes:

> There is a complex relationship between the statement of general principles and the emerging network of services in Kirklees. The principles are set to work in the real world of existing resources and service constraints, where there is a tension between the philosophy and available finances.

In practice

One consequence of the lack of an overall strategy and of the compromises which followed was that all kinds of implicit assumptions came to be made about the nature of the services it was possible to implement. This section examines these assumptions by describing some of the ways the Partnership operated in practice.

The concept of community care

Perhaps the most pervasive assumption operating in the KPCC related to the kind of people for whom community care was seen to be appropriate. Without question it was presumed that the most able/least troublesome people would move first. For example, when asked to nominate candidates for inclusion in the first round of moves, the two DHAs automatically selected those who presented the fewest management problems.

Within an incremental framework it may well have made sense to start with those who were the easiest to move. It is certainly true that most of the social services hostels, as they were then organized (e.g. no waking night staff), would have found it difficult to cope with people who were very profoundly handicapped, had significant additional physical handicaps, or who presented very challenging behaviour. The whole framework of the plans, with those leaving hospital all bound for places in hostels, was based on the belief that provision in ordinary housing would be inappropriate for this group. Yet by 1985 the principles enshrined in *An Ordinary Life* (Kings Fund 1980) were well established, and there was well-documented research evidence available showing that schemes based on ordinary housing could provide both a viable and a desirable environment for people with profound handicaps or challenging behaviour (see, for example, Mansell 1980; Felce *et al.* 1984b). In Kirklees the arguments for community care were rarely expressed in terms of a right to a life outside an institutional setting, but rather in terms of implicit beliefs about the effectiveness/feasibility of such placements.

Joint planning

Another characteristic of the KPCC was the nature of the inter-agency relationships. As we have already noted, the 1985 position statement had backed away from joint management of KPCC developments, proposing instead that a number of Project Teams be set up, staffed by full-time secondments from the Social Services Department and supported by NHS staff on a part-time basis. Similarly, it was intended that the multi-disciplinary Resource Teams would play an important role in the move. In the event, the Project Teams did not materialize and the involvement of the Resource Teams remained fairly marginal. With the exception of one voluntary sector house, all the new developments were developed and managed by social services staff, who were also primarily responsible for organizing the moves.

The position statement had not been precise about future plans, but had implied that at some future date everybody would leave hospital to take up places in 'jointly planned' provision. It soon became apparent that the health authorities held a different view. Early on in the process they had screened their populations for people who would be suitable candidates for community care. At this stage the future provision was unknown, and the purpose of the exercise was simply to identify a group of the most suitable people for a pilot project. Over time those selected metamorphosed into the 'official candidates' for community care. At that point the DHAs (Huddersfield in particular) made it clear they viewed the remaining hospital patients as in need of 'NHS nursing care' and that they themselves intended to develop the future provision for this group. Four years on (1989) Huddersfield is in the process of opening (in the grounds of a long-stay hospital) a 28-place purpose-built scheme, with its own day centre, for people with profound learning difficulties or additional physical handicaps. Part of this specialist provision is a 10-bedded 'behavioural' unit.

The form of the liaison between the different agencies might more properly be called parallel rather than joint planning (Hunter and Wistow 1987). As we suggested above, the focus of most of the early discussion was on the orderly transfer of people between agencies, rather than on hammering out a consistent and coordinated approach to all the different services. Things did change as the Partnership initiative developed. The relationship between the agencies improved markedly over time, largely as a consequence of the perceived success of the earlier limited collaboration. A degree of trust was established resulting in, among other things, the initiation of joint training exercises. In these respects Kirklees would appear to be fairly typical, having achieved no more and no less in this direction than most areas in England (see, for example, Booth 1981a; Hunter and Wistow 1987).

Financial arrangements

Another key feature of the local context was, almost inevitably, the issue of funding. At bottom the process of resource allocation was based on a straightforward 'dowry' system. For each person transferred from NHS to social services provision, the health authorities made a payment of approximately £10,500 per annum (1985/6 figure). This was based on the average cost of a residential and day care place in a hostel at the time.

As the hostels (with one exception) already existed, this revenue was to be used for funding the alternative community placements. However, since the money could not be transferred until the move out of hospital had actually taken place, and since few hostel places would have been vacant prior to these alternatives getting off the ground, a bid to the Yorkshire Regional Health Authority for bridging money was necessary.

Back in December 1985 there was considerable confidence about the financial situation. A number of bullish statements were made to the effect that even if the bid for bridging money failed, the development money would be found elsewhere. As time went on, confidence waned somewhat and attitudes towards the issue hardened as a consequence. The Region's decision on the allocation of bridging money had been expected in March 1986, but in the event was delayed until July when at last it was announced that they had been allocated £207,000, almost all of their original bid. This figure was reported to represent 80 per cent of the Region's bridging money for that year. The outcome was seen in Kirklees as a considerable success. This had the immediate effect of confirming people in their belief in a pragmatic approach. It was argued that by basing the bid on the offer to the health authorities of existing places rather than prospective (and therefore 'risky') developments, the local authority was making an offer that was unlikely to be turned down. There were some deft sleights of hand during this period. For example, there were frequent references in the documentation (KSSD 1986b) to the hostel places being 'immediately available', even though so far nobody had moved anywhere and therefore those places were still occupied.

Although the scheme may have started with a financial boost, there were other financial constraints looming. In a period of general shrinkage of local authority grant support from central government, Kirklees was incurring financial penalties for 'overspending'. Even so, the local authority made considerable efforts to protect and even increase spending in the relevant budgets. For example, with the aid of the joint funding money it was able to increase expenditure on mental handicap services by over 20 per cent between the years 1985/6 and 1986/7 (KSSD 1986c).

Nevertheless, possibilities for expansion over and above joint funding were limited.

Voluntary sector involvement

One consequence of these financial limitations was that 'benefit planning' became important, i.e. the planning of services so as to offset the costs of people's accommodation against their social security entitlement. We have already noted that one of the houses opening in the first year of the KPCC operations was run by the voluntary sector – the Homes Foundation (MENCAP) – and in subsequent developments almost all the ordinary housing schemes have been set up by voluntary organizations. Residents in these placements could attract (provided that they were not working) up to £150 per week in social security benefits, representing a considerable shift of the financial burden from the local authority to central government.

The arguments for these changes were not entirely financial. During these early years of the KPCC the local voluntary groups became markedly more vocal and insisted on playing a more active role. For example, one group set up a small day activity scheme designed to act as an alternative to a conventional Social Education Centre. This innovative scheme emphasized the use of ordinary community facilities and the value of maximizing participation. During this period the role of the voluntary sector was transformed. It moved away from mainly pressure group activities to become a mainstream service provider.

Problems in implementation

During the early years of the KPCC a number of difficulties arose. Many of these problems were either directly or indirectly a consequence of the approach adopted by the Partnership and give additional insight into the context in which the developments took place.

Slippage of time-scales

Delays in the Yorkshire Region's decision on the bridging money fed through into the implementation of the scheme, contributing to the considerable slippage of time-scales that occurred. This five-month hiatus in funding made some delay inevitable but did not account for all of the problem. The moves out of the hostels, initially scheduled to start in April 1986, did not begin until October and remained a trickle until well after Christmas. No one left hospital until February 1987, and the bulk of the hospital movers only finally made the move during April and May 1987.

The delays were the focus of much argument within the Partnership, and considerable criticism was directed against the Social Services Department who effectively controlled the process of moving. Such delays seem endemic in this kind of process. For example, among the projects in the three-year specially funded 'Care in the Community' initiative, only 44 per cent of those planned to move had actually made the break by January 1987, just two months from the end of that part of the programme (PSSRU 1987). In retrospect, given the problems, Kirklees does not seem to have done too badly, but surprisingly little allowance for the financial bottleneck was made by either side to the argument.

To some extent, the Social Services Department brought the problems on itself. Perpetually optimistic in their estimated schedules, officers created expectations they could not meet (some of those statements about 'immediately available' hostel places did not help). Although there were mistakes (e.g. missing appropriate meetings in the council planning cycle), the pace of the moves also reflected a genuine desire on the part of management to ensure the quality of the services. Some otherwise suitable properties were rejected because of doubts about their location, and keyworkers were allowed to move at a speed they thought to be in the best interest of the users.

Lack of management control

In addition managers were forced at times to justify a process they did not always directly control. Traditionally, the management of residential provision has been essentially *laissez-faire* (Booth 1985). Kirklees was no exception, the individual hostels in particular retaining a fair degree of autonomy. Management would provide the basic infrastructure (e.g. acquire property), but the details of how precisely to achieve short-term aims were largely left up to each unit. Indeed, in the absence of a clearly defined strategy there was some debate about what those aims were.

As a result, the pace and style of change tended to be determined by the hostel staff, and varied both between and within establishments. In one hostel, staff seized the opportunities enthusiastically, moving twelve people into ordinary housing in the first phase of developments. In another the senior staff had far more reservations about the whole process and, initially uncertain how to proceed, managed to move only four people during the same period. Although generally aware of what was happening on the ground, management could influence but not dictate the pattern of events.

Differing perceptions

The arguments about the pace of the moves also reflected genuinely different perspectives both within and between the agencies. Many of the senior officers on the NHS side saw the process of moving as essentially an administrative matter. Asking the patients if they wanted to go, consulting the relatives, and organizing the physical move were all seen as straightforward tasks to be ticked off one by one. They tended not to see them as complex processes. On one occasion the efforts of the Social Services Department were likened to 'ten men pushing an open door'.

Although naturally somewhat piqued by this criticism, the Social Services Department did not respond in the obvious way: by explaining what they were doing and why. Rather than go into details, the operational managers regularly fell back on clichés: 'We are doing it sensitively' and 'at the clients' own pace'. This in turn enraged some of the operational staff on the health side who were convinced such platitudes were a cover for sloppiness. In time these arguments faded as some trust began to develop, but an opportunity early on to resolve some of the doubts and mis-understandings was lost.

Failure to document the process

These initial attempts at communication were not aided by the remarkable lack of documentation. Operational plans for individual projects were few and far between, and those that did materialize were sketchy. There were no guidelines on how to tackle particular tasks, what to aim for, what to avoid, and little attempt to document the process for future reference. In view of the emphasis laid on an incremental, learn-from-our-mistakes approach, this is a significant criticism. Even where individual staff gained important experience, that knowledge was not widely disseminated and, subsequently, was all too frequently lost when they changed posts.

Characteristics of the Partnership approach

In summary, the KPCC had a number of distinctive characteristics:

- *It was not radical:* The options that would have provided the greatest challenge to services organized along traditional lines (e.g. shared living schemes, placements for people with profound handicaps or challeng-ing behaviour in ordinary housing) were either dropped from the original plans or, because of implicit assumptions about appropriate provision, never considered.

- *It was only marginally innovative:* Most of the ideas pursued in Kirklees were already well tried and tested. The use of large hostels was a feature of the existing pattern of services, and nationally the successful use of semi-independent living schemes for more able people was already commonplace. So both the main elements of the residential side of the initiative can scarcely be said to be original. Some aspects of the day services that were developed were more innovative, notably the voluntary sector day scheme and the flexible use of adult education services. Also, to be fair, there is remarkably little available information on the processes involved in implementing a significant relocation programme, and in many cases staff, forced to operate in the dark, showed considerable ingenuity.

- *The developments were service-led:* The form the developments took was determined largely by the fact that the hostels existed and, in political and financial terms, had to be used. Both the hostels and the day centres remained largely unaltered. The mainstream services were left unchanged, with the developments occurring around the margins.

- *It was pragmatic:* This was not a programme based on a well-articulated philosophy. 'Idealistic' approaches were consciously eschewed. Working out a common philosophy would have forced discussion of contentious issues. It was easier to settle on practical acts (which to some extent were open to differing interpretation). There was a belief that agreement on a more radical approach would never be reached. Better to start with a much less ambitious programme, so the reasoning went, than never get anywhere.
- *There was no comprehensive strategy:* The focus of the Partnership was not on a global reformulation of services for people with learning difficulties, but on the achievement of a very specific practical objective: the relocation of people from hospital. This is not to say that the needs of other groups were not recognized, particularly those already living in the community with their families. However, people in hospital were seen as a particular priority group for whom it was suddenly feasible to do something.
- *It was incremental:* All the objectives of the KPCC were framed in the short to medium term. In keeping with the pragmatic nature of the exercise, the intention was to learn from the initial experience and develop the programme accordingly.

Throughout these early developments there had been a rejection of 'rationalist' planning and an emphasis on the 'art of the possible'. Most of those involved would be among the first to acknowledge there had been problems and that the approach had flaws. Nevertheless, within its own terms, the early developments were perceived as a great success:

> Although we should be self-critical, and rightly we should engage in debate about the respective role and responsibilities of each member of the Partnership, we should also note there has been tremendous progress. . . . In the coming year, the Partnership will be in the forefront of developments within the Region, with a good chance of creating excellent services within a realistic financial strategy.
>
> (KPCC 1987)

While events in Kirklees undoubtedly did act to break an organizational log-jam and morale was certainly high, there remain two important unanswered questions. First, accepting for the moment the case for an incrementalist approach, did those achievements represent the optimum possible in the circumstances? Without clear aims and objectives there are no well-defined yardsticks against which to measure change. There is a danger that any progress is seen as success. Second, how do the achievements in Kirklees measure up to wider notions of good quality services? We hope this book will enable the reader to make some kind of judgement on these issues.

2

Ways and means: the study design

This chapter outlines the aims, design and methods of the study. It explains how the information on which this book is based was obtained, by what means, when and from whom. We have tried not to belabour the details, suspecting that most of our readers would prefer us to get on with the story. Nevertheless, a proper understanding of the strengths and limitations of our study and of the data it presents presupposes some knowledge of its methodology and how it was undertaken. Research, after all, should always be read in a doubting frame of mind. The purpose of this chapter is to provide just such a necessary background and to assist our readers in judging for themselves what weight to give to the results of our research.

Our aim has been to write a book that will hold the attention of policy-makers and practitioners as well as other researchers. This is not an easy task. In many ways these two groups occupy separate worlds of discourse. We have tried to strike a balance between the demands of rigour and methodological adequacy on the one hand, and the requirements of utility and policy relevance on the other (Booth 1986, 1988). Where these two sets of criteria have seemed to pull in different directions, we have generally opted for the path of relevance. Among other things this means that we have sought to make our study useful and comprehensible to potential end-users in the field and to focus on issues and problems that they can do something about. It also means that we have tried not to shy away from drawing out what we see as the implications of our work for policy and practice.

We have described the study as an evaluation of a community care programme. This calls for some clarification. It was not conceived or designed primarily as an evaluation of the particular model of service introduced in Kirklees by the Partnership in Community Care between the health and local authorities and voluntary agencies. As the previous chapter pointed out, the pattern of services devised to accommodate the people moving out of hospital is based largely on existing facilities and old ideas; it represents nothing new or innovatory. Rather the study was intended as an evaluation of the process of relocation itself, and of its effects on the lives of the movers and their families.

Evaluations come in all sorts of shapes and sizes. Broadly speaking, we have seen our project as comprising two strands: a *formative evaluation* of how the moves were planned and handled and of the workings of the process of relocation, and a *summative evaluation* of the outcomes of relocation for the movers and their families.

So far as the process element of our research is concerned, we were interested primarily in two areas of investigation: the management of the moves and how our subjects and their families coped with the stress and upheaval of the transition. The sort of questions we set out to explore covered a range of issues.

- *The management of the moves:* How were people selected for relocation? To what extent were they party to the decision to move? How were they prepared for the move? What steps were taken to introduce people to their new placements? How were they helped to settle in? What system of review was set up and how did it work? How were relatives involved in the decision and what efforts were made to consult them?
- *Coping with the transition:* What did the movers and their relatives think about how the moves were handled? What did they feel about the new placements? Were they satisfied with their involvement in decisions? Did the stress of relocation affect the relations between movers and their relatives? Did the movers themselves show any short-term problems of adjustment or adaptation? How did they feel about their new homes?

We wanted to see if we could identify some dos and don'ts from the experience in Kirklees that might guide others going down the same road.

The part of our project concerned with the evaluation of the outcomes of relocation focused on five broad types of indicators:

- *Developmental indicators* for monitoring any changes in the adaptive behaviour, skills or personal functioning of the movers following relocation.
- *Social indicators* for monitoring any changes in people's lifestyles, their integration into the wider community, the pattern of their relationships or their social network.
- *'Quality of service' indicators* for monitoring any changes brought about by the move in people's living environment; in the opportunities they had for self-determination, personal choice and participation in decisions about their lives; and in the availability of specialist services suited to their individual needs.

- *Activity indicators* for monitoring any changes in the level and type of people's daytime activities and their participation in social and leisure pursuits.
- *Subjective indicators* for monitoring people's own feelings and perceptions about the move and its impact on their lives.

Together it was hoped that these indicators, along with other material and information collected as part of the study, would enable us to throw some light on the promises and pitfalls of community care for people with learning difficulties.

The study design

The key features of our research design are easily summarized. It is a *longitudinal* (follow-up) study involving *three groups of respondents* which explores the process and outcomes of relocation for *two sets of movers* living in a *variety of different placements*. Here we shall outline briefly each of these key features in turn.

The longitudinal approach

The study comprised three distinct phases of interviewing. The first (pre-move) phase – sometimes referred to as Phase I in later chapters – was carried out shortly before the initial moves took place. The purpose of these interviews was twofold: to gather baseline information about the pattern of people's lives in their original (pre-move) placement and to tap respondents' feelings and expectations about the prospective move.

The second (settling-in) phase of interviews – also referred to as Phase II – was completed in the months immediately following the moves. These interviews focused mainly on issues relating to the process of relocation, including how the moves were handled and how well the movers were settling in and adapting to the change.

The third (follow-up) phase took place about a year after the moves. These Phase III interviews were designed to replicate the pre-move baseline measures and to compare how perceptions had changed with the course of events.

Such a follow-up approach has a number of strengths. It avoids the dangers in retrospective studies of dulled memories, selective perception and people confusing the past with the present. It facilitates the study of change by providing a baseline for making comparisons. And, finally, it makes the business of unravelling the processes involved in these changes easier.

Complementary points of view

Three groups of respondents were involved in each of the three phases of the study. We interviewed the movers themselves, their relatives where they had any, and their keyworkers or other direct care staff.

From the outset these three perspectives were regarded as equal and complementary. We did not expect them always to coincide; nor did we see it as part of our job to judge between them. Each group of respondents had a different stake in the relocation process, and each could be expected to view it from a different angle. We simply wanted to bring these views together in the hope of obtaining a more rounded picture.

The same movers and relatives were followed up in each phase of the study. However, in most, though not all, cases the staff respondent changed when the moves took place. In such instances the pre-move interviews were conducted with the relevant keyworker in the original placement, while the Phase II and Phase III interviews were held with the equivalent member of staff in the new placement.

A comparative ingredient

The study involved two sets of movers. One is made up of people who left long-stay hospital to take up places in social services hostels. The other comprises people who moved out of social services hostels into a variety of community placements including flats and houses (with staff support) and family placement schemes. Throughout this book these are referred to respectively as the 'hospital movers' and the 'hostel movers'. None of the hospital movers went directly into community placements.

Having two such groups going through the process of relocation at the same time enabled us to exploit the possibilities for internal comparisons and so address questions we would not otherwise have been able to ask. Did the hospital movers, for example, meet with more difficult problems of adjustment than the hostel movers? Were there any differences between the two groups in their feelings about moving before and after the event? Was the process of moving handled differently for the two groups and, if so, with what results? How did the relatives' views of the new placements compare? Did families find the move out of hospital harder or easier to come to terms with than the move from hostel to community living? By making use of the comparative method in this way, we were able to extract more insights from our data, and to untangle the challenges presented by certain specific kinds of move from those more properly seen as part-and-parcel of the process of relocation itself.

A cross-placement perspective

Our study embraced a wide variety of placements and settings. The hospital movers originated mainly from one NHS mental handicap hospital (just two people moved out of a second unit for people with a mental handicap linked to a large psychiatric hospital scheduled for closure). This hospital was divided into sixteen physically separate, mostly self-contained villas. Each villa had its own character and its own unique social environment. Our movers were drawn from eight of these villas. They left to take up placements in five different hostels varying in their size, location, physical amenities and regime.

The hostel movers transferred from three of the same social services hostels into a range of types of accommodation. The majority moved into four houses with daytime staff cover. The others were placed variously in a staffed house with 24-hour cover, warden-controlled flats, their own flats in ordinary housing and a family placement scheme.

In its broadest sense, the concept of relocation refers in this study to these two sorts of move: from hospital to hostel, and from hostel into a community placement. Reality, however, is a little more complicated. These three settings in fact subsume a range of different social environments. Hospital villas and social services hostels differ not only from each other but also among themselves as places in which to live. Community placements too are by no means all of a type. It cannot be assumed that a move from hospital always brings with it a less institutionalized pattern of living.

Accordingly, we set out to compare the social environments of the placements in our study in order to find out what changes, if any, had been brought about in the opportunities and constraints faced by our movers following relocation. Did people enjoy more privacy? Did they have more control over their own lives? Were they allowed more say in day-to-day decisions? Did they become more integrated into the wider community? Were they given more scope for expressing their individuality?

Research instruments and methods

The previous section has outlined the key features of our study design showing how it involved three groups of respondents (staff, relatives and movers) in three lots of interviews (before the move, during the settling-in period, and twelve months on); how it included two sets of movers (from hospital and from hostels) and a variety of placements; and how it focused on both the process and the outcomes of relocation. This section describes in more detail how we went about collecting the information we wanted.

In the case of both staff and relatives data collection was carried out primarily by structured interviews using schedules with a mix of pre-coded and open-ended questions. The interviews with the movers were arranged as conversational-type encounters guided only by an 'aide memoire' of topics and tape recorded for transcription later.

The staff interviews

Each interview was about a specific mover and was conducted with either that person's keyworker or the member of staff who was considered to know them best. Where the same member of staff was involved with more than one mover, they were interviewed separately about each. While the form and focus of some of the questions were changed to reflect the changing situation at each phase of the study, the broad core of topics and issues covered remained much the same across all three interviews.

The Phase I interviews explored seven main areas of interest: health and physical disability, services and supports, community involvement and social activities, friendships and family relationships, benefits and income, the predicted outcomes of the move, and behaviour problems. Our approach in this last area is worth describing in more detail.

Problem behaviour – or challenging behaviour as it is now widely known – has been viewed as an important mediator of placement outcome as well as a response to the stress of relocation. We felt it was an issue that had to be examined with staff for this reason.

The questions we developed were based on what are known as ABC charts. These are an assessment method derived from behavioural principles (Mansell *et al.* 1987) and designed to help staff unravel what lies behind these episodes. Any incident of difficult behaviour is logged on a chart. As well as describing the behaviour (B), both the antecedents (A) and the consequences (C) are also noted. In behaviourist terms, the purpose of such a process is to demonstrate how what appears to be irrational or bizarre behaviour can often be seen as an understandable outcome of a particular situation.

We were unable to log people's behaviour over a period of time. However, our pilot interviews indicated that staff often had quite clear ideas about factors and contexts that seemed related to the occurrence of problem behaviour. Accordingly, we devised a ten-fold classification of different types of challenging behaviour based on that used by Wing (1981). This referred to behaviour that was aggressive, destructive, self-injuring, objectionable, antisocial, disruptive, persistently uncooperative, stereotyped, elaborately routinized or bizarre. For each type of behaviour we established whether it was exhibited by the individual and, if so, asked for a description of a typical incident. We then asked when and where this behaviour usually occurred, how often, whether staff could identify any triggers and how they usually responded in each case.

The Phase II interviews were designed to replicate much of the baseline information collected before the move. Their main aim was to establish what changes had taken place following relocation. The section on community involvement was omitted because we felt that movers would not yet have found their feet in their new neighbourhoods. Also, in place of the predictions exercise, we included a range of questions focusing on issues related to the move itself, such as how the movers were helped to settle in, how well they had adapted to their new routines, what changes had taken place in their behaviour or outlook since their arrival, how happy they were in the new placement and whether staff would judge it a success so far.

Phase III had two purposes: to find out how people had developed in their new placements and to sum up the changes brought about in their lives by relocation. The same broad framework of questions was used as in the pre-move interviews, except for those about benefits and income. These were dropped because it had proved hard to obtain reliable information in Phase II. Few staff, especially those attached to the community placements, were sure about what benefits people were receiving or what other sources of income they had. The section on community involvement and social activities was reintroduced to provide comparable data with the pre-move phase. Finally, staff were asked to make a series of summary judgements about how successful the placement had been to compare with the predictions made in Phase I.

The adaptive behaviour scale (ABS)

We used the American Association of Mental Deficiency's Adaptive Behaviour Scale (Nihira *et al.* 1975) in its Anglicized version (Thomas and Webster 1974) to measure the developmental changes in our movers following relocation. The ABS is a structured, pre-coded scale made up of two parts: Part One is designed to assess people's 'adaptive behaviour' (that is, their competence in daily living skills); Part Two is designed to assess 'maladaptive' – or problem – behaviour. It is commonly used as both a clinical tool and a research instrument.

We completed Part One *only* of the ABS for our movers, using staff as respondents, at the same time as the Phase I (pre-move) and Phase III (follow-up) interviews. We chose not to administer it as part of Phase II on the grounds that most staff in the new placements would not have known the movers long enough to answer all the questions accurately.

We decided against using Part Two of the ABS for two reasons. In the first place, sections of it show low levels of reliability (Nihira *et al.* 1975). Also, we were unhappy with some of the moralistic undertones implicit in its make-up. For example, individuals are given a negative score for 'homosexual tendencies'. There seems to be an underlying confusion between behaviour that simply fails to conform to a fairly narrow set of norms and that which is genuinely disruptive or presents problems of management. We felt that these things were better dealt with by our section on behaviour problems.

The ABS covers a wide range of everyday skills grouped under ten main headings: independent functioning, physical development, economic activity, language development, numbers and time, domestic activity, vocational activity, self-direction, responsibility and socialization. The skills under each heading are broken down into a series of tasks representing different levels of competence, each of which is assigned a score. These scores can be summed within each heading or 'domain' and across all domains to give a measure of a person's development.

Despite the fact that the ABS is a widely used instrument which has been thoroughly tested and validated, we still found in our pilot interviews that staff respondents had difficulty with the section on 'vocational activity' and the questions on 'passivity' and these were subsequently dropped.

The relative interviews

Wherever meaningful contact still existed, we sought to interview a member of the mover's immediate family or some other close relative or surrogate. Often these interviews involved more than one person, for instance where both parents participated. In some cases it was found that our initial contact (usually obtained from staff or case records) was not the best informant and that some other relative was in closer and more regular touch with the mover. Where this happened the new lead was followed up and, if possible, another interview arranged. For the purposes of later analysis this person was usually regarded as the principal respondent. All the interviews were held in the relatives' own homes.

As with the staff, the pre-move (Phase I) interviews were designed to provide baseline information against which subsequent changes could be measured. This included relatives' opinions and perceptions of the current placement; their views about unmet needs and service deficits; the extent of each mover's involvement in the use of community facilities when visiting their relative's home; their feelings about the general policy of community care, about how it was being implemented locally and about their involvement in the planning of the move. Finally, the relatives were asked to complete the same predictions exercise that staff had undertaken.

The Phase II interviews focused mainly on relatives' first impressions of the new placement – its amenities, staff and the kind of care and support that was provided – as well as on how well people had settled in following the move. We were also interested in finding out whether they had seen any changes in the movers and whether any new problems had arisen.

The relatives' contribution at this stage was especially critical in the case of the hospital movers. Where regular contact had been maintained, they were better placed than anyone to observe any immediate behavioural consequences of relocation. Our staff respondents in Phase II had rarely had any contact with the movers in the hospital. For the most part all they knew about them was what they had picked up from the introductory visits prior to the move or what was written in their case files. At this point the relatives provided a crucial link with the past.

The follow-up (Phase III) interviews covered ground initially explored in both the previous phases. As in the staff interviews, we were wanting to investigate the changes that had occurred between the two placements as well as within the new one. Key areas for questioning and discussion with the relatives included: changes in their opinions about the new placement since Phase II, their relationship with staff, problems that had arisen in the new placement, their views about the kind of care and support provided, and what changes they had observed in their relative since the move. Also, they were asked to assess the outcomes of the move in terms directly comparable with the predictions they gave in Phase I so as to provide an indication of how far their hopes and fears had been realized and whether things had turned out better or worse than they had anticipated. Lastly, we sought to find out what the relatives thought was the 'ideal' placement.

The interviews with the movers

An initial review of the literature (see Chapter 7) had suggested that a largely informal, unstructured approach to interviewing the movers was likely to be the most successful. Also, some of them had little speech, or serious speech impediments, so we had to find some method of enabling them to act as respondents.

While the use of life-story books (Frost and Taylor 1986) seemed to offer great potential, such an approach required more time and resources than were available. In the event, some features of this method were borrowed and adapted for our purpose, along with features of the 'visual question' technique described and used by Conroy and Bradley (1985; see also Willcocks 1984).

From our early days in the field it became clear that we would have to put time and effort into developing our relationships with the movers before interviewing could begin. Fortunately, delays in the start of the relocation programme allowed us an extensive lead-in period. We were able to use this time to get to know the movers and their peers.

Also during this time photographs were taken of all the movers, their friends, other residents and staff, as well as their current and prospective placements. Wherever possible these were made up into a photograph album which the mover kept. The photographs were then used in the subsequent interviews as a focus for discussion.

Most people enjoyed having their photographs taken and looking at and talking about them. Their use in the interviews seemed to help make the situation more relaxed and informal. Also, for people with little or no speech, the opportunities for pointing at, manipulating and ordering the photographs greatly increased the potential for communication. For example, they could often point to or pick up photographs in answer to direct questions (such as 'Who do you like/don't you like?'). Similarly, where a person's speech was difficult to understand, the photographs aided the interviewer's comprehension by providing important textual clues.

The interviews were almost always conducted on a one-to-one basis on the respondent's home ground without staff present. Although the interviewer would have a pre-established range of topics to cover, the wording of the questions used and the order in which the topics were introduced were allowed to vary. Throughout, the emphasis was on illuminating the feelings and perceptions of the movers in terms of the choices they made between known, concrete options. To avoid any appearance of a test, the interviewer did not carry any pens, paper or a clipboard. All the interviews were carried out in a conversational style and recorded on tape. Care was taken to ensure that genuine consent was given, and at any sign of stress the interview was promptly terminated.

As well as providing a focus for the interviews, the photographs were also used in conjunction with a set of pictures depicting happy/sad faces to ask simple questions about the movers' feelings about their placements. At each phase of the study the respondents were presented with the photographs in turn (present and prospective placements in Phase I, old and new placements in Phases II and III) along with three stylized drawings depicting a happy, smiling face, a sad, weepy face and a face with an 'in-between', neutral expression (see Figure 2). They were then asked for each photograph, 'What sort of face would you have if you lived here – a happy one, a sad one or sort of in-between?' Tone of voice, intonation and gestures were used to reinforce the meaning of the question, and the order of the prompts was varied randomly. The resident was then encouraged to select a face and place it on the photograph. Finally, the respondent was shown both photographs together and asked to point to the one showing the place where he or she would most like to live. A full evaluation of these methods is provided with an account of the results in Chapters 7 and 8.

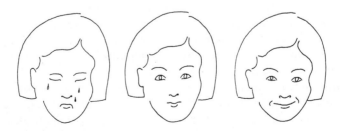

Figure 2 The happy/sad faces

The Unit Practice Questionnaire (UPQ)

Moving people out of long-stay hospitals is often described as a process of deinstitutionalization. We have preferred the term 'relocation' partly because it is a little less ugly but also because it does not carry the same loading. We do not think it can be assumed that hospitals are necessarily more institutional than other settings. Rather it is an empirical question that must be put to the test. The Unit Practice Questionnaire (UPQ) was designed with this aim in mind.

Broadly speaking the UPQ sought to weigh up the characteristics of the regimes in the hospital units and hostels in terms of staff attitudes and caring practices. More particularly, it was used:

- To compare the social environments (or regimes) of the hospital villas, from which many of our movers came, with the social environments of the hostels into which they were discharged. In this context, the social environment of the units was conceived and defined in terms of the rules, procedures and practices which regulate the daily routine.
- To appraise the attitudes of senior nursing and residential staff in relation to current notions of good practice and to see how far their attitudes are reflected in actual caring practices and in the running of the units.

The UPQ is a self-administered, pre-coded questionnaire comprising 34 multiple-choice questions each referring to different aspects of everyday life and the daily routine of the units. The questions were chosen to cover five key dimensions of the institutional environment: personal choice, privacy, personalization, segregation and participation. The design was adapted from an earlier schedule developed by the Joint Unit for Social Services Research (Booth 1985) in connection with work on institutional regimes in homes for the elderly.

Each question was made up of a series of 'practice statements' (about, for example, arrangements for getting up in a morning, bedtimes, bathtime supervision, locking bedroom doors, etc.), and respondents were then asked to place a tick in the box next to the one most accurately describing the *actual* practice or arrangements in their unit. Additionally, in a separate column, they were also asked to tick the box next to the statement denoting what they considered to be the most *desirable* practice. Space was included on the questionnaire for respondents to add any supplementary comments or otherwise to elaborate their replies to each question, and they were encouraged to do so, especially where actual practice diverged from what they regarded as desirable practice.

The UPQ was completed and returned by the nursing sister on each of the hospital villas from which our movers had come (except one which had closed by the time we went back to do the exercise and another where we failed to establish contact), by the second hospital involved in the study, and by a senior officer at each of the hostels into which the former hospital residents moved, including a voluntary home with 24-hour staff support. It was not administered in the community placements so we have no comparative evidence about the kind of environmental change experienced by the hostel movers as a result of relocation. There were a number of reasons for this decision. The instrument itself was not adapted for use in unstaffed settings. Collecting the data by observation would involve too gross an intrusion into people's privacy. And in any case the community placements varied across dimensions different from those tapped by the UPQ, whose content was keyed to the managed environments of the hospital and hostels.

Our respondents

The relocation programme got underway in October 1986 when the first moves took place. Between then and June 1987, the cut-off date for inclusion in the study fixed by our research timetable, 24 people had moved from hospital into hostels and 24 people had vacated hostel places for community placements. In the event, three of the hospital movers presented special complications and were excluded from the study. This left us with a total of 45 hospital and hostel movers.

The staff

Pre-move interviews were completed successfully with the keyworkers of all but three of the movers. One person had moved before we were notified, and in the other two cases it proved impossible to find a member of staff who admitted to knowing the individuals well enough to give an interview. In addition, an interview was also obtained about someone whose name was later removed from the list after he had absconded from hospital in an attempt to see his mother while waiting to take up a hostel place.

In Phase II a full set of interviews was completed during the settling-in period with the direct care staff of all 45 movers. In most cases the staff respondent after the move was not the same person we had interviewed in Phase I.

By the time we entered the follow-up phase of the study, three of the original movers had returned to their former placements (one to hospital and the other two to hostels). These people were excluded from Phase III. Otherwise staff interviews were completed for all the remaining 42 movers.

Many members of staff acted as keyworkers for a number of movers. Consequently, the 130 individual interviews spread over the three phases involved just 50 different respondents. Overall a complete set of staff interviews covering all three phases of the study is available for a core of 39 movers.

The movers

Five movers were unable to take part as respondents in the study because we were unable to find ways of communicating with them. All five were hospital movers.

Pre-move interviews were completed successfully with 37 of the remaining 40 movers. One woman refused to take part, largely we suspect because of the stress and upset occasioned by her impending move, and the other two were missed for logistical reasons. These omissions were again from the hospital group.

In Phase II all 40 people who were able to take part did so, including our earlier refusal. Two of the respondents had returned to their original placements by this time, but interviews were still conducted in order to establish their feelings about the apparent failure of these moves.

In the follow-up phase, 37 interviews were undertaken although two were not very successful. In both cases (one involving the same person who refused in Phase I) the individuals concerned appeared not to recognize the interviewer and would not answer direct questions. The two returnees were excluded from this phase, and one of our earlier respondents was too ill to take part.

All told, then, we have a complete set of three interviews with 35 of the 45 movers in our study, including 23 of the hostel movers and 12 of the hospital movers.

The relatives

Only 37 of our movers – 18 from the hospital group and 19 from the hostel group – still had close living relatives or surrogates (such as a dutiful trustee or a caring, honorary 'Auntie'). Initially we sought to elicit the co-operation of relatives by means of a letter outlining the project, requesting their help and inviting them to return a prepaid slip notifying us when they would be available for interview. This approach turned out to be misguided. Almost half of our first batch of contacts either refused or failed to respond. Thereafter we relied entirely on personal contact, either telephoning or calling round and asking for an appointment. This way was altogether more successful. We retrieved some of the original refusals and only met with one more rejection.

In Phase I, interviews were obtained with the relatives of 25 movers. In 12 cases they either declined to talk with us when approached or could not be contacted. In addition, we also interviewed the relatives of three

Table 1 Number of interviews by respondents and stage of study

Stage		Direct care staff	Relatives	Movers
I	Pre-move	43	28	37
II	Settling-in	45	26	40
III	Follow-up	42	24	37
Total		130	78	114

hospital residents who were due to move but, for one reason or another, did not then do so.

In the second phase of interviews two new relatives, and a very close, longstanding friend of another mover, agreed to join the study. We ran through a shortened and adapted version of the Phase I questionnaire with the two relatives prior to the full Phase II schedule. At the same time, two respondents from the first round dropped out. One had moved house and could not be traced, while the other declined to see us because her daughter had returned to her original placement. We did not attempt to interview the relatives of the three non-movers again. This left us with 26 successful interviews and 10 refusals in Phase II.

In the follow-up phase, relative interviews were completed for 24 movers. We lost two respondents from the earlier phases: one who was too ill to see us and another whose daughter had gone back into hospital.

Looking across all three phases of the study, we have a full set of interviews for 21 of the 37 movers with close living relatives. Table 1 summarizes the information presented above about our three groups of respondents.

Summary

This study presents the findings from an evaluation of a local community care initiative. The core of this initiative was a relocation programme aimed at moving one group of people with learning difficulties out of long-stay NHS hospital care into local authority hostel accommodation and another group out of these hostels into various forms of ordinary housing.

The evaluation focuses on both the process of relocation and the outcomes of the move. The research involved interviewing three main groups of actors: the direct care staff, relatives and the movers themselves. Each group was interviewed three times: before the move, during the settling-in period and about twelve months later. In addition, the study explored the hospital and hostel regimes and compared the daily routines and caring practices in these different settings.

3

Out of step: issues of process and adjustment

Moving house, starting a new school or changing jobs are well known to be stressful events – times when we all may lean a bit harder on those closest to us for support. For the people in our study the upheaval in their lives brought about by relocation was more traumatic and far-reaching than any of these happenings. Indeed, it might best be seen as something closer to a mixture of all three. For the hospital movers in particular, the changes were especially dramatic. They left behind everything familiar, including most of their friends, for what must have seemed like a new world. In many ways they may be compared with emigrants in the challenges they faced – with the added burdens of disability and 'enforced dependence' (Townsend 1981) to compound their problems of adjustment. The next chapter examines the handling of the moves and the measures taken to smooth the process of settling-in. This chapter focuses specifically on two interrelated issues affecting the short-term outcomes of relocation: transition shock and the involvement of families.

Relocation, stress and adjustment

Much research on the effects of deinstitutionalization, especially in the USA, has fastened on to the question of whether it enhances developmental growth – usually measured in terms of adaptive behaviour. While changes have generally been found in people's post-relocation behaviour, they have not been entirely consistent from one study to the next. There are few, if any, behavioural domains in which all investigators have found the same change taking place (Kleinberg and Galligan 1983).

Uncertainty too hinges around the phasing and persistence of the changes that may occur. One strand of research reports a pattern of significant gains in the short term after relocation – especially in the areas of personal functioning, socialization, domestic activity and language development – followed thereafter by a levelling off in performance. For example, Schroeder and Henes (1978) in a matched-control comparison of 19 residents transferred from a mental handicap unit to four group homes found 'that the greatest gains in performance were exhibited immediately after placement and the rate of gain due to learning new skills decreased subsequently'.

Another strand of research, however, while similarly showing the impact of relocation to be strongest in the period immediately after the move, reports a pattern of short-term *decrements* in positive behaviours usually followed by a gradual return to former levels. Heller (1982), for instance, reports that most of the initial deterioration in behaviour observed in a sample of severely disabled children had corrected itself within 4 to 6 weeks of their transfer to a new setting. Heller and Braddock (1985) attribute the sleep disturbances, toileting problems and withdrawn behaviour exhibited by residents in their study to the disruption in familiar routines and relationships occasioned by relocation. They speculate that 'it takes at least a few months for residents to accommodate to the novel setting.'

These short-lived behavioural deficits have been said to comprise a specific syndrome associated with relocation known as 'transition shock' (Macy 1984). In the literature, transition shock is widely seen as a stress reaction whose common symptoms include emotional, behavioural and mental health changes. Cohen *et al.* (1977) suggest that relocation involves many of the same stresses as initial institutionalization. Following Sarason and Gladwin (1958) they identify some of these as separation from loved ones, the pressures of adjusting to a new physical and interpersonal environment, confusion and resentment regarding helplessness, and anxiety about the future.

Transition shock in perspective

In this section we explore the nature and extent of transition shock as evidenced among the movers in our study. We begin by comparing two assessments of the impact of relocation based on the differing perspectives of staff and relatives.

Staff perspectives

During stage two of the study (coinciding with the post-relocation, settling-in period) the keyworkers or other direct care staff in the new placements were asked if they had observed any signs that the movers had found the change stressful. A total of 22 out of the 45 movers were reported as showing some measure of behavioural disturbance.

However, this figure cannot be taken at face value. The majority of our respondents would have known very little about the movers' past. None would have been able to foresee how they might develop in the future. In other words, when interviewed they could not be sure whether the problems they attributed to the stress of the move were indeed of a transitional nature or a continuation of previous maladaptive behaviour or a functional response to their new environment.

In order to weed out the cases properly belonging in these last two categories, it was necessary to compare, for each individual mover, the staff assessments from stage two of the study with the baseline data from the pre-move assessments and the follow-up data from stage three. As part of this process of validation, staff reports were also checked against the extensive case files built up on each of the movers over the three years of the study (from direct observations, professional case reviews, individual programme plans, official records, conversations with relatives, personal contacts, etc.). In the light of this additional evidence 7 cases were excluded from the list of movers whom staff had identified as showing symptoms of transition shock, so bringing the number down to 15 people.

At the same time as some movers were incorrectly identified as exhibiting transition shock, others initially were incorrectly discounted as finding the move stressful. At each of the three stages in the study, staff were asked whether the movers presented any behaviour problems. Questions specifically covered behaviour that was aggressive, destructive, self-injuring, antisocial, disruptive, persistently uncooperative, stereotyped, or objectionable. By comparing staff responses for each individual at every stage, it was possible to identify those who presented these problems during the settling-in period but not before the move nor 12 months afterwards.

Altogether, 11 cases showing transitional behaviour problems were identified by this method. In the event, six turned out to be among those already listed by staff as having found the move stressful. Adding the remaining five to this group of 15 gives a total of 20 who, on the basis of evidence from staff, may be said to have experienced some degree of transition shock as a result of relocation.

Relatives' perspectives

At least one family member belonging to 26 of the 37 movers who still had close living relatives or surrogates was interviewed during the post-move, settling-in stage of the study. Each was asked if any problems had arisen since the move, how well their relative was settling in (what staff had told them and what their relative had said as well as what they had observed themselves), and whether they had noticed any behavioural changes following relocation. All these respondents had maintained contact with their relative since the move, either visiting them in the unit or having them home to visit.

Analysis of these interviews showed that eight people were described by their relatives as exhibiting behaviour consistent with a stress reaction to the move. It is not surprising that relatives should have seen less evidence of transition shock than staff as they saw less of the movers and spent less time with them in the unit. Of this group of eight people, six were among those also identified by staff as experiencing a traumatic reaction to the move. The other two cases were as follows:

> *Lyn Bell* moved from hospital into a local authority hostel. For about the first month in her new placement, her mother said, 'She wouldn't eat and they had to give her enemas. I think she was frightened as much as anything. She wasn't used to the house or the people. She would freeze if anyone approached her.' By the time her three month review came up, her mother could see 'the vast improvement' in Lyn compared to how she had been in hospital.

> *Jill Ridley* also moved into a local authority hostel from hospital. She was found a place at the local day centre but failed to settle, fighting a lot and arguing with the other trainees. Her aunt could not understand the cause of the trouble: 'I've never had any bother with her in the whole of my life.' In the end her place was withdrawn. After a break she was gradually introduced back into the centre, a day at a time, and has now settled in without any further problems.

When these two people are added to the cases of transition shock identified using the evidence from staff, they bring the total number to 22, or just under half (49 per cent) of all the movers in the study.

Features of transition shock

These 22 validated cases all fell into two broad categories: those whose symptoms were mainly *outer directed* and those where they were mainly *inner directed*. Interestingly, the former category was made up overwhelmingly of men whereas the latter category mainly comprised women.

When transition shock took the form of an outer directed reaction to the stress of relocation, it generally showed itself either as an explosion of feeling against other people or things, or as aberrant behaviour. Uncharacteristic fits of anger ('John showed signs of anger and shouted at Margaret. He gets quite red in the face when he's under stress'), personal aggression ('He was a bit aggressive towards Fred at the beginning but he isn't now'), destructive behaviour ('He smashed up a lot of things') and bullying were the most frequently cited symptoms of transition shock.

Michael White moved from a local authority hostel into a family placement. His carer reports that 'when he came he was very excited, relieved to leave the hostel. As a consequence his behaviour was very different from normal. He does have difficulty expressing his emotions which tend to come out as bizarre behaviour. He bullied the others and was more demanding.'

The incidence of aberrant behaviour was low but included petty pilfering within the hostel and shoplifting as well as problems with money and drinking.

Transition shock as an inner directed response to stressful change likewise showed itself in one of two ways (or sometimes a combination of both). One was in physical symptoms or upsets, and the other was in emotionally disturbed behaviour. Physical symptoms were usually non-specific aches and pains or just feeling under the weather, though there were one or two episodes of enuresis and soiling.

There were times when he said he wasn't happy, or not well, and physical symptoms when things were not all right with the world. We put the stresses down to him not being able to get out as much as he did. He felt his routines were disrupted – the club and church – but he didn't want to move back to the hostel.

There were crying episodes in the first month to six weeks and she complained of various aches and pains. When she does cry it's spectacular and quite difficult to cope with. We'd give her a vitamin C tablet which would 'cure' it.

When she first came here she would often soil herself. She also had a very bad body odour which I think was a result of nervous stress but she seems all right now.

Emotionally disturbed behaviour was the most common manifestation of transition shock after aggression. It took many forms including self-injury ('She would slap the side of her head all the time, very hard, and tears would roll down her face'), nightmares and sleeplessness, wandering, weepiness and withdrawal.

She wasn't settled at all at the beginning. When she came she was anxious and withdrawn, picking at her clothes. She refused to eat at times, was very stubborn. She didn't talk, she spoke very little, for about 3–4 months. She's settling very well and talking more now.

The first night she came she wandered around all night. She's also wandered outside of [the hostel]. She was always being brought back. Some nights too she seemed to go without sleep but it didn't make any difference to her. Also she used to take her clothes off but has since stopped.

The first two weeks there were no problems. Then we had a phone call from work [Remploy]. He was falling asleep, shouting, being aggressive. He had a period of being paranoid, thinking people were trying to break in, shouting at staff, disturbed nights. He was really quite disturbed and showing a number of strange behaviours. He was expelled from the adult education class and got a written warning from Remploy. Once his 3-month introductory period [in his new placement] was over and his place here was made permanent, things improved a lot.

Although there was some overlap within this classification – as the extracts from the interviews and case notes show – the majority of cases exhibited unambiguous features of just one of the four types of transition shock described above.

Within the limits of the study design, some tentative efforts were made to identify possible antecedents of transition shock. A higher proportion of people moving from hospital into a hostel (14 out of 21) as against people moving from hostels into community living schemes (8 out of 24) experienced some problems of adaptation. This lends some support to the importance attributed to the degree of environmental change and to the 'novelty explanation' of post-relocation adjustment. On the other hand, there was no difference in the mean pre-move scores on the Adaptive Behaviour Schedule (ABS) of the stressed group and the non-stressed group, suggesting that adaptive skills and personal competence are not mediators of successful adjustment. The last avenue to be explored was people's subjective feelings about the move itself.

Transition effects and mover preferences

Using data from the resident interviews, we looked to see if there was any relationship between people's subjective feelings about the move and the incidence of transition shock.

As explained in Chapter 2, part of the resident interviews involved a 'visual game' using photographs of the old and new placements. Each respondent was shown three line drawings depicting a happy, smiling face, a sad, weepy face and a face with an 'in-between', neutral expression. They were then presented with the two photographs in turn and asked to point to the sort of face they would have living there. Afterwards, as a consistency check, they were asked to choose the photograph of the place where they would most like to live. Table 2 compares the distribution of happy–sad faces among the transition shock group and the rest of the cohort before the move took place.

Those people in the group which subsequently showed a stress reaction to the move were both less happy in their current placement and less happy at the prospect of their new placement than the other movers. At the same

Table 2 Mover preferences prior to relocation by outcome group

	Current placement		Prospective placement	
	Shock group	*Others*	*Shock group*	*Others*
Happy face	8	15	10	19
Neutral face	2	3	2	2
Sad face	5	3	2	1
NA*	7	2	8	1
Total	22	23	22	23

*Includes those who failed to record a choice, refused to choose, or chose inconsistently.

time, the majority of those registering a preference expressed themselves as being happy in their current placement, while slightly more said they expected to be happy in their new placement – a pattern that mirrors the one among movers showing no signs of transition shock.

When asked where they would most like to live, all but 4 of the 36 movers who expressed a choice in stage one of the study selected the photograph of the new placement. Of the four people apparently not wanting to move, three belonged to the stressed group. On the other hand, an outright majority (12 people) of those experiencing relocation stress – an overwhelming majority if the people who did not make a choice are excluded – opted for the new placement.

On the basis of this evidence the hypothesis that transition shock is predominantly a function of involuntary relocation must be rejected. While those who did not want to move (although the numbers are small) were more likely to encounter problems, most of the people who encountered problems chose their new placement in preference to their old.

Overview

The phenomenon of transition shock has received scant attention in the British literature. It has been much more a concern of American researchers. Initially, we were inclined to see this as a result of differences in the American and British situation. Certainly these differences cannot be ignored in making comparisons. In the United States deinstitutionalization often means moving people many hundreds of miles, away from places and people they know, with little chance of retaining contacts, and without the opportunity of preparatory visits. Frequently, hundreds of residents have been moved in a very short space of time, in many cases as the result of timetables imposed by court-ordered closures, allowing little opportunity for them to be prepared for the move. Also, people have often been moved from very big state institutions into big community facilities (by UK standards) accommodating up to 200 and more residents. The size of these units makes it more likely that people would have difficulty in reorientating themselves. A final point to be taken into account is that the frequency of moving between institutions throughout the life-cycle is lower in the USA; it is more usual for people to stay put. Consequently, relocation may entail a greater upheaval for the individual than in Britain where people commonly move about a lot more.

In the beginning these differences encouraged us to think that transition shock might be a feature of the deinstitutionalization process in the United States rather than a feature of relocation itself. This view turned out to be unfounded. Almost half the movers in our study exhibited behavioural signs indicative of transition shock. By close examination of these individual cases we identified four main types of transition effects, but efforts to pinpoint the differences between the stressed group of movers and those who showed no obvious problems of adjustment were less successful. A higher proportion of hospital movers than hostel movers experienced relocation stress, suggesting that perhaps the extent of environmental change may be a precipitating factor. Beyond that, however, no relationship was found between transition shock and people's subjective feelings about the move, the efforts made to prepare them for the move as reported by staff, or their level of adaptive behaviour. Clearly this area calls for further research in order to identify the antecedents of transition shock.

In the meantime, perhaps the most important lesson to be drawn from this study is that practitioners should be attuned and responsive to the stress which relocation may entail for people, alert to its symptoms and manifestations, and mindful of ways by which it might be allayed. This means that transition shock should be anticipated and prepared for as part of the planning for any relocation project; front-line staff, especially keyworkers, should be trained to recognize it; and full individual case reviews involving staff from the previous placement should be arranged within six weeks of the move taking place to ensure that signs of unusual behaviour are picked up and dealt with. Among other things such an approach calls for a carefully worked out programme of preparation, induction and support tailored to each individual's needs and covering the period *after* as well as before the move (one of our keyworkers, when asked if anything special had been done to help a mover settle in, replied, 'We bought him a mug with his name on it'). It calls for continuing liaison and collaboration between staff from the old and the new placement (so that, for example, aberrant behaviour is not mistakenly assumed to be habitual). And it calls for the involvement of families.

The involvement of families

The part families should play in relocation decisions and in the process of moving is a question of policy and practice that must be confronted seriously and not fudged. Ultimately, as our study suggests, the answer may affect how well individuals adjust to any move and the outcome of the new placement. Here we explore some of the reasons why it is important to involve parents or other relatives in all stages of the relocation process, and highlight some of the dangers of not doing so, using evidence from our own research.

From our lengthy interviews with relatives, it became clear that the majority were alerted to the changes afoot in the pattern of local services long before anything definite happened to involve them personally. The policy of moving people out into the community was being talked about on television, featured in local and national newspapers and rumoured at the hospital. Over half the people we interviewed said that this had been a worrying time for them:

> I began to take an interest in programmes about it and there were some awful tales of people being left to wander the streets.

> It was upsetting – wondering where they would be going, whether they'd like it and whether they'd settle.

> I was bothered they might move her further away.

This phase – when plans are in the air but before they have taken shape – is always a difficult one to handle for all concerned. Officials may feel the need to tread warily through the myriad of interests involved, aware that a false step might lead to all kinds of trouble – from staff unrest and union problems to neighbourhood opposition, inter-agency conflict and the closing of options by political gamesmanship. Perhaps not surprisingly their instincts might be to keep things under wraps until the details have been sorted out before going public.

For relatives, on the other hand, the uncertainty induced by such secretiveness is likely to breed only insecurity and anxiety. The inevitability of leaks and the efficiency of the rumour-machine ensure the word will soon get around that changes are in the pipeline. Misinformation, half-truths and guesswork will quickly fill the vacuum. The real danger is that concerned relatives will align themselves on the basis of their inadequate knowledge in anticipation of a worst-case scenario. In the short term such a stance may produce needless stress and worry and foster a lack of trust in the professionals making the decisions. In the longer term, as we shall show, such attitudes can influence how successfully the new placement works out.

There is probably no way of completely avoiding these problems. At this early stage in the relocation process, the concerns of officials and relatives inevitably seem to pull in different directions. Nevertheless, there is a strong case for proceeding in a manner that is likely to minimize worry and misunderstandings. The essential ingredients of such an approach are active consultation, direct personal contact and straight-dealing. This calls for a deliberate and well thought-out policy on the involvement of relatives with procedures to match.

The evidence from our study suggests that such an agenda was lacking. Instead, things were handled in a piecemeal and haphazard way case by case. Accordingly, families' reports of how and when they were told about the decision to move their relative varied widely, as did their feelings about the experience. Some families were formally told many months before the move was scheduled to take place; others received no formal notification of any kind. Of those we interviewed (excluding two cases with insufficient data), 10 recall having had a letter informing them of the impending move and most of these then received a follow-up visit to discuss the proposed new placement; a further three families also reported being visited at home. Six were told over the telephone by a hospital consultant, a social worker or a member of staff at the hostel where the relative was then living. Two found out from staff on one of their regular, weekly visits.

At the same time, fully eight of our families (five involving parents) said they heard first hand about the transfer from their son, daughter or relative (in a few instances only after they had actually moved). While most of these families were contacted later by the agencies or pursued the matter themselves, three profess to having had no official word at all about the move. Indeed, in two cases our contacting them was their first intimation of what was happening. All the eight cases in this last group involved people who were moving out of hostel accommodation into ordinary housing or independent living schemes.

Indeed, closer analysis of the data points to a marked difference between the involvement of relatives in the process of moving people out of hospital as against moving people out of hostels. When we asked families if they felt they had been consulted about the move (in the sense of having their views listened to or taken into account), over half answered they did not. This crude total, however, masks a more significant finding. Families whose relatives had moved out of hostels were disproportionately represented among those who were dissatisfied. Twice the number of hostel relatives as hospital relatives voiced such concerns, and altogether two-thirds of them expressed some criticisms either about being sidelined or about feeling their opinions did not matter.

> They listened but I don't think they took much notice. The staff said they would be having more meetings to discuss the move but if they have then we haven't been invited.

I think they had already made an assessment and the decision was cut and dried.

Some of the hospital relatives similarly met with attempts to bounce them into going along meekly with professional decisions – sometimes of a heavy-handed kind:

[We were told] that if we didn't agree to Sandra moving to a hostel, then we could take her home for good and they would refuse to take her back.

For the most part, however, there were fewer complaints. Two-thirds of the families said they were happy with how they had been consulted. As one mother told us, 'I think they've been very thorough. They've had meetings where I could ask anything and they've answered everything to my satisfaction.'

The undervaluation of families

The reason why these two groups reported such different experiences calls for explanation. The easy answer is that more effort was put into consulting the relatives of people moving out of hospital because the process was seen as more problematic from an agency perspective. From the perspective of the families themselves, however, the hostel relatives were if anything more concerned about the risks of transfer because of their fears about the loss of supervision and support in more independent types of living accommodation (see Chapter 10). This interpretation suggests that the feelings of dissatisfaction voiced by the relatives of hostel movers arose from an undervaluing of their needs for information and reassurance on the part of professionals.

Our close dealings with the relocation team led us to the view that such an explanation presents an undeservedly negative and over-simple picture. Although correct in its details, it nevertheless casts events in a misleading light. The hostel relatives were given less attention usually not because of some omission but as a consequence of social workers seeking to apply what they saw as principles of good practice.

These principles of good practice were grounded on two basic assumptions: that the hostel movers are adults and should be treated as such, and that in each case the individual mover should be regarded as the client. The upshot of this line of thinking was to exclude the families from the process of decision-making and leave it up to the movers themselves to keep them informed of what was going on. Our research shows that this approach, though well intentioned, is also misguided. Two case studies from our files illustrate the dangers.

Gary Smart is in his late 30s, a founding member of the local People First group. For a long time he had wanted to move out of the local authority hostel where he had lived for a number of years and into a place of his own. He knew he could cope and the hostel staff shared his confidence. When the opportunity of moving into a single flat came up, he grabbed the chance. Any reservations that his parents might have had if their opinions had been sought would not have influenced his decision. It was something he wanted to do for himself and rightly so.

It was some weeks after he had moved into his new flat before his parents found out where he was living. Social services staff had left Gary to tell them himself and he had not done so. The Smarts were angry and deeply upset at being left in the dark. The relationship between Gary and his parents is close but volatile at the best of times; this episode almost caused a permanent rift. When Gary had been living at the hostel he would walk up to his parents' home often twice a week, but following his move he only visited once in two months.

His parents harboured genuine worries about him. Gary had a history of epilepsy and some violence, and the idea of him living alone with minimal supervision caused them real anxiety. Yet they felt they had been excluded altogether from the process of the move. They did not understand how it was now possible for him to cope on his own when in the past they had been led to believe he would always need daily supervision and care. They were also fearful of what might happen to him if things did not work out and where he would live then.

These frustrations spilled over into the Smarts' relations with social services staff where their attitudes had already been coloured by previous disagreements – most recently over the wisdom of allowing Gary to take his cycling proficiency test despite his poor balance, lack of road sense and the possibility of fits.

For a while, communications between Gary and his parents broke down. For Gary especially, this rift was an added strain on top of the pressures of settling into his new home and adapting to his new way of life. The strain brought problems in its wake. He became incontinent, left his bed unchanged for months and stored piles of newspapers in his bedroom.

Over time the relationship between Gary and his parents got back on to an even keel, and he again visits them on a weekly basis. He is now managing quite adequately in his flat. The Smarts, however, remain bitter about their lack of involvement and have rejected subsequent attempts by social services to repair the breach.

Janet Pringle, in her early 40s, had lived with her parents all her life. When her mother died she and her father, by then in his 70s, managed the house together and Janet had a job during the day.

Last year her father suddenly fell seriously ill and was rushed into hospital where he made a slow recovery over a period of four months. Meanwhile Janet was taken into the local hostel and there she found a new freedom and met new friends. When the possibility of moving into a staffed house with some of her friends was offered to her, she decided to go and settled easily and happily.

Back on his feet again, though frailer and prone to lapses of concentration Mr Pringle had to learn to live on his own. When we interviewed him about Janet's move, he told us she was nothing to do with him anymore and was very reluctant to talk about her. He knew very little about her circumstances and understood only that she didn't want to return to him. There was no bitterness in his feelings, only hurt, especially about her not visiting him since leaving the family home a year ago.

The second time we called to see him there had been a sea change. Janet had visited recently and had taken two of her new friends with her. Mr Pringle had been thrilled and eagerly told us how well she had looked with a new hairstyle and bright, fashionable clothes. It looked as though their unhappy estrangement, which only ever came about for want of a go-between, was over.

Why involve families?

These two vignettes show how the failure to ensure that relatives are involved in relocation decisions can bring about a whole series of problems over and above those stemming from the pressures of moving. Broadly speaking, these problems fall into three main categories:

1 Feelings of exclusion, rejection, anxiety, anger and fear on the part of parents and families. As one of our parents said, 'It's the lack of recognition of us that hurts.' Such feelings may simply fester in the lives of these families or foment their opposition to the new placement. Either way they can seep through and affect the trauma of moving for the individual and how well he or she adjusts to the change in environment.
2 Breakdowns in the relationship between families and professionals. When this happens, the individual caught in the middle can be seriously disadvantaged from having no one outside the system, but with a stake in it, to represent their interests or speak up for them.
3 Upsets or severance in the relationship between parents and their (now adult) children or between the wider family and their relative. For people whose family ties often represent the only stable and continuous close, personal relationships they have, or might ever have, in their lives, such an outcome can offset any conceivable gains accruing from their new life-style.

There are positive reasons also for involving families over and above the fact that the risks of not doing so are too great.

Research suggests that family involvement in the relocation process and family approval of the placement are critical factors in successful community integration (Schalock *et al.* 1981). Indeed, the quality of the community support system has been identified as more important to the success of community living schemes than the characteristics of the people who move into them (Heal *et al.* 1978). The family is often a key source of such support.

The family too can help to ease or prevent transition shock. The disruption of familiar social relationships is just one of the triggers that has been suggested may produce an adverse effect on personal adjustment. In this context, families offer stability and continuity; they are a fixed point of reference for movers when everything else around them is in a state of flux. They can provide the emotional security needed to fill the void before new friendships are formed and before new bonds of trust and affection are built up with other residents and staff in the new setting. Moreover, knowing that their families support the move and being able to talk it over with them can help individuals into the right frame of mind.

The reasons for family opposition to community placement are rarely selfish or deliberately obstructive. Usually they are expressions of love and concern (Fairbrother 1983). Parents may feel their son or daughter is being pushed into a situation for which they are not ready. The family may have fears about harassment, intimidation or exploitation. Such qualms can almost always be lessened or allayed when they are addressed directly and when families are drawn into the relocation process early enough for them to feel their views have been taken into account. This cannot be done where the job of informing their family is left to the movers themselves. By then the crucial decisions have all been made and the opportunities shut off for meaningful family involvement. The kind of worries mentioned above have no outlet, and in many cases the chance of teaming up with the family to smooth the passage into the new placement will have been lost.

Relocation and family stress

There are other equally powerful arguments against professionals treating the individual mover as the client to the exclusion of the family in relocation decisions. While the thinking behind this approach may seem to accord with the principle of normalization, it actually masks bad practice by staff.

Leaving the people who are moving to pass on the news conveys three coded messages: that the decision has nothing to do with the families, that their opinions don't matter, and that staff know best. It also puts the movers in an impossible position: having to cope with questions they can't answer or feeling they have upset their parents or facing the brunt of their family's opposition.

There are a host of questions that parents might reasonably want to ask about any transfer. Will their son or daughter be able to manage 'in the community'? Who are the other residents? What will they have to do for themselves? How much staff supervision and support will be available? Will it affect current day care arrangements? What will happen if the placement doesn't work out? What extra responsibilities, if any, does community care place on the family? The movers themselves cannot be expected to answer these questions, and the deference shown by so many families to professionals will inhibit them from pursuing the matter. The onus must be on staff to take the initiative in communicating with families and in creating the opportunities for them to have their say. Equally, the movers cannot be expected to cope with the emotional loading their relocation in the community might hold for their families. Indeed, relocation should be seen as a potential crisis for families. Many will have built up a rationale for why their relative needs a sheltered and protective environment which comes crashing down on his or her moving out (Crine 1986). Some may not believe their relative can possibly manage in a home of their own when before they had been told the only realistic prognosis was a lifetime of dependency. Avis (1978) captures the conundrum for many parents caught between wonderment and confusion that:

> their now-adult child, duly labelled as in need of life-time protection and lacking in judgement, was now granted the status to make such important decisions. The person who was now an adult was viewed as capable of making choices when the family had been assured that theirs was an eternal child.

Stedman (1977a) similarly points out how relocation is often a cause of stress for families. He invokes the notion of 'family undoing' to describe the sometimes painful revisitation of earlier decisions to let their child go which often occurs at this time. In the process old wounds may reopen. Parents in particular might again begin to question whether they did the right thing. Long suppressed feelings of guilt about rejecting their child might be reawakened. Some may experience anger about what they now see as wrongful advice they were given in the past.

Families need help to cope with these emotions and work them through, and the surest way of doing so is by involving them in all stages of the relocation process. Families may also need help in coming to terms with their relative's new status and identity. As our two case studies show, trouble and strife can arise when families fail to understand how their relative's greater independence and new way of life might reshape their routines and the relationship between them. An episode involving the Smarts is worth reporting.

Gary Smart usually called in to see his parents once or often twice a week. After one of his visits he did not show up again for over a week, and his father decided to ring the hostel where he used to live before moving into his own flat to see if he was all right. The Smarts allege they were informed that Gary had been told not to visit them, and if they wanted to know how he was, they should go and see for themselves. (Mr Smart the elder is almost blind and partly paralysed from a stroke.) Some days later Gary rolled up again at his parents' house, only to be told by his father to go away because the hostel staff had instructed him not to visit. Gary was dumbfounded by his father's behaviour. When his mother put him in the picture, Gary explained that he hadn't visited in the past two weeks because he'd had a cold and didn't want to infect his dad. He then became angry too, and told his parents that he'd 'give a piece of my mind to that lot at [the hostel]. They aren't going to tell me when I can visit my dad'.

Subsequent enquiries at the hostel revealed a different story. The Smarts had indeed rung up, but according to the member of staff who'd talked with them, he'd merely said that hostel staff were not in a position to tell Gary when he should visit them, that it was up to him to decide.

This misunderstanding arose mainly because the Smarts had not grasped that their son was now much more his own agent, that the role of hostel staff had changed accordingly, and that, as parents, their expectations too would have to change. Many families – like the Smarts – need themselves to be carefully prepared for the move and to have its implications for them pointed out sensitively.

A strategy for involving families

Three main arguments have been put forward for ensuring that families are fully involved from an early stage in the relocation process:

1 because failure to do so can cause problems for the person who is moving;
2 because families can ease the transition for the movers and assist them in the process of adjustment to their new life;
3 because relocation often places the families themselves under stress.

These points bring to the fore an issue running throughout this discussion; an issue that has long absorbed social workers in many fields of practice. It is perhaps best summed up in the oft repeated question, 'Who is the client?'

In the case of the hostel movers in our study, the agency response was unequivocal: the individual mover is the client. We have set out to show that this approach is too narrowly circumscribed and should be widened to take in the families both as *clients* where they need advice and support concerning the reasons for the move, how it might affect them and any worries they may have; and as *partners* where they can help in preparing their relative for the move and in settling-in afterwards.

The ambiguity of this dual role as clients and partners is more apparent than real. In fact both roles require essentially the same struts: easy access to the professionals managing the move, involvement in the preparation of individual programme plans, and a say in the outcome of case decisions. How might such involvement be ensured?

Our own study families and evidence from the wider research literature (Braddock and Heller 1984; Atkinson and Ward 1987) suggest a number of practical steps or principles:

● *'Before hospitals are shut down they should consult everyone involved rather than just being told.'*
  'Gary told us three or four years ago that some other people were moving. We never heard anything about Gary before he moved.'

The families of likely candidates should be informed in writing of the general plans for relocation, their rationale, the stage reached and the proposed timetable.

- *'They've taken her over now, and we haven't really any say, but I think we should have been asked. We would have liked to know before the decision was made.'*

They should be given an assurance that no decision about the placement of their relative will be made without full consultation with them.

- *'I think parents should be informed more. I sit here worrying and worrying on my own.'*

They should be given the name and telephone number of a contact officer in the Relocation Team who thereafter will act as their personal link with the agency.

- *'After initial contact another year elapsed before I heard anything again. In fact I had to ring [the social worker]. They should keep parents informed more.'*

A home visit should be arranged within a fortnight of first contacting the family.

- *'I would have suggested that I would have liked Robin to have been in some sort of sheltered housing so that if anything happened he could just press a button.'*

The types of placement available and considered suitable should be explained to the family and any options they might put forward should be welcomed.

- *'There should be more involvement and discussion in a group of those affected by the move.'*

Families should be offered the chance of visiting placements similar to those being considered for their relative and, if appropriate, the opportunity of talking with others whose relative has made a similar move.

- *'I think they could let us know sooner and perhaps have regular meetings to discuss how things are going.'*
'I would like to have been involved more while she was being discussed.'

Families should be invited to all programme planning meetings concerning the placement of their relative, which should be arranged to facilitate their attendance.

- *'I think we should have been listened to before the decision was made.'*

While parents or families should not have a veto over the new placement, no decision should be made about relocation without them being given the opportunity to participate. Although conflicts of interest might be expected occasionally, and parents' wishes may sometimes differ from those of their son or daughter, this cannot justify ignoring the parents' views (Conroy 1985). When decisions have to be taken without their approval, the onus is on those concerned to ensure that not taking such a step would do more harm than will be done by flouting the parents' wishes (Fairbrother 1983).

- *'Nobody has really let me know that she's moved. In fact on the 4th July I rang to say I wouldn't be coming to see Amy because I would be going to a wedding [and] then they told me she wasn't there. They hadn't let me know.'*

Irrespective of whether they attended the placement meeting, families should be formally notified by letter of the move and when it is to take place without delay.

- *'I think they should have let us know, let us look around his new flat.'*

  Families should be encouraged and helped to visit the new placement before the move, to meet the staff (if any) who will be working there and any other residents – where possible with their relative.

- *'There was a meeting at [the hostel] and it was then that they told me. There was going to be another meeting but it never happened. I had a letter to say they were moving on the Thursday and Deidre rang me on the Wednesday to say they were in.'*

  Families should be enabled to attend the actual transfer if they and their relative wish.

- *'There should be more contact at every stage with parents. They want to know what's happening to their children.'*

  Where appropriate during the settling-in period, arrangements should be made for families with transport problems to visit their relative and vice versa.

- *'I think they ought to keep in touch with relatives. We want to show our appreciation.'*

  A home visit should be arranged by the family's contact officer within six weeks after the move to discuss any problems, anxieties or queries.

- *'I rang to speak to the Officer-in-Charge [at the hostel] about the plans and there was a case conference regarding Guy's move – but they wouldn't have included me if I hadn't phoned.'*

  A full review should be held in each case not more than six weeks after the move to which the family should be invited. Where no one can attend, a home visit should be arranged by the contact officer to report on and explain the outcome.

Even following these steps it is unlikely that all friction between professionals and families will be avoided or that the fundamental asymmetry in their relationship (Gliedman and Roth 1981) can be corrected and overcome. Families who have learned over the years to live with the barriers erected against them by institutional practices may take a while to gain confidence in a more open, sharing type of approach. At some time in the past most will have been let down, misinformed or excluded. Such experiences may understandably lead them to take a very sceptical view of agency intentions, the promises of professionals, or their readiness to deliver. The practical steps outlined above may not go all the way towards surmounting the backlog of poor communications, but at least they would show a measure of good faith.

4

Handling the move

We have talked about the situation before the move and how things were after it, yet so far have said little about how people got from one place to another. It is reasonable to assume that people's experiences during the move will be important in forming their early perceptions of their new placements. The degree of sensitivity and understanding shown by staff may well be crucial in helping them to adapt and in mitigating the inevitable stresses associated with such an upheaval.

However, many aspects of the *process* of relocation have been entirely ignored in the literature. Perhaps the issues are thought to be self-evident, but they certainly did not seem that way to the staff in Kirklees. There were frequent references to being 'thrown in at the deep end', and with no obvious models to follow each establishment tended to evolve its own way of doing things. In many ways it is easier to focus on measuring outcomes and ignore the processes in between. From the initial preparation, through the physical move, and extending into the settling-in period, there are all kinds of subtle, interrelated influences that might be critical. However, an exclusive focus on outcomes is of limited help to others looking to implement a similar move; they will want to know how things were *done*. The limitations of our research design mean that we cannot clearly and systematically link the events with particular outcomes. However, during the considerable formal and (particularly in this case) informal involvement in Kirklees, we were able to observe and discuss many of the issues that arose and the strategies that were adopted. Although we cannot definitely say which worked and which did not, we can at least throw some light on the topic and make some tentative suggestions for good practice.

Selection for the move

For most people, the first brush with the idea of the move came as the agencies started to select candidates for the new services. Most of the people who eventually moved out of the hostels had already been identified by the time we began the research. Attempts to establish what criteria were used revealed a variety of approaches. At least one hostel claimed to have started by holding a meeting with all their residents and establishing, regardless of ability, who liked the idea of moving into a house in the community. In other hostels various pragmatic combinations of ability and compatibility were used. For example, the redecoration of one hostel had led to four residents being temporarily established in a training flat. When it was found that the four got on well together, they were nominated as candidates for a move, even though at the time there were many doubters as to whether one member of the foursome would manage. Many of the hostel movers had lived together in small groups prior to the move and so knew each other well.

To their credit some hostels did not put pressure on people who did not like the idea of moving. One woman in particular, although an obvious candidate for a move to a more independent life (being extremely able), had made it clear she wanted to remain where she was. Eventually, having seen what life was like for those who did make the break, she became an enthusiastic convert to the idea and is now looking for someone with whom to share a house. Although ability was still an important factor in determining who moved, both the desire to try a new life and existing relationships certainly played their part.

The situation was very different for the hospital movers. With a much larger population spread out over many hospital wards, the process was perhaps inevitably more bureaucratic. A small team of health and social services staff identified a total of 100 of the least dependent people through discussion with the hospital consultants. They tended to eliminate the most behaviourally disturbed or multiply handicapped people. A short assessment schedule was then developed, briefly touching on topics like paramedical services used, mobility, incontinence, behaviour problems, communication skills, medical history, basic self-help and domestic skills, etc. At this stage the kinds of provision that would be available were not at all clear, and the intention was simply to screen the population for 50 of the least problematic people for possible inclusion in a pilot project. An internal report on this exercise made it clear that this was meant to be just the first step.

> The Preliminary Assessments provide a general indication of the services the residents will require. Detailed case planning cannot be carried out from the Preliminary Assessments, and case conferences are strongly recommended.'
>
> (Unpublished report, Kirklees 1985)

In the event things did not happen this way. As we have already indicated, when the proposal hardened up, the various pressures resulted in plans that meant all those leaving hospital were destined for a place in a social services hostel. Those people who had come through the screening process were considered the official candidates for community care. From these lists the health authorities were asked to nominate people for inclusion in the first phase of the developments.

A series of case conferences was held, but this was intended to assess whether the individual would fit one of the available hostel places rather than to develop plans for the services that each would require. The main criterion appeared to be based on a straightforward judgement of whether the individual would present any problems. For example, since the hostels did not at this stage have waking night staff, anyone able to get up and wander in the night was rejected.

The report on the preliminary assessments suggested there were at least 15 people with friends who came from other Districts or who had not been assessed. In at least one instance, due to the prompting of the hospital staff, plans were adapted to take into account the friendship between two movers. However, the system of filtering people through these selection phases resulted in them being seen very much in isolation, without much weight being given to their existing relationships. By default it was assumed that there were no friendships unless demonstrated otherwise. Unlike the situation with the hostel movers, whether people wanted to move was not an acknowledged criterion for selection. Indeed, by administrative accident (the health authorities were not sure who was responsible for him) one able man who very much wanted to leave hospital was left off the lists until a hospital manager drew attention to his situation.

Individual planning

Currently there is great interest in the use of Individual Programme Plans (IPPs) as a mechanism for ensuring that services are focused on, and geared to, the requirements of each particular service user. They have been described as the 'cornerstone' in ensuring high quality services (Ward 1986). Descriptions of an ideal system vary slightly depending on the version used (see for example Blunden 1988 or Jenkins *et al.* 1982), but all have a number of features in common. At their heart is the concern to provide opportunities for users to make meaningful choices, along with a focus on growth and development and the coherent, coordinated delivery of services. Central to these systems is the meeting at which the main decisions are made. Typically an IPP meeting would be attended by the user, their relatives and/or an advocate, as well as direct care staff and managers. Opportunities should be provided for the user and their family to participate in the meeting as much as possible, and negative judgements about the user should be avoided.

During the study we attended more than 50 case conferences, case reviews and IPP meetings. In general, few of those we attended conformed to the outline given above. The small minority that did mostly occurred later on in the project when staff had undergone some training in the principles underlying IPPs and had some experience of the new services. Relatives were absent from nearly all the meetings we attended and the users themselves, even when present, were rarely invited or enabled to contribute to the proceedings.

This was particularly apparent with a number of the case conferences held to assess the suitability of people living in hospital for the move to a hostel. Here, typically eight or nine professionals (plus a researcher) would be present. There would be no preamble, introductions or explanation of the purpose of the exercise. The meeting would begin with the consultant reading out details from the hospital case file, often stretching back many years. Negative judgements often expressed in the pejorative terminology of 20 years ago were recounted out of context and without comment. The purpose of this seemed to be to identify potential problems that might occur, but the effect was to produce a continuous string of people's worst moments. The subject of the meeting would be called in for a short while and interrogated by the consultant. It was always clear that their presence was more about a chance for the assembled professionals to view the person in question than for the person to give their views or participate in the meeting. There were few references to the issue of relationships or to the feelings of relatives (who invariably were not present). Not all those attending these meetings were happy with this process. However, in the absence of any agreed format for individual planning, they felt they had to accept the compromise and participate.

IPP systems are often seen as a potentially powerful mechanism for initiating change. Almost all new projects in the field of service provision for people with learning difficulties now claim to be based on individual plans and Kirklees was no exception. However, where genuinely partici-pative, individually based work arose, it was usually as a *consequence* of better quality services rather than a catalyst in their development. This point echoes the findings of Laws *et al.* (1988), who concluded it was much harder to implement an IPP system in a hospital than anticipated.

The decision to move

The majority of the movers were asked if they wanted to move at some point in the proceedings. However, the extent to which each individual could genuinely be said to have been involved in making the decision varied immensely. As we show in the chapters dealing with movers' views, there was a small minority of people who indicated to us they did not want to move, and there were doubtless others who, although quite happy, simply fell in with the plans made for them.

This is a complex issue and it is worth disentangling some of the strands. For example, there was a tendency to see agreement to move as a one-off act. Having accepted the *idea* of moving, a number of people, particularly those in hospital, were swept along on a conveyer belt of events. Having set off, only those with the self-confidence to assert themselves forcibly stood much chance of switching lines or jumping off altogether. In a number of cases no attempt (formal or informal) was made to check that the mover was still happy with the proceedings. There was an assumption that since the movers were not voicing concerns, things must still be all right. In fact it is unlikely that many of the movers would *spontaneously* express reservations, except possibly to people they knew and trusted. The onus should be on those organizing the move to ensure that there are opportunities for people's feelings to be monitored throughout the process. People must have the opportunity to change their minds, particularly when they have had some experience of the new placement, for example after they have spent day or weekend preparatory visits.

There is a clear difference between agreeing to a move *in principle* and being willing to go to a *particular* placement. Certainly almost all the movers in Kirklees had some kind of chance to find out what life would be like in their new home. However, there was a marked divergence between the experience of the hospital and hostel groups.

Most hospital movers were going to existing establishments. Usually they, and a member of staff from the hospital, would initially visit the hostel for tea. This would be followed by a programme of overnight stays, weekend visits, often leading up to an extended period of a week or more. By and large these were positive developments, a chance for both the mover and the hostel to see how things might work out. However, there were some staff who had reservations. In particular, the keyworkers of two of the more profoundly handicapped younger people felt that the long drawn out introductory period had been counterproductive, that the movers involved had shown marked signs of being very unsettled both during and on their return from each visit. It was said on a number of occasions that people 'don't like change' and that it would have been better to have moved quickly, allowing them to settle down sooner.

At the same time they were also said to enjoy immensely and respond positively to the experience of going on holiday. This seems a paradox, since this would have involved equally significant changes of environment. It gives us a clue that some kinds of changes are more disturbing than others. What is the difference between a week's stay in a hostel and a week in a holiday camp? In the latter case there would have been continuity in the staff involved. There were a number of proposals to allow staff from the hospital to move across temporarily with movers, but under the pressure of maintaining the staffing levels in hospital, this proved impossible to organize. If the intention is to minimize the stress of a move by providing a gradual transition between settings (particularly for people who may have difficulty understanding the changes), much more thought needs to be put into maintaining continuity amongst staff.

Because those leaving the hostels were not moving to established units, a wide range of new possibilities arose. As soon as a likely house was identified, the potential movers were taken to view it in its uncleaned, undecorated state. Many of the movers were then involved in a whole variety of tasks from cleaning through to stripping wallpaper and painting, giving them a chance to see and understand the process of preparing the house. There were many opportunities to participate in all kinds of decisions about their future lives: choosing the wallpaper and colour schemes, deciding how the house would be organized, even helping to choose and order all furniture and fittings. This was always a time of great excitement. Gradually people could see an abstract idea take concrete shape in a way which allowed them at least some degree of control.

Inevitably there were hiccups. There were a series of running battles between administrative staff (who wanted to control the budget) and care staff (who wanted to maximize the choice for the movers). One particular incident illustrates the different perspectives. The local authority had a discount arrangement with the Co-op necessitating the use of special order forms rather than cash. One group of residents went on a massive shopping expedition in the local Co-op department store, along with their key-worker and someone from the administrative section. They chose a whole range of equipment from beds to saucepans, including an attractive set of crockery. However, several weeks later, when they were unpacking in order to make their first cup of tea in their new home, they were somewhat bemused to find a different set of teacups to the one they had chosen. It turned out that there had been some problem with the order, and so the woman from administration had 'nipped out' and 'got something similar'.

A small point perhaps, but it did lead to some confusion on the part of the movers and similar problems cropped up regularly. Many staff argued that if they had simply been given a fixed budget within which to operate without restriction, they would have been able to maximize the extent to which movers could have determined their own lifestyles, rather than end up with the rather bland 'new three piece suite style', as one person put it. It was not that the administrative staff did not mean well. They were particularly concerned that everything supplied was good quality and reliable, since it was not clear who was going to provide replacements in the years to come. However, setting up a home for a small number of individuals is a different kind of process to equipping a large institution. Opportunities to make choices should not be lost for the sake of things being a little more organized.

The issue of participation did not stop with the physical environment. A number of the hostel movers, for example, were offered adult education opportunities focused as much as possible on their particular interests. Gardening and bricklaying were two of the topics chosen, and indeed one house now boasts a brick barbecue in a well-tended garden. All these points serve as a reminder that the involvement in the decision to move, while important, is just one of many steps in involving users fully in planning their lives.

Those people who had the most opportunity to express choices tended to be the most able or those with the best communication skills. While it is understandably difficult to establish whether someone who has problems in communicating or answering direct questions is capable of making an informed choice, there was a clear tendency to underestimate the extent that people could participate if offered the chance *on their terms*. Some ingenuity and commitment on the part of staff are required. Being asked formal questions in front of strangers in an inquistional-style meeting is not the best way to establish someone's true feelings, regardless of whether they can speak or not. Felce *et al.* (1987) advocate working through a hierarchy of approaches to establish preferences until the most suitable method is found:

> People can be asked what they want; they can be shown pictures or models to augment the explanation; they can be asked several times to check the consistency of their preferences; they can be given samples of the choices available and then asked which they prefer; or they can be given both choices for as long as it takes until they either indicate a preference or staff notice a clear preference from their behaviour. In the last resort, representatives such as advocates can be used to make a proxy decision.

Giving people a choice also implies being prepared to respect their decision, even if it might prove to be the wrong one. We all learn best through our own mistakes. At the same time, mistakes do not have to be catastrophes. Expressing preferences and making decisions are skills that can be learnt, and are best acquired with support and encouragement.

Preparation for the move

One of the other strengths of the way the moves out of the hostels were organized was the fact that the staff involved in setting up the houses were already known and familiar to the movers. Even where new staff were appointed, there were chances for them to get to know the movers in the hostel before the moves were made. This had two main advantages. First, staff had a good idea of what was going on, and some kind of vision of what life would be like in the house. They were able to answer people's questions and provide assurance where necessary. Second, it meant there was usually someone known and trusted by the movers with whom they could talk through all these changes.

When we asked if people had been prepared for the move, all but one of the hostel movers' keyworkers reported having discussed the move in detail:

> The emotional side was carefully monitored. . . . Things have been very positive but we would have picked up any hesitation. We have made definite efforts to make sure more was understood.

> We regularly used to discuss the move as a group – about getting on with each other, and being able to talk about problems when they arise. They went to see it [the house] before deciding to go, and they were asked what they thought of it.

This was true of just seven of the hospital movers:

> Yes, I have talked to her about the move. Discuss any problems. We talk over her visits, what she likes and dislikes. For example, she was a bit scared of being on her own in the bedroom. We discussed whether she wants to go.

It is not immediately clear why hospital staff were so much less likely to have talked over the issues with the movers. One possible explanation may lie in the fact that they were much less involved in organizing the moves, with the hostel staff making most of the running. Many of the hospital staff acknowledged frankly that they had little idea of what the hostels would be like and found it difficult to answer questions from movers. There is a sense of events being outside their control:

> [The hostel] took her a few times and she went for an overnight stay and then she was gone within a fortnight.

In the circumstances many did the best they could:

> When he visits the hostel I involve him in getting the case ready – not just packing him off.

Another factor working against the hospital staff was that many had not been working with the movers long enough to really get to know them. Since most people had been in hospital for a number of years, this conundrum needs some explaining. The answer lies in the fact that movement *within* the hospital was common. As larger numbers began to leave, the remaining population was regularly reorganized, allowing wards to be closed and facilitating the optimal use of resources. Six of the potential hospital movers alone came from a villa which had only opened in the previous November. Many of the staff there had never previously worked with this group of individuals.

Familiarity can be a two-edged sword. It can easily lead to a kind of blindness where staff fail to see beyond the limitations imposed on people by their particular environment. They cease to question why this person lacks teeth, why that individual has stopped developing. Nevertheless, many of the real success stories in Kirklees involved situations where staff had some special empathy derived from insight into the mover's background and experience.

There was the example of Jenny whose career in hospital had consisted of an unremitting series of outbursts of difficult and aggressive behaviour. She moved to a hostel where the officer-in-charge took a particular interest in her case. His wife had worked in the hospital a number of years previously and had always felt that Jenny had got a raw deal. In her new home, care was taken not to put pressure on her and to give her time to adjust. The hostel has never had any of the problems recorded in hospital. There was a hiccup when Jenny first started going to the Social Education Centre (SEC). Here she was expected to conform quickly to the patterns and routines. Within a few days she was banned from attending, the SEC staff describing her as 'murderous'. The hostel staff felt the situation had been completely mishandled and insisted on Jenny being slowly eased back in. At first she went for just short periods and was always accompanied by her keyworker. Jenny now goes to the SEC full-time without problems. Throughout there was an understanding of how the services had failed Jenny in the past and a determination to put things right. Her difficult behaviour was not seen just simply as a problem to be contained, but an indication of feelings Jenny was otherwise unable to express.

It is impossible to legislate for empathy. However, there are things that can be done to promote its development. Assessment should arguably be less about determining whether people can boil a kettle than about gaining a sense of the person as a whole, as someone with a history and a set of experiences that will be important in determining how they react to new challenges. The *Getting to Know You Process* (Brost *et al.* 1982) is one example of a format that is less concerned with technical performance than developing the basis of a relationship between staff and user. Another strategy would be the use of life-story books (Frost and Taylor 1986) to try and put the person in some sort of context in which they themselves have a major input.

Despite the assessment procedures used in Kirklees, there was an almost universal complaint from staff in the new placements that the information travelling across with the movers was inadequate. A closer examination of these situations showed that a number of factors were working here. For example:

- *There were situations where important information was not passed on.*
  Staff in one hostel noted that Jenny appeared to have lost contact with

her father. In one of the rare examples where relocation was seen as an opportunity for rebuilding bridges between the movers and their families, they started to try to contact him. They were shocked when they subsequently discovered that there was a care order in force, for Jenny's protection, preventing her father from seeing her. We should add that the same set of events reoccurred much later on when Jenny moved on from the hostel into a voluntary sector placement.

- *There were situations where the information was sent on, but either the file was not read or the significance of the information was not realized.*
  Deidre occasionally experiences bouts of a very severe form of epilepsy known as status epilepticus: a series of grand mal attacks following immediately after one another which can be fatal unless intravenous medication is quickly provided. Indeed, her parents had already lost one child from the same condition. Although the staff at the hostel where Deidre moved were aware that she suffered badly from epilepsy, they were unprepared for these complications. Thus when Deidre had nearly 60 seizures in 24 hours, they failed to realize the seriousness of the situation and omitted to call in medical help as soon as they should have done. As a result she ended up at the local District General Hospital where fortunately she received the treatment she needed. The information that Deidre was liable to go into status was in the file that was sent to the hostel.

- *There were situations where the complaints seemed to reflect a difference in perspective between placements, rather than a failure to provide information.*
  One woman, Gemma Molloy, returned to hospital quite soon after the move to the hostel. In the 'post-mortem' held to determine the reasons for the failure, the hostel staff intimated that the hospital nurses had overstated Gemma's skills, making her appear more able than they had found her to be. In particular, hostel staff said they had been told that Gemma could 'do everything' for herself. While there is some confusion over precisely what skills they thought Gemma lacked – it was apparent that while she was capable of some tasks she would often refuse to do them – it is true that hostel living placed rather more demands on its residents than did Gemma's original hospital ward. In the latter she would have had no access to the kitchen, and so no experience of preparing food or drinks, or of washing up. In this context, doing 'everything' for herself would mainly be about eating, dressing and personal hygiene. The complaints of the hostel staff highlight the fact that a brief nursing report completed in one environment may not adequately predict how a person will manage in a different context.

Some of the complaints about inadequate information seem justified, but others reflect an overly passive attitude towards getting to know the movers. There is an argument that the information transferred with people should be minimal and should not include judgemental or impressionistic material; the move should be a chance to wipe the slate clean and for people to escape their reputations and some of the limitations of their past. Almost inevitably, though, attitudes to people leak between placements. It is therefore doubly important that any assessment is not just of the person but of their original environment (in its widest sense) as well. Understanding how services have – or more probably have not – met people's needs in the past is a crucial part of understanding how they may react in the future. It is never enough to rely on the face value of information from files or reports. Assessment has to be an *active* information gathering process drawing on as many sources as possible. Having a checklist, no matter how comprehensive, cannot cover all circumstances. The aim should be to build up a rounded picture of the person so that, even if they are not liked, they can be treated with empathy and understanding.

While the preparation of people emotionally has largely been ignored in the literature, the issue of training for a move has been the focus of much attention. At times this borders on the bizarre. For example, Staite and Torpy (1983) have described situations in which success in a 'simulated' post-move set-up was used as a method of weeding out 'unsuitable' candidates. Similarly, Kerr (1982) describes how users had to move to a separate unit over 60 miles away to get their 'pre-move' training. In each of these situations the pre-relocation period would have been characterized by change and uncertainty, simply adding barriers for the potential movers to leap over.

Fortunately, nothing of this kind occurred in Kirklees. Two-thirds of the hostel movers were said to be involved in training programmes specifically designed to help with the move. These mostly consisted of simply having the opportunity to start doing some of the things they would later do in their new homes whilst still in the hostel. For example, some were given their own pension books and started to cash their own benefits and pay rent. Others started to shop for their own food at the local supermarket.

In contrast, only three of the hospital movers were involved in training specifically for the move. All of these three lived in what was notionally described as the hospital pre-discharge unit. Actually a move into this unit was not a condition of leaving hospital, nor did all those living in it necessarily move on. It differed from the other villas in that, being converted nursing staff accommodation, it was much more domestic in design and scale. Its occupants lived in groups of five, each with their own kitchen, lounge and dining room. Here it was possible to try out new skills like cooking or making a drink. In almost all of the other hospital villas, such opportunities simply did not exist.

The move itself

> I mean it's a big change. It's a big change from here. I shall miss them
> down here, going out.

Many of the movers were aware of the magnitude of the changes facing
them, yet for some of those leaving hospital the actual move passed off
almost without notice, with little official attention being given to the
significance of what was happening for the individuals involved. One
afternoon (determined by someone else) they would simply be told not to
go to occupational therapy, their few belongings would be packed up by a
nursing assistant, and they would wait until somebody from the hostel
came to collect them. Since many did not have suitcases, they would sit
patiently surrounded by a few black plastic bags. Life in the hospital would
carry on as though nothing special was happening.

For others, staff recognized that this was an event of importance. They
went to great lengths to organize leaving parties, would give the movers
mementoes of their time in hospital and would make sure they were there
to say goodbye. The leaving parties were often emotional affairs ('I feel full
up – choked') with their own rituals of presentations and hugs. Here the
movers were being treated as human beings and not simply objects in an
administrative exercise. Above all they increased the sense of the move
being a positive event to be *celebrated*.

By and large a similar pattern of events occurred for the hostel movers,
with the added opportunities for housewarming parties in the new home.
However, there were a number of problems. In one house the moving date
was suddenly brought forward by two days when the administrative staff
objected to a fully equipped home being left empty. In another instance
one keyworker was greatly upset by an intervention from the same source
which pre-empted her carefully laid plans.

> I came back from holiday and found that [a member of the adminis-
> trative staff] had moved him – no party, no card. He didn't know her at
> all.

In another house the suppliers failed to deliver the cooker on the appointed
day. This crisis was faced with equanimity by one of the movers.

> She was the most philosophical about it all. When the cooker didn't
> arrive and all around were panicking, it was Mary that said let's go and
> get some fish and chips.

This was an instance where a practical problem proved to be less of a
disaster than expected. While logistical issues are important, there is a
danger in giving them priority over the feelings of the movers.

Settling-in

For the most part, staff did not see settling-in and adjusting to the new environments as much of an issue. By the first of the post-move interviews, 17 out of the 45 movers were said to have adapted very quickly, with all but six of the rest judged to have fitted in after just a few initial problems. Yet, as we have shown, the issue of negative reactions to the stress of moving – transition shock – was more prevalent than we had expected.

For just under a quarter of the movers (11 out of 45) staff were unable to identify anything that had been done specifically to help the mover settle in. Often the suggestion seemed to be that something special only had to be done in response to a 'problem'.

> If he wanted something, or needed help, he is the kind of person that would come and ask, he wouldn't just sit there.

However, in other cases staff showed great ingenuity and insight in developing strategies to help movers feel at home, some of them obviously very carefully thought out. A number of themes emerged.

High on many people's list of priorities was ensuring that the movers had their personal possessions around them.

> She has some pictures and ornaments in her room. She has a blue and white rabbit her mother gave her and it seems to calm her down.

There has to be a word of caution here. There was no problem with certain kinds of possessions, but other things tended to get dismissed as worthless.

> A lot of it was pure rubbish – sweet wrappings, the lot. It looked as if the drawers had just been emptied into black plastic bin bags.

Soon after one move we encountered a hospital mover who was highly indignant because some of the old clothes he had brought with him had been thrown away.

There were a number of attempts to provide additional reassurance. In one house staff slept on a mattress on the lounge floor on a temporary basis because one of the movers had been convinced she would not be able to manage if there were no staff there at night. The staff were immensely pleased when the woman herself decided it was no longer necessary.

There were often attempts to develop a special relationship with the mover.

> I spent a lot of time with him in the evenings when I knew he would be feeling vulnerable.
>
> I would go out of my way to spend time with her. I changed my rota to fit in with her visits. I wanted there to be a familiar face.

Some staff reported that they simply tried to make the mover feel welcome by paying them extra attention, 'finding out what they like or don't like' and making 'a great fuss of them the whole time'.

Similarly there was sometimes a conscious decision not to put pressure on the person and give them space to adjust, perhaps taking time out to walk around the local area to help them become familiar or simply to see what it was like. In some circumstances, individuals were allowed to continue their old routines and practices in their new home, and for a few there was a decision to avoid imposing too many changes at once. For example, not everybody who moved from hospital immediately took up a place at an SEC. In many cases this was because of a shortage of places, but there were instances where it was done that way to allow the mover to settle into the hostel first.

In only the odd instance were relatives involved (for example, in helping a person unpack). Staff professed not to understand why this sort of thing did not happen more often ('I think his mum could have come up when he first moved here to look around. I think he would have liked that'), although this issue is obviously bound up with the broader failure to involve families in the relocation process discussed in Chapter 3.

Guidelines for practice

As we indicated earlier, it is impossible for us to identify any particular strategy as the most successful or the most effective. Nevertheless, on the basis of our evaluation of the experiences of people in Kirklees, a number of observations may be made which together comprise a checklist of precepts or guidelines for others planning a similar relocation programme.

First steps

The first points are not directed at the movers but those organizing the move. Before anything can be done, a number of questions have to be resolved. These relate to:

Vision
Why are the changes happening? If it is to improve people's quality of life, then be prepared to say how this will happen. Go out and sell the ideas, not just to the movers, but to staff and families. Be prepared to give people a picture of what life might be like.

Strategic thinking
Do not just react but have a coherent strategy. Work out and agree beforehand mechanisms like Individual Planning and case conferences. Unless there is an urgent need to rescue someone from a desperate situation, the likely aim is to provide a gradual step-by-step transition.

What does this imply? In particular, will there be a need for staff to move with the people to provide that extra degree of continuity? Could friends and family be involved to help ease the change?

Selection/planning

Who wants to move?

There is a good argument for starting with people who want to move. It may be tempting to begin with people who look 'easy' to move, but motivation may well be just as important as ability or the absence of difficult behaviour.

Get to know people

Use tools like life-story books to get to know people. Assessment must go beyond a tick-list of skills. Aim to develop an understanding of the person and their experiences. What do they want out of life? This is easiest if the individual concerned is involved. Recruit people they know and trust – do not leave them marginalized.

Friendships

Start with the assumption that people have important friendships unless demonstrated otherwise. Do not simply take the staff view of who is friends with whom – ask users and relatives as well. Make group compatibility a central issue, and where people have not lived together before, give them a chance to spend time together in a variety of settings beforehand.

Individual planning

Establish what kind of individual planning mechanisms are to be used. As a minimum, both the users and their families should be invited for the whole of the meeting and encouraged to take part. A meeting is more likely to work when people are introduced to each other and have some idea of what the meeting is for and what is expected of them.

Choice

It goes without saying that people should be asked if they want to move. Do not do it formally in a meeting or in the office. Minimize the pressures on people. The initial approach should be by someone known to them, and done in a relaxed, informal way. Finding out people's thoughts on the subject should be part of the *preparation* for the meeting.

Give people a chance to change their minds

Do not just assume people are still happy about the move; actively check out their feelings regularly. Make sure these feelings are fed back into the planning process. There are plenty of opportunities for reversing decisions which seem not to be working out as planned. Do not regard having to do so as a failure.

People who cannot communicate their feelings
There are none. There may be people who cannot articulate their views in the conventional way. In this case use a number of strategies. Find out how the individual indicates pleasure/stress behaviourally and monitor them in the different placements. Take care to provide continuity of carers and make a particular effort to involve advocates.

Experience
Do not expect people to commit themselves until they have sufficient experience of the new placement. To make an informed choice they must have a good idea of what everyday life will be like. As a minimum, arrange a series of visits, including longer stays. Ensure the people themselves have some control over this process and are not passed backwards and forwards like a parcel.

Participation in establishing the new placements
The best way to develop understanding of what a home will be like is for people to be involved in its creation, either through choosing materials or doing some of the work. The opportunities are only limited by people's ingenuity. As a minimum, think about the following areas: decoration, furnishings, equipment, choice of rooms and house rules (or lack of them). Make sure that priority is given to the principles of choice over administrative considerations.

The pace of change
Moving at the user's 'own pace' is a good principle but tends to get pre-empted by all kinds of pressures. Be clear on how you will decide the person is ready to move.

The move

Packing up
Make sure the mover is involved in packing their things and that they and their belongings are treated with respect. Do not just empty drawers into a few bin bags.

Rights of passage
If the move is a step in the right direction, then celebrate it. If it is not, then why is it happening? Organize leaving parties, provide mementoes and make sure everyone is on hand to say goodbye. Do not let people simply disappear as though they never existed.

Involve friends and family in the move
A familiar face to people at the end of the journey can help a lot.

Settling-in

Recognize the stresses of moving

Moving home almost always brings its own stresses, particularly when someone has been living in the previous home for many years. Recognizing this and accepting that people may need some extra help to adjust is the first step.

Possessions

As soon as possible establish people with their own possessions around them. Make it a golden rule that nothing they bring with them is discarded or thrown away unless the mover approves, no matter how apparently worthless the object.

Avoid pressures to conform

Do not expect people to fit in instantly with a strange set of routines and rules. As much as possible let people do things in their own ways. Do not be dismissive of what is often described as 'institutional behaviour'. Doing things in the way they used to do before may well be a source of security.

Excessive change

Do not pile change on change unless the person involved is lapping it up. To move to a new home and a new day centre at the same time may be too much. Delaying the start at the latter will give people more space and may well allow for extra individual attention during the day.

Orientation

Show people around. Not just the unit but the local area. Introduce them to people. Help them find out what kind of place they have moved to.

Reassurance

From time to time people will need additional reassurance. Do not dismiss their fears. In many instances lack of confidence rather than lack of ability is the disabler. Be aware of periods when they will be vulnerable, and try to ensure someone sympathetic will be on hand.

Keep contacts with previous placement

Give people opportunities to keep in contact with their old friends, if that is what they wish, either by visits, telephone calls or letters.

Ultimately the success of relocation will be determined by a whole combination of factors. On the way there probably have to be many compromises and fudges. However, in many ways the key to the process is empathy and commitment to the person moving. The object of the exercise has to be to adjust the environment as much as possible to the individual, and not the other way around.

5

New homes for old?

Deinstitutionalization involves more than just moving people out of long-stay hospitals. Properly speaking, it describes not merely a change in *where* people live (a process we call relocation) but also a change in their *way of life*. The importance of recognizing these twin aspects of change is illustrated by experience in the United States where many patients discharged from large state hospitals have been rehoused in nursing homes and board-and-care homes containing upwards of 100 beds (Scull 1985). Although often referred to as 'community facilities', these places in fact display most of the characteristics of the full-blown institution with locked doors, inflexible routines, lack of personal space and loss of individuality. Instead of liberating people from the corrosive effects of institutional living, some critics maintain they have served only to extend the institution into the community in a process more akin to one of decentralization than deinstitutionalization. Others have contended that the process might more accurately be described as one of 'transinstitutionalization', meaning simply the movement of people from one institutional setting to another (Morrisey and Goldman 1981). Unless relocation brings about a fundamental change in the essential characteristics of people's living conditions, it creates only the illusion of deinstitutionalization (Halpern *et al.* 1978).

Viewed in this light, deinstitutionalization takes on a more complex hue. At one and the same time it may be seen as:

- a *policy* geared towards the run-down or closure of large institutions, the prevention of admissions and the rehabilitation of former residents in settings responsive to their individual needs (Vitello 1986);
- a *philosophy* emphasizing the variety of needs among people with learning difficulties, their right to individual treatment, their value as individuals, their rights as citizens and the importance of integration as a guiding principle in the planning of services (Lerman 1985);
- a *process* leading to a shift in human and financial resources from

institutionally based services to community support systems and the movement of people from larger to smaller living units, from more to less structured and restrictive environments, from dependent to independent living situations, and from segregated to integrated facilities (US Comptroller General 1977);
- *practices* which promote autonomy and personal development, minimize the care-induced aspects of dependency and help to create a responsive living environment.

Over and above these four meanings, deinstitutionalization may also be conceived in more everyday terms as a *frame of mind* (Stedman 1977a) calling for changes in long-held attitudes and notions on the part of parents and professionals (Avis 1978), a reappraisal of old fears and deeply rooted prejudices by the wider public, and a new set of survival strategies on the part of the movers themselves (Dokecki *et al.* 1977).

Against this background, the task of drawing up anything like a balance sheet of the effects of relocation on our movers is made more difficult. For the implication is that we need to take into account not only the changes in *people* associated with relocation but also the changes in their *milieu*. If community care is more than just institutional care writ smaller, then it must bring about a qualitative change in the opportunities and constraints built into the residential environment: in particular, a change towards less restrictive management practices and daily routines, more responsive attitudes to the rights and needs of people as individuals, and greater control for residents over their own lives. This chapter sets out to explore how far such objectives were met for the hospital movers in our study.

Sizing up residential environments

Residential environments are complex and subtle things. Getting the measure of them for the purpose of making comparisons is a tricky business. This difficulty may not always be so apparent in everyday life where people are used to judging the relative qualities of, say, different pubs, restaurants and hotels. Indeed, staff within different hospital and social services settings generally operate with implicit views about which are the 'better' wards or the 'better' homes and hostels in their areas. Such common-sense assessments, however, usually rest on values and criteria which are intuitive rather than explicit. People are rarely asked to articulate the standards which inform them or to spell out the facts on which their impressions are based. Consequently, they cannot be checked or verified; nor can it be assumed that different people's judgements are comparable.

Our aims called for more precision than this. Specifically, we required some method for evaluating and comparing the characteristics of residential environments using clearly defined criteria based on a common scale of values. The research literature presents many examples of instruments designed for this task which fit these specifications (Johnson 1978; Raynes 1988). A crucial point to emerge from the literature is that any investigator seeking to compare different residential settings is faced with three key choices when deciding how to proceed:

1 Across which dimensions of the residential environment are comparisons to be made?
2 Who is going to supply the information?
3 What system of assessment is going to be used?

Readers who are not interested in the technicalities of how we resolved these choices should skip to the next section at this point.

Which dimensions?

Residential environments are made up of a number of interlocking dimensions or levels of reality (Booth 1985). First, there is the *intrapersonal* environment which is shaped by the characteristics of the individuals (both residents and staff) who live and work there. A second layer comprises the *interpersonal* environment of formal and informal relationships that exist between them. Third comes the *'suprapersonal'* environment (see Lawton 1970) as defined by the dominant, shared characteristics which identify the residents as a group. Fourth, there is the *social* environment composed of the norms, rules and procedures that regulate the daily routine, as well as the attitudes and approach which staff bring to their job. Finally, there is the *physical* environment formed by the design, location, fabric and amenities of the place. It is the mix of all these features that together creates the distinctive atmosphere of different residential environments and gives to each its own special character.

Faced with choosing on which dimension(s) to compare the movers' pre- and post-relocation placements, we opted to focus on the social environment or regime. By regime we refer quite specifically to the way a unit or establishment is run. In this sense, it covers both the organization of the daily routine and the attitudes of staff. For the moves to be considered successful, we should expect to find, in the light of the reasoning outlined earlier, a shift towards less restrictive practices and a closer alignment between staff attitudes and current notions of good residential practice.

Whose judgements?

There are three ways of obtaining information about the daily pattern of life inside residential units: from residents, from staff or from outside observers. Each of these sources has its own strengths and weaknesses.

Listening to what users themselves have to say about where they live is important for a variety of reasons. It works against the tendency to stereotype people who are segregated in institutions. It also throws light on the sort of institutional deprivation that arises when the needs and wishes of residents are subordinated to the demands of the communal routine. Listening to users is important too if we are to give due weight to their subjective feelings and experiences in the planning and evaluation of services instead of trusting the interpretation put on them by others.

At the same time many obstacles to eliciting residents' opinions are deeply ingrained in the nature of residential life itself (Booth 1983b). The pervasive control exercised by staff over the daily lives of residents tends to instil a sense of powerlessness and dependence which in turn fosters passivity, submissiveness and compliance. The processes of institutional socialization lead residents to enact the roles they are assigned and to internalize the expectations held of them by staff. Once again the effect is to encourage them in an uncritical acceptance of their lot. The encompassing and often insular routine of residential life itself can so shape residents' expectations as to leave them unable to conceive of anything different to which they might aspire. Residents may in any case be reluctant to voice their criticisms of complaints either because of fears about 'biting the hand that feeds' or because of loyalty to the staff who look after them. For all these reasons, residents themselves may not always be well placed to provide a balanced appraisal of the quality of their residential environment.

Similarly, relying on staff as respondents has its disadvantages as well as its advantages. The senior staff play a crucial role in determining the style or orientation of the regime in residential establishments (Evans *et al.* 1981; Sinclair 1971). Among this group, however, the leadership and influence of officers-in-charge are usually paramount. More than anyone else it is they who are responsible for translating principles of care into actual organizational practices and for managing the daily routine. Certainly, no other single person has the same grasp or command of day-to-day, round-the-clock operational concerns. These considerations obviously make officers-in-charge prime candidates for the role of informant in a study such as this.

On the other hand, their position as key actors may also be seen as possibly compromising their objectivity. Quite naturally they might be expected to present their unit – and themselves – in the most favourable light. This could lead them into putting more stress on their aims than their accomplishments (on what they would *like* to do rather than on what they *actually* do) or into allowing their replies to be influenced by what they think others may see as good practice. The point is that staff cannot be regarded as neutral reporters. They have a personal stake in any data which researchers ask them to supply about the regimes in their units, and these vested interests might realistically be expected to colour the answers they give.

One way of avoiding the potential bias from relying on residents or staff as informants is by using outside observers or external evaluators. Their judgement is not compromised by their status as participants. At the same time, they do not share the latter's first-hand experience of the residential environment. Other problems too arise. External evaluation is a costly and time-consuming business that becomes increasingly impracticable for research purposes as the number of units involved in a study increases. It is hard for outsiders to penetrate the backstage areas of residential life or to grasp the way regimes may subtly alter as between day and night shifts, weekdays and weekends, summer and winter. Access itself may not always be easy to negotiate. Also, importantly, in the end there remains a measure of uncertainty about how far the presence of an observer may itself have influenced people's behaviour and their daily practices and so changed the nature of the regime under scrutiny. In brief, observer methods may succeed in overcoming the main deficiencies of using insiders as inform- ants, but only at the cost of introducing other shortcomings of their own.

There is no single best method of researching residential environments. The secret is to choose the one best fitted to the purpose at hand, and then try to moderate its defects. In fact, few studies in the learning difficulties field have sought users' views on their living environment, presumably because of preconceptions about their likely competence as respondents. We did not share any such reservations, and an important part of our attempt to evaluate the outcomes of relocation was to listen to what the movers in our study had to say about their old and their new placements and how they compared the two. This material is presented and discussed in later chapters. Our aim here is somewhat different. Rather than seeking to compare the social climates of different settings (as delineated through the experience of residents), we wanted to compare their regimes (as conceived in terms of organizational practices and staff attitudes). With this aim in mind, it was more appropriate to use staff, whose job it is to run and manage the units, as our primary source of information about the regimes, supplemented or qualified as necessary by our own direct observation.

What system of assessment?

A fundamental problem of comparing the qualities of residential environ- ments is the lack of any commonly agreed system of assessment and classification. Broadly speaking, the methods most often used fall into two main types: standards or scales.

Standards generally take the form of a checklist of criteria relating principles of good practice to the services actually provided. Facilities may then be evaluated in terms of their success in achieving the targets spelled out in these guidelines. There are many off-the-shelf sets of standards in existence. Among the better known or more widely used examples are, from the USA, the *Standards for Services for Developmentally Disabled Individuals* (the AC/MR-DD Standards) and the *Standards Manual for Rehabilitation Facilities* (the CARF Standards) and, from Britain, the National Development Group's *Checklist of Standards* and the *Stamina* checklists produced by Mencap.

The use of standards as a means of evaluating residential environments is mostly geared to very practical ends. In the United States they are widely employed for accrediting privately operated facilities as a condition of eligibility for public funding. Johnson (1978) reports that 37 states require fulfilment of the CARF Standards before facilities can qualify for licensing and vendor reimbursement. Similar applications might be expected to increase in this country with the growth in private care. *Home Life: A Code of Practice for Residential Care* (CPA 1984), for instance, was produced as a set of standards partly for the guidance of local authorities when vetting private and voluntary homes under the Registered Homes Act 1984. More commonly, however, checklists of standards have been used in Britain as an aid to improving services, as a baseline for measuring progress, as a framework for planning and as an educational resource for staff. From a research point of view, though, they suffer from a number of defects. They can be time consuming. A minimum survey using the AC/MR-DD Standards, for example, takes two evaluators at least three days. Some, like the CARF Standards, call for specialist evaluators who have passed through an intensive training course and completed a period of apprenticeship. Also they can be demanding of staff cooperation and goodwill and risk being seen as intrusive. Lastly, and perhaps most important of all, there is not usually a way of aggregating the information they provide in order to enable comparisons to be made between different facilities. Checklists may be used to show whether or not, say, a particular residential unit successfully attains the prescribed standards of good practice, but they cannot easily be used to make judgements about *degrees* of success or the *relative* performance of different units. They do not enable distinctions to be made (among units reaching the defined standards) between the good, the better and the best or (among those falling short) between the poor, the bad and the worst. The system of measurement on which standards are based is basically one of all or nothing rather than more or less: about absolutes rather than degrees.

Where standards are useful mainly as practical tools for service development, scales serve more analytical functions. Unlike standards, which basically comprise a set of external criteria for evaluating the characteristics of environments, scales are built on the assumption that there are intrinsic or underlying dimensions – such as privacy, participation, engagement, control – along which residential environments may be ranged. By collecting the right sort of information, the position of a unit along these dimensions might be plotted and its resulting profile compared with that of others.

For our purposes, a broad distinction can be drawn between two types of scales: what might be called criterion-referenced scales and norm-referenced scales. A norm-referenced scale classifies residential environments relative to each other and assigns them a position on a continuum which reflects their comparative standing. A criterion-referenced scale classifies them relative to a specified set of environmental characteristics or features so as to yield comparisons in terms of these objective yardsticks.

This distinction may perhaps be illustrated using an example familiar to most people. The AA 'star' classification of hotels comprising a scale ranging from one to five stars belongs to the norm-referenced type. Travellers know that a three-star hotel will generally be better appointed than a two-star one and that a four-star hotel will not be as luxurious as a five-star one, but the precise differences between them in terms of services, facilities and accommodation remain unspecified. By contrast, the English Tourist Board's 'crown' classification (a six-point scale ranging from a listed category to a highest rating of five crowns) belongs to the criterion-referenced type. Each ranking on the classification is defined in terms of the minimum level of facilities and services provided, and with every additional crown the extra facilities to be expected are spelled out.

Faced with the choice of which of these three systems of assessment to use, we opted for a criterion-referenced scale. The next section explains from where we derived the principles or criteria of good practice on which it was based and what they were.

Criteria of good practice

Over the past 15 or 20 years a great deal of work has been done in developing and setting out the principles on which residential services for people with learning difficulties should be based. As a result, much progress has been made in breaking the hold on thinking exerted by tradition, prejudice and sentiment and in building a new consensus around the vision of people's rights and needs which these principles embody.

The Jay Report (1979) played an important part in spreading awareness and acceptance of these new ideas and in giving them leverage. It put forward a model of care grounded on a coherent philosophy which emphasized people's rights to enjoy as normal a life-style as possible, to be treated as individuals, and to receive the support they needed to turn these principles into practice. Services should enable people to live, learn and work in the least restrictive environment they could manage, facilitate their integration into the wider society, ensure their involvement in decisions affecting their lives and guarantee the availability of choice.

The Jay Committee argued that these broad principles could in turn be interpreted more specifically to provide guidance on basic questions such as what kind of living environment residential care units should provide. Their answer goes some way towards outlining the rudiments of good residential practice. After underlining the importance of personal space for residents, the Committee went on to say:

> The climate of experience for adults, depending on their personal, social and physical development, would be one in which personal competence and personal identity were continually strengthened; in particular, in making decisions, as much freedom as possible would be normal. The practicalities or difficulties involved in making it possible for mentally handicapped adults to decide when to go out and when to return, who they should be friends with, how they should spend their money and what they should eat would be seen by residential care staff as exciting problems to be solved, rather than as barriers to progress.

A similar conception of good practice had earlier been endorsed by the Personal Social Services Council after being invited by the DHSS to prepare and publish guidelines on the principles and practice of care in residential homes. In responding to this brief, the PSSC produced two reports which together set out 'the kind of policies that should determine a home's practices' (PSSC 1975 and 1977). Caring for people, they declared, 'involves more than ensuring that they do not come to any harm or that they are given shelter, food and warmth.' It also involves caring practices which help to fulfil individual needs within a group setting, especially the need for personal identity, for making decisions and choices, for forming relationships, and for interacting with the physical setting of daily life. With these objectives in mind, the PSSC defined the 'essential components of a satisfactory residential life' as:

> A respect for privacy; encouragement to independence; availability of choice; stimulation; recognition of emotional needs; opportunity to participate in organising the pattern of life.

The same basic principles were affirmed in the code of practice for residential care produced by a working party under the chairmanship of Lady Avebury (CPA 1984). Although devised mainly as part of the Government's measures for regulating the private and voluntary sector, it contains nothing 'which should not also apply to the setting up and running of homes in the statutory sector'. The code delineates certain basic rights which 'should be accorded to all who find themselves in the care of others'. These rights are defined in terms of concepts such as fulfilment, dignity, autonomy, privacy, individuality, esteem, choice and responsible risk-taking and freedom of emotional expression. It is these concepts which are held to 'provide the foundations and reference points for good practice', and their observation 'in all possible circumstances is in itself good practice'.

Most recently these ideas have again found expression in the report of an independent review of residential care commissioned in 1985 by the Secretary of State for Health and Social Services (Wagner 1988). The review team was charged with investigating how the residential sector might best respond to changing social needs. Its report sets out a vision of residential care becoming a 'positive experience' in which 'the needs and wishes of the user must be paramount'. This goal, the report says, will only be achieved if residential practice is informed by a set of clear aims and common values. Among the important values endorsed by the review team are: the preservation of human dignity, a respect for individuality, a recognition of the need for privacy, freedom of choice in matters of life-style and relationships, and the right of residents to exercise as much control over their own lives as possible and to be involved in all decisions affecting their well-being. These basic principles were held to 'provide the yardsticks against which services and practice can be tested and evaluated'.

What gives these several statements of principle an overlay of legitimacy is the fact that they accord broadly with the things self-advocates say make services better for them. For instance, the published report of the 1984 International Self-Advocacy Leadership Conference puts forward five crucial points that matter to people and can be used as a basis for their own evaluation of services: 'going places and doing things in the community'; 'making choices and having responsibility'; 'increasing self-respect'; 'developing new abilities'; and 'meeting and knowing other people' (People First and the Self-Advocacy Project 1985). Each of these areas finds an echo in the standards outlined above, so giving some confidence that they are attuned to the views and aspirations of users themselves.

In devising our scales for comparing the hospital and hostel environments, we sought to tap the prevailing consensus on principles of good practice in residential care as revealed by these (and other) authoritative sources (see also, for example, CMH 1978; King's Fund Centre 1980). By drawing together their common threads, we identified five key dimensions of the residential environment and used the Unit Practice Questionnaire (UPQ) (see Chapter 2) to construct a scale for measuring each of them. These key dimensions related to the opportunities provided by the environment for satisfying residents' needs for personal choice, privacy, personalization, integration into the wider community and participation in the running of the unit.

UPQ data were obtained for all ten hostel living units involved in our study and for seven of the nine hospital sites from which people were relocated. As we explained in Chapter 2, the community placements were excluded from this exercise. On the basis of their experience in the

Pennhurst study, Conroy and Bradley (1985) concluded that it is probably a mistake to use the same instrument for both institutional and community settings. Doing so, they say, is likely to result in either unrealistic standards for institutional environments, unnecessarily low expectations of community placements, or a combination of the two.

The regime scales

The purpose of the scales was to classify the hospital and hostel units in terms of the similarities and differences in their caring routines and practices across the five key dimensions of the residential environment.

Personal choice

The PSSC (1975) argued strongly that individuality and independence are expressed through choice: residents 'cannot live full and interesting lives if all choice and responsibility is removed from them'. The *Home Life* code of practice similarly affirms that 'the provision of choice is an essential principle'. Domestic routines, it adds,

> need to take into account both individual needs and preferences and the desirability of a lifestyle which is as normal as possible, especially in relation to bathing, getting up, going to bed and mealtimes. Routines should be applied in a friendly, understanding way and offer maximum possible choice.

In this context, choice is conceived as more than just the absence of restraint. It also necessitates positive measures by staff for enabling or encouraging residents to express their wishes.

The *personal choice scale* classified the units on the basis of their flexibility and the degree to which individuals were enabled or permitted to express their wishes and preferences in such matters as getting up at weekends, bedtimes, bathing, choosing new shoes and clothes, mealtimes, menus, using the kitchen and making snacks, and looking after their own spending money.

Only two hospital and three hostel units were assessed as having routines flexible enough to allow residents the scope for exercising personal choice. Two units – a hostel and a hospital villa – were rated as having structured routines that were too inflexible to accommodate resident choice. The remainder fell into an intermediate category where choice was provided in some areas and denied in others. Within this category, comprising the majority of the units in our study, there was little to distinguish the hostel from the hospital settings in terms of the opportunities they gave to residents for making choices in the areas of daily living covered by our scale. Indeed, the differences among the hospital units on the one hand,

and the hostel units on the other, were every bit as marked as those between them. The inference is that the residents who left the hospital were just as likely to move into an environment offering them less choice as more, but most likely to experience no significant change at all.

Privacy

Privacy is important in a residential setting for at least two reasons (Kelvin 1973). First, it helps to safeguard a person's independence in situations where otherwise they might be vulnerable to the intervention or power of others. Second, it gives people a measure of personal autonomy which otherwise would be restricted by the constraints and pressures of residential living. Also, as *Home Life* stresses, a respect for what is personal and private in such things as beliefs, feelings and relationships is important for the preservation of self-respect and individual dignity (CPA 1984).

The Wagner Report (1988) saw privacy in the residential context as partly a matter of design and partly of practice. The major design feature helping to sustain privacy was held to be 'a room of one's own where one may live as one pleases'. Only two of the hospital units provided single bedrooms for all residents. The others had just a few individual rooms, but most of their sleeping accommodation was in the form of dormitory bays (holding about five beds) or large, open-style wards. By contrast, most hostel residents had their own rooms, although there were also doubles in four of the units.

Our *privacy scale* classified the units in terms of the presence or absence of amenities and practices aimed at securing some personal space for residents and upholding their dignity in the following areas: bathtime supervision, locking bathroom doors, toileting, locking toilet doors, access to bedrooms during the day, locking bedroom doors and having a private lockable place for personal valuables.

A word of caution is necessary about the interpretation of this data. In the residential context, the notion of privacy only takes on a meaning relative to the overwhelmingly public and communal nature of institutional life. It is intrinsically a scarce commodity. To describe a particular setting as responsive to the demands of privacy may simply imply that less is done to erode it than elsewhere.

In this light, we found three of the hospital and five hostel units were supportive of the need for privacy as measured by the criteria used in our scale. Only one (hospital) unit was rated as unresponsive: with routine bathtime supervision and toileting of residents by staff, no locks on bathroom and some toilet doors, restricted use by residents of their bedrooms during the day – for which they had no keys (indeed, there were no doors either) – and the only positive feature being the provision of a personal, lockable place (although we could not verify that the residents in fact retained the keys). All the remaining units were classified in an intermediate category.

Closer examination of the UPQ data for the individual units showed that perhaps three of this intermediate group – two hospital units and a hostel unit – were near the borderline for being rated as unsatisfactory. Otherwise they were much of a muchness.

Overall, then, it seems fair to conclude that the hostels offered movers more privacy simply because of the greater likelihood of them having a room of their own. On the other measures tapped by our privacy scale, the differences, if any, between the hospital and hostel units only slightly favoured the latter. An individual mover was almost as likely to find himself or herself with a little less privacy as with a little more. In any case, aside from the provision of single rooms, the differences in the amount of personal space given to residents were mostly too small to have an impact on the quality of residential life.

Personalization

It is widely held that good residential practice is built on a respect for people as individuals. Both the Jay Report and *An Ordinary Life* embraced this principle as a touchstone of service provision. The Wagner Report too observes that 'caring is about treating people individually', and the *Home Life* code of practice urges the importance of regimes which are 'responsive to the needs and requirements of individual residents'. As Sinclair (1988) notes from her examination of personal evidence submitted to the Wagner review, people seemed to be unhappy with residential care where, among other things, it failed to show respect for individual personality.

Nurturing a sense of individuality and self-awareness among residents in the face of the pressures to conform exerted by group living calls for the avoidance of any sort of block treatment and for positive measures aimed at bolstering personal identity. Clearly, in this area both personal choice and privacy have some part to play, and a degree of overlap with the two previous scales might properly be expected. Accordingly, our *personalization scale* classified the units on the basis of the support they gave to the maintenance of personal identity in matters such as toiletting practices, the possession of one's own toiletries, locking bedrooms, choosing new shoes and clothes, managing one's own spending money and having a personal savings account.

On balance, the hostels showed themselves to be slightly more resident-orientated in these routines than the hospital units. Three of the four best rated units were hostels, the majority emerged at the top end of the scale, and none were classified as institution-orientated for showing too little regard for individuality.

The hospital units were characterized by greater variety. Although three stood comparison with the better hostels, the same number were assessed as having institution-orientated practices that did not reflect enough concern for people as individuals. Overall, where the hostels scored an average of 4.8 good points as against 1.8 bad points on the personalization scale, the hospital units averaged only 3.3 good points compared to 3.0 bad points.

Once again, there is no clear-cut divide between the hospital and hostel units, only a tendency for the latter to provide more scope for individual expression. From the point of view of the residents themselves, while they seem likely to be better off *as a group* in this respect, it is still possible that particular individuals ended up in a less resident-orientated environment as a result of relocation from hospital.

Integration

The PSSC (1975) noted that a close relationship with the local community is a vital ingredient of successful residential care: 'Relations should be such that residents are able, as their abilities and inclinations allow, naturally and without formality, to take part in the activities of the local community.' The *Home Life* code of practice spells out in more detail what this might involve. Residents, it says, should be able to go out freely for trips, meals and longer visits with relatives, friends or volunteers; they should be encouraged and enabled to take holidays away; families and friends should be encouraged to visit regularly or to keep in contact by letter or telephone; visitors should be welcomed at all reasonable times. Using these indicators as a guide, our *integration scale* assessed the openness or closedness of the regimes in the units in terms of the following variables: visiting arrangements, residents' access to a telephone, the extent of their involvement in outside social activities, away visits to relatives and friends, holidays and outings (including participation by relatives), and whether the front door was locked during the day.

The majority of both the hospital (5) and hostel (8) units were rated as having an intermediate status – neither good nor bad – on the integration scale. All of them could have done more to further their links with the wider community and to overcome the problems of access faced by their residents, but equally none seemed to have given way entirely to the inward-looking pressures of institutional life. Just three units (two hostels) were assessed as having a qualitatively more open environment than the others, and one hospital unit was classified as being a closed regime.

Despite most units falling into the intermediate category, there was some evidence that the differences between the hospitals and hostels were slightly more pronounced on this scale than the previous three. Looking at the pattern of responses across the individual variables making up the scale, it is evident in terms of the balance between good and bad features that, even within the middling category, the hostels were placed towards the more open end of the range while the hospital units clustered more towards the closed end. For our purposes, however, such differences may be more apparent than real. Although they show up on a computer print out, their human effects are likely to be too small to leave a mark on the experience of residents.

The one area in which all the hospital and hostel units markedly underperformed was in the involvement of relatives and the maintenance of links between residents and their families. Only one (hospital) unit said it was normal practice to invite people's relatives or friends along on day trips or holidays. Similarly, only two (hostel) units reported that about half or more of their residents *sometimes* stayed overnight with friends or relatives. While many reasons were cited for the absence of such links, it remains the case that almost none of the units put any serious investment in keeping them open or building them up, and none saw this task as either a duty or a priority.

Participation

The last key dimension of residential living on which we compared the unit regimes concerned the opportunities they provided for the participation of residents. The PSSC (1975) and the Jay Report (1979) both insisted that residents should not be regarded merely as the passive recipients of care or as passive users of services. On the contrary, they should be construed as people who would make choices given the chance and who are entitled to be involved in decisions affecting their daily lives. The *Home Life* code of practice states squarely that residents 'should be involved as much as possible in making decisions concerning the way in which a home is run'. For people with learning difficulties in particular, participation in the running of the home is urged as a way of acquiring independent living skills by learning through doing (CPA 1984). The extent to which such principles are carried through into practice is, according to Wagner (1988), 'one of the tests of the quality of care'.

Our *participation scale* classified the units into three categories on the basis of their involvement of residents in the running of things and the making of decisions as shown by: their part in the planning of menus, their access to the kitchen or other facilities for making snacks, their role in the preparation of meals, the serving of food, washing up and other domestic jobs, and the arrangements for staff and/or resident meetings.

The differences between the hospital and hostel regimes were more marked on the participation scale than on any of the other environmental dimensions we measured. Fully six of the hostel units were rated as providing an enabling environment in terms of opportunities for resident particiption. The remainder (4) were all classified in the intermediate category – although two were on the borderline of the top ranking. By contrast, three of the hospital regimes were found to be restrictive in their practices: doing things *to* or *for* residents rather than *with* them. Another three were placed in the intermediate category, and one of these only narowly missed being classed as restrictive. Only one hospital unit was ranked alongside the best hostels. Indeed, the positioning of the units on the scale was such that if the best hospital regime and the worst hostel regime are excluded, then all the hostels were more enabling in their practices than the hospital units.

There was, of course, still a lot of room for improvement even among the hostels. The PSSC (1975), for example, strongly recommended the setting up of regular residents' meetings as a necessary step towards greater participation. The importance of such a forum emerges clearly from the growing achievements of the self-advocacy movement (Williams and Shoultz 1982). Among the things that self-advocates say hurt them most in services are 'staff getting together without me to decide what I will do' and 'staff not asking what I want – choosing for me instead of checking with me' (People First and the Self-Advocacy Project 1985). Yet only four of the hostels (and one hospital unit) held regular, formal meetings of staff and residents to discuss together common affairs relating to the running of the unit.

The gulf between the two settings was widest in their practices and routines bearing on menu planning and the preparation and serving of meals. In only one of the hospital units were residents involved in the planning of menus; in none were residents involved in the preparation or cooking of main meals; and in all but one the main meal was served to residents on plates by staff. These restrictive practices owed less to staff attitudes than to the centralized system of hospital catering: menus were decided by the central catering department, food was cooked in the central kitchens and meals were delivered to the villas in heated trolleys from which they were served already plated by staff.

On this dimension of the residential environment, then, most people leaving hospital to live in the hostels were likely to find themselves better off – in the sense of having more opportunities for involvement in the daily routine of living.

Overall scale profiles

In this section we try to pull together the information presented by the regime scales in order to arrive at a summative assessment of the changes in the quality of their living environment experienced by people as a result of the move from hospital to hostel.

So far we have looked at how the 17 hospital and hostel units compared on each of the five regime scales independently. These scales divided the units on the basis of their daily practices and organizational routines into three broad categories: more liberal-type regimes, intermediate ones, and more restrictive-type regimes. The next task is to see how the units performed across all the scales taken together in order to provide an appraisal of their regimes in the round.

Only three units (including one hospital) were ranked in the more liberal category across all five regime scales. Highwood Lodge – the hospital chart-topper – was as its rating suggests quite different in character to the other hospital villas. Occupying former student nurses' accommodation, it was designated as a 'pre-discharge' unit and had only been opened a few months before our study began. The main block contained three groups of five residents, each with their own kitchen, lounge, dining room and bathroom. The bedrooms were all single and located on the first floor. All the rooms (except the kitchens) were carpeted throughout and individually decorated with lots of pictures, ornaments, stereos and other personal touches evident everywhere. Attached to the main part of the building were several self-contained flats accommodating up to three people. The unit had a number of domestic washing machines which residents were encouraged to use but no separate food budget. Most meals were brought across from the central kitchens in orange plastic insulated boxes. Unlike all the other hospital villas, Highwood Lodge did not have separate toilets or rest rooms for staff. There was an office, but the residents had free access to it except during meetings. The nurses were all young and committed and more aware of normalization principles than direct care staff in any other hospital or hostel unit. None of them wore uniforms and most were known by their first names. Although Highwood Lodge had been given a separate postal address, it was still clearly located as part of the hospital campus and the buildings looked similar to the rest of the hospital.

Loosening our criteria slightly to include among the best-rated units all those having liberal regimes on four scales and an intermediate ranking on the other adds only one more (hostel) unit to the three identified above.

At the other end of the scale no units were assessed as being restrictive in their practices across all five dimensions of the residential environment, and none also were found when the criteria were relaxed to take in any with an intermediate and four restrictive ratings.

Looked at in the round, then, most of the hospital and hostel units were neither clearly good (in the sense of more liberal) nor clearly bad (in the sense of more restrictive) when assessed against current notions of good residential practice. Mostly they fell somewhere in-between. Indeed, an overall majority of the units (three hospital villas and six hostels) were classified in the intermediate category on three or more of the regime scales. All this evidence indicates a strong underlying continuity among the hospital and hostel units in the routines of daily life to the point where, in many areas, their similarities outweigh their differences.

As a way of exploring this issue further, we devised a simple method of scoring the units on the basis of their rankings across the five regime scales. On each of these key dimensions of residential living – personal choice, privacy, personalization, integration and participation – units assessed as providing an opportunity-rich environment scored two, an intermediate rating scored one, and an opportunity-sparse environment scored zero. These scores were added to create an eleven-point scale ranging from 0 (the most restrictive regime) to 10 (the most liberal regime). Table 3 presents the results.

The overlap in the scores of the hospital and hostel units is further evidence of the similarities in their regimes discussed above. Also evident, however, is a tendency for the hostels to show up as slightly more liberal in the way they are run and slightly more opportunity-rich in the quality of their environment. This tendency is expressed in the higher average score of the hostels (7.1) compared with the hospital units (5.1) and the mean regime score (6.3). Once again though, as has been said before, we cannot be sure that differences of such a magnitude are enough to have an effect on the lives of residents.

One last point emerges from Table 3. Any differences between the hospital and hostel units in the nature of their regimes are more than matched by differences among the individual units in each of these two settings. The data behind the table show, for example, that where the hospital scores ranged from a maximum of 10 to a minimum of 2, the hostel scores varied from 10 to 4. The implications are twofold. The first is that hospital environments cannot be assumed to be more institutional than hostel environments. The second is that whether or not relocation brings any positive benefits of the kind measured by our regime scales depends very much on where people move from and where they move to in each individual case.

Staff attitudes

The Wagner Report (1988) was emphatic that a residential service can only be successful if it is informed by a set of clear aims and a shared philosophy,

Table 3 Regime scores by hospital and hostel units

Regime scores	Hospital units	Hostel units
Most liberal (8–10)	2	4
Medium (5–7)	1	5
Most restrictive (0–4)	4	1
N =	7	10

and if these common values are adhered to consistently by staff in their daily work. A key factor in ensuring such a commitment, the report adds, is the leadership offered by the most senior member of staff. Sinclair (1971, 1975), for example, found that wide variations in the nature and effectiveness of probation hostel regimes were related to the attitudes and approach of the staff in charge. Against this background, we set out to establish if the hospital and hostel units were marked by what Cawson and Perry (1977) have called distinct 'attitude climates' as shown by the orientation of their senior staff to the common values underpinning current notions of good residential practice.

For this purpose we followed closely the approach developed by Booth *et al.* (1990) in their study of staff attitudes and caring practices in old people's homes. Using material from the UPQ we constructed a *good practice schedule* comprising a series of ten statements, each describing what is widely held to be an example of good practice. The ten statements we selected were as follows:

- Residents should be able to choose what time they go to bed.
- Residents should have a choice of main course for their evening meal.
- Evening mealtimes should be flexible.
- All toilet doors should be fitted with locks.
- Residents should have their own savings account.
- Residents should have a lockable place for their personal valuables.
- Residents should help to plan menus.
- Residents should be involved in the preparation of meals.
- Residents should have the opportunity to take an annual holiday.
- Residents should regularly participate in social activities outside the unit.

These statements were looked on in two ways. First, they were seen as a set of *standards* describing ways of working that are important in their own right. Second, they were regarded as a set of *indicators* pointing to the underlying values that staff bring to their task, especially in relation to the five key areas of personal choice, privacy, personalization, integration and participation discussed earlier. If, for example, senior staff do not think it desirable that residents should have a choice of main course for their evening meal, or choose their own bedtimes, then their commitment to the principle of personal choice must be queried. Equally, if staff demur about residents helping with the planning of menus or the preparation of meals, then their acceptance of the value of participation may similarly be questioned.

Using the UPQ data, the hospital and hostel units were compared in terms of (a) the number of respondents who said the good practice statements described how things were *actually* done in the unit and (b) the number who said the statements constituted a *desirable* guide to practice.

As our earlier analysis of the regimes would have led us to expect, proportionately fewer hospital units than hostel units were actually following the good practices listed in the statements. Only for two statements was this relationship reversed (choice of main course for the evening meal and access to a lockable place for personal valuables). Otherwise, across the good practice schedule as a whole, the proportion of hospital staff endorsing the statements as accurate descriptions of their current operational practice averaged 28 per cent compared with 53 per cent among the hostels.

The pattern of responses on the second issue looked very different. For every good practice statement there were more staff among both the hospital and hostel respondents who put it down as desirable than put it down as operational. In other words, for each one there were more who thought it should be done than who said they did it. Indeed, the evidence points to a widespread awareness among senior staff in hospital and hostel settings of what constitutes good practice and encouragingly high levels of agreement with the good practice statements. Six of the ten statements were endorsed unanimously by the hospital respondents and two by all the hostel respondents (although a further five were accepted as desirable by all but one of them). Averaging the responses to the good practice statements as a rough measure of their support showed that hospital respondents gave them a 92 per cent endorsement compared with 91 per cent from senior hostel staff. In short, while there were differences in the actual practices followed in the units by these two groups of staff, there were virtually no differences in their attitudes about what should be regarded as good or desirable practice.

The tendency, observed again here, for adherence to good practice principles to tail off between their endorsement and their implementation has been termed the 'cooling effect' (Booth *et al.* 1990). Several reasons – what Wagner (1988) calls 'impediments to good practice' – might lie behind this phenomenon, including:

- *design-related reasons* such as the absence of doors on the toilets, or the lack of lockable cupboards and drawers in residents' bedrooms, or the reliance on meals supplied from central kitchens;
- *policy-related reasons* such as regulations forbidding personal banking or requiring that residents' finances are handled only by authorized officials, or rules prohibiting residents' access to the kitchen, or having all meals planned by a central catering department;
- *resource-related reasons* such as not having enough money to ensure all residents get away on holiday, or enough staff to escort everyone to outside activities;
- *resident-related reasons* such as severe disabilities or the 'learned helplessness' associated with years of institutional living;

- *staff-related reasons* such as inflexible duty rotas that mean residents have to be in bed before the shift changes, or simple self-interest leading to the avoidance of practices which might make their job more difficult.

The evidence from the good practice schedule showing a more pronounced 'cooling effect' in the hospital units than the hostels suggests these 'impediments to good practice' may be more serious and entrenched in the hospital setting. So far as the main question posed in this section is concerned, however, we are led to the conclusion that there was no apparent difference in the 'attitude climates' of the hospital and hostel units when judged by the views senior staff in leadership positions held about the ingredients of good practice.

Overview

Our main aim in this chapter has been to establish whether the move from hospital to hostel brought with it a change for the better in people's living environment by way of less restrictive daily routines, more responsive attitudes to their rights and needs as individuals and greater control over their own lives. Our conclusions on the basis of the evidence we have presented are unavoidably ambivalent.

When looked at as a group, the hostels tended to offer more opportunities for personal choice, privacy, personalization, integration and participation than the hospital units. But these differences were often found to be very small (especially in the area of personal choice) and, with the possible exception of participation, it remains uncertain whether they would have had an impact on the experience of residents. Overall there appeared to be a substantial measure of overlap in the characteristics of the hospital and hostel regimes. Indeed, the variations in liberality or restrictiveness among the hospital units on the one hand, and the hostel units on the other, were just as marked as the variations between them.

The implications of this last point show up in a one-to-one comparison of individual units. People who moved from the lowest-rated hospital villas to the highest-rated hostels undoubtedly found themselves in a more enabling kind of environment. Equally, though, people who moved from, say, Highwood Lodge, mentioned earlier, into one of the more restrictive hostels experienced a loss of opportunities they formerly had enjoyed. Certainly it cannot be assumed the move from hospital was always to a more responsive regime. For the remainder, while the move meant a change in the physical horizons of their world, its social horizons probably altered little. The lesson would seem to be that deinstitutionalization, as opposed merely to relocation, calls for something more imaginative than simply substituting hostels for hospitals.

6

View from the office

Apart from the users themselves, basic grade staff are usually the only people who experience the day-to-day reality of a service. Those we talked to were working very much at the sharp end of the system. The majority were basic grade workers, the most common designation being care assistant or its nursing equivalent, with just the occasional officer-in-charge or ward sister. Three-quarters of the staff in hospital had some form of relevant qualification, but this was true of only about one-third of social services staff.

On average our respondents had been working in their unit for between six to eight years. However, the opening of the new social services and voluntary sector facilities drew in a number of less experienced people. After the moves, 16 of the staff we spoke to for the first time had recently joined the unit in question, and of these 10 had no prior experience of working in a facility for people with learning difficulties. Overall, the vast majority of staff claimed to like working in their unit very much, and most of the rest expressed positive feelings about their work. Nobody said they disliked their job.

Most staff were fairly hazy about the plans for community care in Kirklees, and their comments about the programme inevitably tended to be framed in terms of their personal experience. Nevertheless, virtually no one declared themselves to be against the moves. The hospital staff divided into three roughly equal groups. There were some firm advocates of the principle of community care ('They should have a right to move into the community'). Such a stance was often coupled with criticism of the hospital environment:

I don't think hospitals are nice places to work or live. We can't even provide proper physical care – there isn't enough continuity – and we certainly cannot meet social or emotional needs.

A second group was in favour of community care subject to a variety of qualifications ('If it's nearer the family and it's got the facilities available they should go'). Finally, there was a group of hospital staff who, although frankly sceptical about the philosophy behind the changes, were prepared to look at each case on its merits:

> I've never been a great believer in moving people for just administrative reasons. . . . Can't see any point in moving some of the older residents, particularly if they don't have any relatives. However, in Jane's case . . .

By contrast, the staff working in the hostels and the community placements were much more likely to be committed to the principles they believed underpinned the developments in Kirklees. One respondent spoke for many when she declared herself, 'definitely in favour. . . . I don't see why anybody in the hostel wouldn't like a small house so long as the staffing is adequate.' Some of the hostel staff involved in setting up the ordinary housing pointed to the limitations of the hostel settings:

> I don't think there's an institution anywhere that can replace a home. . . . In the end it's the numbers that dictate what you do. For your own sanity you have to compromise. I dislike the thought that anyone has to come to this sort of life.

Equally there were staff still working in the hostels who felt that such accommodation had 'something to offer', and should remain part of community care in the foreseeable future: 'A group of sixteen *must* be better than 200 to 300. Plus the hospitals are so isolated.'

Despite the generally positive tone of most comments, there was a strong streak of cynicism running throughout the interviews with both hospital and hostel staff. In particular, doubts were voiced before the moves about whether the planned levels of support would actually materialize. One person caught the gist of these worries when he said the plans were: 'Good if done correctly and not just on the cheap, and they keep up to all the promises they have made.'

The changes in Kirklees were not based on a grassroots pressure for reform; they were, by and large, imposed on staff from above with relatively little consultation. Nevertheless, there was little or no resistance to the proposals from those directly involved. Indeed the workforce was broadly in sympathy with the perceived aims of the changes.

Indicators and outcomes

As we have shown in Chapter 1, the policy climate in both Britain and the United States has been marked by growing acceptance of certain core ideas or principles regarding the care and support of people with learning difficulties. Generally speaking, these principles stress their rights to as

normal a life-style as possible, in the least restrictive environment com-
patible with their needs for protection and support, and to such help and
services as they may require to develop their maximum potential as
individuals (Lakin *et al.* 1985; Willer and Intagliata, 1984; Jay Report
1979). These ideas were discernible in the thinking behind the Kirklees
Partnership in Community Care if not always in the initiatives on the
ground. Certainly, the Partnership set out to improve the quality of life of
service users in ways that resonate with these principles. The last chapter
explored how far the new placements surmounted the 'less restrictive' test
for those people who moved out of hospital. (In the case of the hostel
movers, these issues are touched on in Chapter 10.) We now turn to
consider the effects of relocation on people's daily functioning and on
aspects of their life-style using the following key indicators: adaptive
behaviour, behaviour problems, aids and medication, training and habi-
tation, use of community and leisure facilities, visits and contacts with
relatives, and the use of remedial and support services.

Adaptive behaviour

As explained in Chapter 2, we used the Anglicized version of the AAMD's
Adaptive Behaviour Scale (ABS) to measure the developmental changes in
our movers following relocation. The ABS was designed to provide a full
description of the way people maintain their personal independence in
daily living or how they meet the social expectations imposed on them by
their environment. It is used to evaluate an individual's skills and traits in
ten behavioural domains, each comprising coherent groups of related
activities considered important to the maintenance and development of
personal independence. These behavioural domains cover the areas of
independent functioning and self-care, physical development, economic
activity, language development, numbers and time, domestic activity,
vocational activity, self-direction, responsibility and socialization. We
omitted the section on vocational activity for the reasons mentioned in
Chapter 2. For the purpose of drawing comparisons between Phase I and
Phase III of the study, the mean ABS scores of hospital and hostel movers
were expressed as a percentage of the highest scores attainable within each
behavioural domain and across the scale as a whole.

Overall, there was a small gain of between 3 and 5 per cent in the profile
scores of both groups of movers. Table 4 presents the data in full. As can be
seen, the people who left the hostels were generally much more able than
the hospital movers who took their place. Also, though the differences are
fairly small, the hostel movers do show a slightly greater gain in their
aggregate profile score after relocation. Within both groups, however,
there were big variations between individuals with some making giant
strides towards greater personal independence while others seemed to lose

Table 4 ABS profile scores before and after relocation for hospital and hostel movers

Mover group	Phase I before relocation	Phase III after relocation	% change
Hospital (N = 17)	55.8	58.9	3.1
Hostel (N = 22)	82.4	87.5	5.1
All movers (N = 39)	70.8	75.1	4.3

ground. Among the hospital movers, for example, three people recorded improvements of more than 40 per cent in their pre-relocation scores, while at the other extreme one person's score fell by 26 per cent: altogether, 5 of the 17 people in this group for whom ABS data are available showed signs of behavioural regression 12 months after the move. A similar variation in the degree and direction of behavioural change is also evident among the hostel movers (ranging from an increase of 42 per cent to a decrease of 31 per cent in ABS scores), although only 3 people recorded a lower rating in Phase III than in Phase I. Out of the total of 39 movers, 31 registered developmental gains following relocation: 18 increased their score by 10 per cent or more, of whom 11 improved by upwards of 20 percentage points. Table 5 analyses these changes in more detail for each of the behavioural domains on the ABS.

Among the hospital movers the biggest gains were made in the areas of domestic activity, numbers and time, and economic activity (money handling, budgeting and shopping skills). It seems probable that these gains reflect the changes in the structure of opportunities within the post-relocation environment. People were more likely to do things in the

Table 5 Behavioural changes by ABS domains and type of mover

ABS domain	% change in ABS score Phase I–Phase III		
	Hospital movers (N = 17)	Hostel movers (N = 22)	All movers (N = 39)
Independent functioning	3.2	3.9	3.6
Physical development	2.2	1.5	1.8
Economic activity	5.0	9.1	7.1
Language development	2.9	9.2	6.4
Numbers and time	5.9	11.7	9.2
Domestic activity	12.1	0.8	5.7
Self-direction	−1.3	4.6	2.0
Responsibility	−1.0	5.3	2.6
Socialization	−1.0	4.6	2.1
Total profile score	3.1	5.1	4.3

hostels like make cups of tea, tidy their rooms, lend a hand with the washing up or do a bit of hoovering. Hostel life also beats to a different rhythm from life on the ward. In the relatively closed world of the hospital there is little to distinguish one day from the next aside from TV programmes and Saturday visiting. As Bercovici (1980) has noted, residents 'are passive respondents to a time framework established by the institution'. They have little opportunity to develop 'a more active role vis-à-vis the management of time'. Hostel residents, on the other hand, are more attuned to the changing pitch of everyday life because they come and go places, catch buses, attend evening classes, visit the sports centre, keep appointments at the hairdresser's. Most hostels kept a diary recording who was doing what and when. It was not unusual to hear a resident shout, 'Put me in the diary for Friday.' In this context it is not perhaps surprising that the concept of time should acquire a new meaning and a greater significance. People's skills in managing money likewise seem to have increased because the incentive was there. After moving they had a little more money in their pockets, were closer to the shops, visited them more often and were encouraged to buy their own small necessities or treats.

These gains, however, were accompanied by small losses in the areas of self-direction (including initiative, attention and persistence), responsibility and socialization (covering how people relate to others). Possibly these ratings measure the residual trauma of the move itself (discussed more fully in Chapter 3) occasioned partly by the disruption of relationships, partly by the greater demands of the new environment and partly also by their new and comparatively more able reference group of peers. If so, then the reverberations of transition shock may be longer lasting than is generally supposed.

Unlike the hospital movers, the people who moved into the community placements from the hostels showed no setbacks in any of the ABS behavioural domains. Their main advances were in the areas of numbers and time, language development and economic activity. These ratings probably reflect their increased use of adult education (in particular adult literacy), their heightened responsibilities for household budgeting and management, and their greater use of money through shopping and having to pay their own way.

Overall, the relationship between the before-and-after ratings was a linear one. The gains and losses were largely unrelated to people's original ABS scores. The only qualification to these findings comes about because of a certain lack of sensitivity at the bottom end combined with a low ceiling on the ABS. (Some people had such high scores in Phase I there was little chance of them showing any improvement. We suspect this may partly account for the small gains in domestic activity recorded by hostel movers in Table 5.) As a result, there was a slight tendency for the biggest changes to be skewed towards the middle of the range. Nevertheless, the evidence supports the conclusion that, while a number of individuals made significant progress towards greater independence in daily living and a few lost out, there was no one group of people who emerged as winners or losers.

One last point about the interpretation of the ABS data needs to be stressed. Environment and behaviour are intimately coupled. This fact is acknowledged in the definition of adaptive behaviour which underpins the scale and which emphasizes that the term refers primarily 'to the effectiveness of an individual in coping with the natural and social demands of his or her environment' (Nihira *et al.* 1975). From this viewpoint, an increase in an individual's score may indicate either new learning, the acquisition of skills and a growth of mastery, the reactivation of dormant skills or the expansion of opportunities and the improvement of supports. In the same way a lower rating may signify a change in the person, a change in their environment or, in line with the precepts of social ecology, a change in the 'person–environment fit' (Lawton 1970; Lawton and Nahemow 1973).

For example, the young man whose ABS score fell the most (−26 per cent) between Phase I and Phase III had moved from Highwood Lodge at the hospital, one of the three most liberal and responsive units in our study (see Chapter 5), into a hostel offering fewer opportunities and more restrictions. Although he had been assessed as needing male company, the other residents were mostly women and mostly much more severely handicapped than he was. The only male member of staff was the officer-in-charge. There was no SEC place available for him, and no other form of daytime occupation was found. His main source of stimulation was to take himself off for a stroll in the neighbourhood. Against this background it would obviously be a mistake to view his weaker ABS rating merely as a function of his own abilities or as signalling his personal failure to cope with his new way of life or as demonstrating his unsuitability as a candidate for relocation. The deficiencies of the setting must be taken into account as well (Intagliata and Willer 1982). In short, the ABS scores should be read as providing a commentary on the interaction between the characteristics of clients and their placements (Romer and Heller 1983).

Behaviour problems

Problem behaviour has been named as an important factor influencing placement outcomes (Sutter *et al.* 1981). Pinning down its referents, however, is no easy matter. Behaviour which goes unheeded in one context may be labelled as unacceptable in another. For instance, shouting as a normal mode of communication may pass unnoticed against the generally higher background noise levels on a hospital ward, but appear as intimidating in a quieter hostel setting. People accustomed to stubbing out cigarettes on the uncovered floors of hospital corridors suddenly become a nuisance when they persist in doing the same in a carpeted hallway. Once again, as with the ABS, the issue turns on the relationship between environment and behaviour. Bercovici (1981) has argued that people who spend long years in institutions acquire different behaviours based on a different set of assumptions about the world and different strategies for survival and the maintenance of self-esteem. Such reasoning suggests two possibilities. On the one hand, behaviour adjusted to hospital or hostel life might appear as maladaptive in another setting. On the other hand, behaviour problems may be rooted in the environmental press (Davies and Knapp 1981) and disappear once the pressures generating them are removed. In other words, relocation might be expected to lead to an increase or a decrease in problem behaviour depending on which line of thinking one follows.

Despite such inherent difficulties we decided the topic was too important for us to neglect. Accordingly, we asked staff before and after the move whether each individual exhibited any of the following types of behaviour (see Chapter 2): aggressive, destructive, self-injuring, objectionable, anti-social, disruptive, persistently uncooperative, stereotyped, or otherwise bizarre. Chapter 3 explored the changes during the settling-in period after the move in the context of a discussion of transition shock. In this section we concentrate on a comparison between Phase I and Phase III of the study.

As might be expected, there was a much higher incidence of problem behaviour reported among the hospital movers than among the hostel movers before relocation. A year later these initial differences had widened. The changes are best presented for each group separately.

Taking the hostel movers first, the incidence of behaviour problems fell by almost a half (see Table 6) between Phase I and Phase III. Even before the move, none of the named types of problem behaviour was exhibited by more than a minority of people. The most frequently cited examples were physical or verbal aggression (displayed by 5 people), objectionable personal habits (5) and other strange or bizarre behaviour (7) such as faking fits, constantly making funny noises, hoarding knotted wool and compulsively buying babies' dummies. By the 12 month follow-up there had been a decline in 6 of the 9 types of problem behaviour and none had increased.

By contrast, as Table 6 shows, there was an upsurge in problem behaviour among the hospital movers. Outbursts of aggression – manifested by just over half the movers in both phases – were the most frequently cited and recurring cause of trouble. The numbers of people reported as showing objectionable, antisocial or other bizarre behaviour doubled in the same period. Possibly this may reflect a shift in what were regarded as acceptable and desirable norms of conduct. A smaller rise in instances of destructive and stereotyped behaviour was also noted. At the same time, there was a marked drop in the numbers who were said to have been persistently

Table 6 Incidence of problem behaviours by hospital and hostel movers before and after relocation

Mover group	*Mean number of problem behaviours per mover*	
	Phase I	*Phase III*
Hospital (N = 17)	2.94	3.41
Hostel (N = 22)	1.32	0.68
All movers (N = 39)	2.03	1.87

uncooperative or prone to self-injury in the hospital. Overall, looking across all nine types of problem behaviour, more increased (6) than decreased (3) among this group of movers.

Another way of presenting these changes is by looking at what happened to individuals. Among the hospital movers, six people were described as having fewer behaviour problems after the move, another six were said to have more and five the same. The position with the hostel movers was altogether more positive: twelve people showed fewer problem behaviours, eight showed no change and only two presented more (one of whom was subsequently found to be suffering from Alzheimer's disease). Table 7 sets out these changes in more detail.

The single most striking feature of the table is the big increase in the number of people who were reported as exhibiting no behaviour problems after moving into the community placements from the hostels.

Making sense of these findings is quite a puzzle, mainly because there is no way of knowing for sure whether they represent real changes in people's behaviour or incidental changes in staff perceptions. Certainly staff would have seen less of the people in the community placements, so possibly leading them into being less strict or exacting in their judgements.

Table 7 Movers by number of behaviour problems before and after relocation

Number of behaviour problems	*Hospital movers*		*Hostel movers*	
	Phase I	*Phase III*	*Phase I*	*Phase III*
0	2	0	7	16
1–3	8	10	14	5
4–6	7	5	1	1
7–9	0	2	0	0
(N =)	(17)	(17)	(22)	(22)

Equally, those who came out of hospital would have been judged against the expectations of care staff as opposed to nursing staff – although the fact that as many improved as regressed in their behaviour suggests that the changes were not just an artefact of differing standards. Indeed, it would be surprising if the transformation in people's life-styles brought about by relocation did not somehow express itself in how they behaved.

Aids and medication

According to reports, 18 out of the total of 39 people for whom a comprehensive set of staff interviews is available were taking some form of medication prior to relocation. This number was made up of 12 hospital movers (N = 17) and six hostel movers (N = 22). Almost three-quarters of the latter group (73 per cent) were receiving no medication at all, compared with less than a third (29 per cent) of the former.

Hemming *et al.* (1981) warn of the dangers of failing to recognize the stress of relocation and mistakenly trying to control its symptoms by drugs. There was no sign of such a response in our study despite the fact that transition shock affected just under half of all the movers. Most people had their prescriptions reviewed shortly after the move. Three hospital movers had their medication stopped altogether, and two had the brand changed and the dosage reduced. Interestingly, four hostel movers were reported as having been put on medication in their new placements but, so far as we can tell, in each case this was because of physical conditions (including angina and an ulcer) that were only diagnosed after they had moved. Two others had their medication either stopped or reduced.

Subsequently, six movers were either taken off their medication or had their dosage reduced. At the same time, four others were given new prescriptions (in three cases a laxative or a skin cream) and one person had their dose increased.

Overall, the evidence points to very little change in the pattern of medication before and after relocation. The number of people who stopped taking drugs or medicines was matched by the number who started, and the number who had their prescription or dosage increased was mirrored by the number who had theirs reduced.

Before the move most people were said to have no need for any kind of physical aids. The most widely used were glasses and dentures. Three hospital residents had a wheelchair. There is some evidence that staff took a fresh look at their needs after the move. Elizabeth is a case in point. Thirty-five years old, she had spent 22 of them in various institutions. As a teenager, her four front teeth had been knocked out and she had been given a set of dentures. But they did not fit properly and she had found great difficulty in eating with them. At mealtimes she would take them out and wrap them in a paper tissue until she had finished. Two weeks after getting them a domestic assistant had accidentally swept the bundle off the table into a waste bin. She had done without ever since. Four months after leaving hospital, the hostel staff arranged for her to have some new false teeth. Still removable, they were secured to her back teeth by wires. For the first time in 20 years Elizabeth was able to smile with confidence, enjoy apples and crisps again, and no longer make a mess of herself when eating and drinking. By Phase II of our study, five movers had been prescribed new glasses (Phillip was advised to have tinted lenses to mask a defective eye). Also four people were newly supplied with dentures and seven others were identified as needing them. Two of the wheelchair users had found they could manage without their wheelchairs. Such attention to particulars suggests that relocation prompted staff to look at people in a new light, free from the blinkers of habit and familiarity (Booth, W., 1988). Sadly, such an effect did not appear to be long lasting. Twelve months later none of those waiting for dentures had been fixed up with them.

Training and habilitation

Throughout all three phases of the research just over a quarter of the movers were not involved in any kind of training programme. In the case of some of those who left the hostels for community placements, this might have been because they were seen as competent enough to manage without. Certainly there were fewer receiving training after the move than had been doing before. Even more surprising, perhaps, is the fact that the number of hospital movers on training programmes remained about the same after relocation. It might have been expected that they would all have benefited from some help in learning how to meet the demands of their environment.

Almost all the training that was given involved informal, unstructured work which, even when it showed evidence of planning, lacked anything so directive as a clear statement of goals or purposes. There was very little use made of prepared training materials or packs. Indeed, the number of people on structured programmes actually fell after the move although everyone was facing new challenges.

Both before and after relocation the focus of training for the hospital movers was on tasks like personal hygiene, self-care, etiquette (for example, table manners and socially acceptable behaviour) and basic domestic skills. In the case of the hostel movers, a shift of emphasis was observed. Before the move, most attention was paid to developing competence in areas such as personal hygiene, cooking, the use of money and especially domestic skills like household cleaning and laundry. Afterwards greater priority was given to instructing people in social and literacy skills, and in how to use public transport.

Remedial and support services

A comparison was made of the use of services by movers in the old and new placements. Answers were sought to three specific questions: was there any change in the volume of services used before and after relocation? Did people enjoy the same access to specialist and remedial services after the move? Was there any change in the pattern of use of segregated as opposed to ordinary community facilities?

There was a drop in the number of services used by hospital movers (from a pre-move mean of 6.2 per user to 4.8 after the move). Mostly this reflects the ending of any ongoing contact with consultants, a decline in the use of chiropodists (in the hospital many people were sent along as a matter of routine even when they had no problems with their feet), and a fall in the provision of laundry and domestic services (residents were more involved in these tasks in the hostels). There was also a smaller decline in the number of people receiving physiotherapy, but an increase in those getting speech therapy. Perhaps the most worrying was the drop in provision of daytime occupation or day care facilities. Many observers have noted that day activity is a critical component of successful community adjustment. Gollay *et al.* (1978), for example, refer to involvement in day activities as 'one of the keys to normalized living'. As we shall show later, the lack of such an outlet was a major cause of boredom, frustration and unhappiness for many people in our study. In Phase III, two out of every three hospital movers were said by staff to be bored for want of organized activity.

Compared with the picture among the hospital movers, there was a small increase in the overall use of services by people who left the hostels. This was mainly accounted for by a rise in the number seeing a clinical psychologist or attending adult education classes.

One of the concerns sometimes expressed about moving people into the community is that they will lose out on the specialist medical and remedial services available in hospital. We checked to see if there was any significant decline in the use of clinical and rehabilitative services on the part of hospital movers, including consultants, clinical psychologists, physio-therapists, speech therapists, special needs clinics, audiologists, opticians, music/art therapists and specialist workers for the deaf and blind. Although there were some shifts in the balance between these services – a decline in the use of some being accompanied by a rise in the use of others – there was no evidence that the hospital movers as a group were receiving less specialist attention in the hostels than they had done before. Indeed, so far as some families were concerned (see Chapter 9), things began to look up after relocation. Take Colin Halifax for example. Prior to moving into one of the hostels at the age of 25, he had spent the greater part of his life in residential schools and, later, hospitals. As a youngster he was operated on for a cleft palate and harelip. Thereafter he suffered continuously from chronic catarrh. His constantly running nose was both unpleasant for him and unsightly. At mealtimes food used to find its way down his nose. He was also troubled with frequent bouts of sickness which staff always put down to the catarrh upsetting his stomach. It was not until he left hospital that anything was done about his condition. A speech therapist referred him to a specialist for examination. He was found to have a defective epiglottis which could be corrected by surgery. At the same time he was diagnosed as being deaf in one ear and as having a chronic chest complaint. The last we heard he had just started his treatment.

Overall, there were signs of a movement towards greater use of ordinary, public services and facilities and away from segregated or specially designated sessions and from services provided within the units. As might be expected, this trend was more evident in the case of the hospital movers (for this group, the average number of services per user provided in the units dropped from 3.5 to 1.5, while the equivalent figure for the services provided in the community increased from 0.1 to 1.5). Mostly this change reflects the greater use made of local GPs, high street opticians and the regular chiropody services after the move. The small increase in the use of ordinary, public facilities by the hostel movers (up from an average of 1.7 per user to 2.3 after the move) came about mainly as a result of more people attending adult education classes at the local technical college and having places on worklink schemes.

Relatives and other relationships

As we reported above, a number of studies have found an increase in levels of contact with relatives among people who have moved out of institutions (Felce *et al.* 1985; Firth 1986; Beswick 1988). There is a tendency for such an objective to be regarded as a measure of placement success. We explored this topic before and after relocation with both staff and relatives. Our data suggest we may need to look beyond simple comparisons based only on changes in the frequency of visiting.

Relocation seemed to have remarkably little effect on the pattern of visiting by parents (or other next of kin). For the most part people continued as before. Those who had been regular and frequent visitors to the units before the move remained so afterwards; those who had rarely if ever visited maintained the same profile. A number of relatives had thought the move would make it possible for them to visit more often, but these hopes generally did not materialize. Most found it difficult to change their routines and rearrange their commitments, but other considerations too played a part. Mrs Heald, for instance, had always preferred to have her son home to stay for the weekend instead of simply visiting him in hospital. When he moved into the hostel she had tried just popping in to see him now and again. But this had not worked out. As she told us, 'He assumed he was coming home and it was very stressful for us both. It's best if I only go when I'm going to fetch him home.'

The absence of any obvious relocation effect must be seen in its wider context. Rates of visiting in the units were in any case pretty high before the move. Almost half the families interviewed visited once a month or more often, most of them weekly. Just about the same proportion had their relative home for visits monthly or more often: many who seldom or never visited them in the unit belonged to this group. Hospital families were in the majority among regular visitors; the families of hostel residents among those who had people home. Against this background there may have been less scope than is sometimes assumed for relocation itself to exert much of an impact.

At the same time, there was a noticeable increase in the number of people who visited their families after the move, and in the frequency of their visits. This trend was evident among both groups of movers. The number who were said never to go home fell by almost a half between Phase I and Phase III (from 18 down to 10), and there was a proportionate rise in the number who went to see their families monthly or more often. Few people stayed overnight either before or after the move.

Relocation also seemed to result in more fequent contact with a wider network of relatives, especially for the hospital movers. This was particularly so in the case of siblings. Almost twice as many people had some sort of contact with brothers and sisters after the move as had done before (22 compared with 12). Similarly, there was an increase (from 5 to 20) in the number of people with friends outside the immediate company of those with whom they lived. Partly this will have been because friendships were maintained with residents in their former placements. But there was also evidence for both groups of movers that the change in their life-style had broadened their horizons and extended their social circle. One small but illuminating example is given by the jump from two to ten in the number of hostel movers who sometimes had guests round for a meal. Rather surprisingly, very few people were said by staff to have special boyfriends or girlfriends and this did not change after the move – although possibly staff were not aware of, for example, relationships at the SEC.

Finally, and importantly, there were indications of small but significant post-relocation changes in the quality or character of some movers' relationships with their families. Mostly these changes were seen by staff as stemming from people's greater self-confidence and independence. Thus, for instance, Gordon Manchester's relations with his mother and step-father, which had long been fraught with difficulties, were said to have improved after his move from a hostel into a flat of his own: 'I think he feels confident and in a stronger position and he can cope with the relationship.' Similarly, June Rothwell had 'become mature' and had started to look on her mum as 'a bit old-fashioned'. Mrs Rothwell always used to bring her sweets, which June now associates with being a child; 'she has begun to see faults in the way her mum treats her.' Malcolm had been observed answering his dad back. He'd made it clear that if he had to do any gardening, he would not go home. It was the first time this had happened. Other relationships were described as 'far better', 'healthier', 'a bit more reciprocal' and 'mended now'. John Crawford's sister no longer 'smothers him'. Such changes were not always easy for the families to cope with. Peter Snow had become 'less dependent' on his mother but this 'created anxieties' for her. She used to rely on him for company and for doing her shopping. Now she 'sees him as better' and accepts that he should do as he wants, 'but can't help feeling lonely and rejected'.

Overall, then, relocation had little apparent effect on the level or frequency of visits by relatives to the placements (although rates of contact had been quite high anyway before the move). However, according to staff, there was evidence of an increase in the number of home visits by movers and in the extent of contact with relatives other than parents, especially brothers and sisters. Lastly, there were signs that some movers' growing independence had begun to show in the nature of their relationships with their families.

Use of community and leisure facilities

Successful community care means extending the opportunities for people to participate as ordinary members of society. As Bjaanes and Butler (1974) say, 'exposure to the community is an important factor in "normalization".' Among other things this involves improving their access to public facilities, reducing their dependence on special or segregated services, enabling them to get out and about in ones and twos or small groups rather than large parties, and giving them more say over their use of local amenities.

We set out to explore and compare with staff the pattern of community participation by movers before and after relocation. For each of a set of 12 everyday services or activities (shopping, hairdresser, bank, cinema, concert/play, cafe/restaurant, pub, church, sports event, social club, day trips and public transport), we asked about the use each person made of them (in the past month or past year), about their characteristic features (located in or outside the unit, public or segregated), and about the conditions of use (who decides, unaccompanied or with staff, alone or in small or large groups). In addition, we asked the same series of questions about people's leisure activities, focusing especially on their participation in outdoor games, indoor games (like snooker or darts), other sports (like swimming), amateur dramatics, musical activities and dances or discos. The results are presented below for hospital and hostel movers separately.

Community facilities

Overall both groups of movers, starting from a similar base, showed slight gains in the range of facilities used in the new placements, but important differences between them persisted in the way these facilities were used. Although none of the changes recorded were dramatic, they all pulled in the same direction.

So far as the hospital movers were concerned:

- There was an increase in the use of ordinary community facilities (from an average of 4.9 to 6.7 per mover), mainly accounted for by more people going to the local hairdressers, visiting pubs, attending a nearby church or chapel, and using banks, post offices and public transport.
- There was a small drop in the use of segregated facilities either in the unit or provided specially for people with learning difficulties outside. The number of such facilities had been low even in the hospital: films were shown in the hospital; there was a hospital chapel and social club; and a hairdresser visited periodically. After the move people went into town to have their hair done or to go to the cinema. The social club remained the only segregated activity on the checklist.
- There were few signs of any real gains in personal autonomy or self-determination on the part of the movers. Most people were accompanied by staff whenever they went out, and there was no apparent rise in the number going to shops, cafes, pubs, etc. on their own (despite their greater proximity in many cases). Similarly in the hostels, as previously in the hospital, people's use of community facilities was mostly determined by staff who decided when and where they should go.

The people who moved into the community placements were by comparison much more independent in their ways. They used a wider range of checklist facilities, were more likely to use them on their own or with each other, were less likely to be accompanied by staff, and more often than not decided for themselves what they wanted to do. Similar differences, though less pronounced, were also evident when comparing this group as they were in the hostels in Phase I with the people who had taken their places by Phase III. Almost certainly this reflects the higher levels of adaptive behaviour among the hostel movers (see Table 4 above).

Otherwise, so far as the hostel movers are concerned, two main points emerge from a comparison of their use of community facilities before and after relocation:

- Surprisingly the move did not result in people getting to more places without staff. Partly this may be an artefact of their relatively independent life-style in the old placements: in other words, there was less scope for improvement than supposed. Certainly, most people were using hairdressers, local shops, cafes and public transport on their own even before the move. Nevertheless some gains might have been expected, especially, for example, in the area of recreational and entertainment pursuits like cinema-going, having a day out or watching Town play on a Saturday. The fact that people did not participate in such things on their own accord may have been because they lacked the money. At this point, the exclusions brought about by disability are compounded by the exclusions enforced by poverty. Most hostel movers in Phase III still went to the cinema, live shows and concerts or on day trips in organized groups with staff.

- There was definite evidence after the move of people assuming more initiative in running their own lives. For almost all checklist facilities there was an increase in the number of people who were said to decide for themselves when to use them without reference to staff. The only exceptions were the organized activities mentioned above. If these are excluded from the picture, then the average number of facilities whose use was determined by the movers themselves increased from one-half to three-quarters of those listed on the checklist between Phase I and Phase III.

Leisure activities

The level of participation in leisure activities was low among all movers before relocation and remained so afterwards. The most popular events were discos and dances. Very few people played outdoor sports of any sort, and only a handful were involved in pastimes of a musical or theatrical kind.

The major change precipitated by the move seems to have been a shift away from activities based in the unit towards the greater use of outside facilities. Mostly this is accounted for by more people going out to discos and dances, but there was also a rise in the number of hospital movers having swimming lessons and in the number of hostel movers visiting their local for a game of darts or pool. In the main, however, even when people took part in things outside the unit, it was usually in a segregated setting. The dances were organized by the Gateway Club at the SEC; swimming lessons were held in special closed sessions at the local baths. There was almost no increase in the use of public leisure facilities, and generally people relied on staff to organize their activities for them. Even the hostel movers showed only very modest progress towards greater independence when judged against their limited participation in leisure pursuits.

Quality of experience

In an attempt to summarize the nature of the changes brought about by relocation in the use of community and leisure facilities by movers, we devised a scale which aimed to capture something of the relative quality of their experiences before and after the move. The scale was created from four pairs of variables describing the kind of facility used (public/segregated), how it was used (by individuals alone or in a small group/big group; with staff/without staff), and who determined its use (residents/staff). These pairs of variables were combined to form a six-point scale. At one end (low quality) we classified segregated facilities where people went in a big group accompanied by staff who made all the decisions. At the other end (high quality) we classified public facilities used on their own initiative by individuals or small groups of friends without staff being present. The points in-between were defined in terms of different combinations of these positive and negative features. Finally we added a point indicating that the particular facility was not used at all (recognizing that this might be because people chose not to do so or were denied the opportunity). Table 8 summarizes the results in terms of the average number of checklist facilities per mover on each point of the quality scale.

Four main points emerge from a careful reading of the table:

- Overall, the gains following on relocation are scanty even for the hospital movers, among whom it might have been thought the potential for change was greatest.
- There was a small increase for both groups in the use of checklist facilities.
- People's quality of experience rose slightly, marked by the shift in the average use of facilities towards the higher points of our scale in Phase III.
- The hostel movers used more facilities at higher points on the quality scale in both phases of the study.

A similar scaling procedure was followed using the data on leisure activities but, as reported above, the levels of participation were too low to allow any meaningful inferences to be drawn from the results.

Staff assessments of placement success

In this chapter we have reviewed the outcomes of relocation for our movers on the basis of information provided mainly by their keyworkers.

Table 8 Quality of experience of community facilities before and after relocation

Scale points (no. of positive features)	Hospital movers		Hostel movers	
	Phase I	Phase III	Phase I	Phase III
Low (0–1)	2.5	2.4	1.9	1.7
Medium (2–3)	4.0	5.1	2.4	3.1
High (4)	0.5	1.2	4.4	4.7
Not used	4.9	3.3	3.4	2.4
N =	17	17	22	22

Most of our measures so far have been targeted on specific areas of behaviour and activity. It is time we looked at the changes in the round and gave our respondents a chance to say whether they thought the new placements represented an improvement on the old.

We begin by exploring the way in which staff from the original placements viewed the new services. How successful did they think they would be? There is some evidence (Hemming 1982) that staff judgements are one of the better predictors of the outcome of a move, particularly in comparison with more commonly used variables such as IQ and length of institutionalization.

The vast majority of staff (42 out of the 43 we interviewed in Phase I) expected the new placements to be successful. By and large, staff working with the hostel movers were inclined to be more optimistic than their hospital colleagues. This difference may in part be due to a lack of certainty among nurses about what the hostels were like. As one respondent told us: 'I have vague doubts but I'm also not sure what [the hostel] will offer – except that they are nearer the facilities.' The reasons why hospital staff thought the new placements would be better related primarily to the additional resources the hostels were perceived to have which, along with a more able client group, were thought to allow them to work much more effectively with the residents:

Better staff ratio. . . . A different, more homely environment. Staff will be able to do more.

They might be able to implement the normalization philosophies we were taught at nursing school but cannot put into practice on the villas.

At the same time, paradoxically, the hostel staff were stressing the limitations of the hostels. For example one keyworker, referring to a woman who was leaving a large hostel for an ordinary house, said: 'Because Caroline was at home so long, she misses a lot of home life and [the new placement] will offer more home-like features. She won't have to compete with 20 or more people.' Staff also had clear views about the advantages of the new placements: 'It will be her own home. Her self-esteem will grow, she will value herself more.'

In all, staff thought the changes would leave just two people worse off. In one case this was because the keyworker saw the person, who was leaving a hostel for a house with five others, as a potentially disruptive influence: 'Although Terry is a very able fellow, he could present problems. He will create some bother, particularly on the money side.' In the other case, the person was moving out of a flat in the hospital grounds (shared with just two others) into a hostel with some 20-plus other residents, and his keyworker thought this would allow him less choice and privacy.

We also asked staff how happy they thought each mover would be after the move. The overall pattern of replies was very similar. The majority were expected to be happier (23), with a similar number likely to be just as happy (18). Nobody was expected to be less happy. Again staff working with the people leaving the hostels were more likely than hospital staff to predict the mover would be happier. This question elicited some strong responses from hostel staff, underlining both the relatively institutional nature of the hostels and the anticipated opportunities for greater privacy and autonomy offered by the community placements. For example, one woman drew parallels with her own experience as a student:

> I can understand how he feels. I once lived in the halls of residence at college. Moving out in the second year was bliss – being able to have tea when you wanted. Little things like being able to have a sandwich without using a plate will please him. People treating him as a worthy person . . . increased status. If he meets a girl he would hav e felt a right wally saying he lived in [the hostel], now he will be able to invite her back to his flat.

Another, echoing the concerns of the movers themselves, focused on the friction generated in the hostels:

> There won't be the stresses and strains of this place. He won't have to run the gauntlet of Stan, or sense the atmosphere if we are having trouble with Diane. This place can be very intense, and that can rub off.

Others emphasized how the small homely nature of the ordinary housing would itself change people for the better. Asked why she thought Peter would benefit from the move, his keyworker replied: 'Because of the smaller group. Basing it on our experiences of Peter on holiday with a small group, he's a completely different person – more relaxed, joins in more, he's great.' Finally, staff recognized that the movers themselves wanted to move on: 'He's very happy – he's so excited. When you bring the matter up, he always tells you he's looking forward to it.' By comparison, the kind of comments made by the hospital staff were very much more low key: 'His mother might visit him more. . . . He is happy here at the moment so he will probably be pretty similar.'

The general picture that emerges from the predictions is positive. Despite the fact that some staff were sceptical about the principles involved, when it came to looking at the plans for each individual they appeared to approve; almost everybody was expected either to gain from the changes or to be no worse off. However, there were differences between the two groups of staff involved. Those working in the hospital were a bit more cautious in their judgements. In the first place there was a degree of uncertainty over what the hostels would be like. Second, where the hostels were seen to be better, it was primarily because they were judged to be more effective as institutions. More resources, plus fewer pressures from highly dependent residents, were thought to leave the hostel staff better placed to work with people, doing the kind of things they would have done had they had the opportunity.

In the months immediately following the move, we asked staff to give an assessment of any changes in people's outlook or behaviour (both for the better and for the worse), the overall success of the placement and the happiness of the movers. Our respondents were able to identify positive developments in over three-quarters (35) of the movers during the settling-in period. The kinds of changes mentioned covered a range of areas of personal functioning, from the acquisition of skills to shifts in attitude and behaviour. Two broad patterns are discernible.

For the hospital movers the main focus was on behaviour changes, either through a decrease in problems (nine people) or an increase in approved behaviour (six people). By contrast, staff working with hostel movers in the community placements placed much more emphasis on the changes in personal development that had taken place since the move (cited by 12 people). Lucy's keyworker, for example, noted how she was growing in 'self-esteem and confidence, talking a lot more, actually contributing, pitching in ideas, showing signs of disapproval when she's not happy'. With both sets of movers there were relatively few people for whom staff could identify changes for the worse. A few mentioned increases in difficult behaviour (for example, drinking more), while for one man events had precipitated a loss of confidence: 'At first he used to like going out, especially to the pub for a drink, but now he seems nervous and hangs his head down. It's as if he wants to go, but is aware how he looks and feels self-conscious.' On balance, however, the problems were usually minor. With the exception of the two people who had already returned to their original placements, any difficulties that had arisen were usually offset by other changes for the better.

Not surprisingly, therefore, most placements were either considered very successful (26) or fairly successful (14). Many of the predictions made by staff before the move appeared to be borne out, particularly among the hostel movers. Within this group, 17 people were thought to be very successfully placed, and many of the reasons given for this outcome echoed the hopes expressed earlier. The small size of the community placements was frequently emphasized as an important factor: 'As there are only five residents here you are more aware of things, things are more consistent. Because there was nothing wrong with him he tended to get left out at [the hostel]. Here it's possible to cater for the individual.' Other staff mentioned increased autonomy and improved relationships as signs of successful adjustment. For example, Laura's keyworker explained, 'She can do her own thing, which she always wanted to do. Her independence, she loves that, handles all her own affairs.' Similarly, the support worker for one of the community houses said, 'Larry, Jim, Paula and Gary are good as a group living together. They don't just get on, they balance each other. They have a lot in common.'

Just four placements (all hospital movers) were thought to have achieved only mixed success. The only person whose placement was deemed unsuccessful was a woman who had returned to the hospital shortly after the move. She was also the only person described as being unhappy. Almost all the other movers were thought to be settling happily or fairly happily in their new homes. Some of the staff were very articulate about why they made these positive assessments:

> He's very appreciative, as though things are being done *personally* for him. A superb laugh. He will tell who he's met in town, who's getting married, where they live and what they were called before they got married – fabulous.

> He doesn't want to go back to [the hostel] even for a visit. He entered a fancy dress competition and the compere interviewed him. He wanted to know who I was. . . . 'One of the family' . . .

Others found it harder to spell out the ingredients of success, relying on general impressions ('No specific reason, just a general feeling about her'), and a number wondered if they knew what the individual mover was truly feeling. The prevailing air of optimism about the moves at this stage is highlighted by the fact that nearly three-quarters of the staff thought the placements would become more successful as time went on.

Twelve months after the move we again asked staff their views about how well the new placements had turned out. Their responses broadly confirmed the assessments they had given at Phase II with just a few subtle changes of emphasis. The great majority of placements (37 out of 42) were again described as successful, and all except 3 of the 22 hostel movers were said to be very successfully placed. Staff were a little more cautious in their appraisal of the outcomes for hospital movers and slightly less upbeat than they had been in Phase II. Only a third of these placements were rated as very successful, and more staff were ready to give them only a qualified endorsement. The three main reasons given for harbouring reservations referred to the lack of daytime activities ('not enough to do – she needs occupying during the day'; 'There's not enough activities for her'); problems of relationships ('No one that she can be close to – no friends. She has all the home comforts but that's not enough on its own'; 'Lack of male friends of his ability'); and the institutional nature of hostel life ('No matter how homely we try to make it, it is still an institution. She is living in a group which she doesn't like'; 'He's still in an institution, and while people are still living in large numbers, they can never have everything they need').

Collectively, staff reaffirmed their opinion that almost everyone was happy in the new placements. Compared to Phase II, however, they were less inclined to describe the hostel movers as very happy ('Is anybody *very* happy?'), more guarded about the meaning of happiness ('Content, really, rather than happy'), and more aware of the ups and downs of people's moods and feelings ('She's happy some of the time'; 'Just sometimes I feel she's not that happy'; 'Sometimes he does get depressed'). These more muted comments seem to signify a change in people's frame of reference. Immediately after relocation the comparison was with how movers had felt about their lives in the hostels. As we have seen, most were delighted with the change. A year later this had not altered ('None of them wants to go back'; 'There is no way he would ever want to go back'; 'I don't think she could see herself anywhere else'), but some of the feelings associated with making the break had begun to wane. Staff were sensitive to the fact that other considerations were now having an influence on how happy they seemed to be in their new placements.

As a final measure we asked staff where they thought the ideal placement would be for each mover. Nearly three-quarters of the hostel movers were felt to be ideally placed in the accommodation they were now living in. The remainder were thought to need either less supervision, such as might be provided in an unstaffed house ('In an ideal world I would like to see him living with a friend, particularly a girlfriend, getting some support from staff') or a family-type environment ('He needs a mum and dad figure'). No one was thought likely to benefit from a return to a hostel such as the one they had left.

By contrast, only a quarter of the hospital movers were felt to be in their ideal placement. The preferred options split evenly between a staffed house ('It would be a smaller group. He would have the staff to relate to, but there might be a chance of developing relationships'; 'He would feel more secure in a close-knit environment') or a family placement ('I think she'd enjoy a family placement because they'd concentrate on her'; 'June puts great store by families and people who are close to her'; 'I've seen her at home with a family where she doesn't show the bizarre behaviour she does in the institutions'). In short, only a year after leaving hospital most people were seen as potential candidates for some form of ordinary housing. No one was regarded as having been better off in a hospital environment or as needing to go back.

Summary

The findings outlined in this chapter present us with something of a paradox. For the most part, all the objective indices we have used for measuring the changes concomitant with relocation among our movers have yielded, at best, only small gains or benefits. While improvements usually were recorded on the various indicators – more so among hostel than hospital movers – they were also mainly incremental in nature. There was no giant leap forward, no runaway progress, no transformation in people's behaviour or the extent of their involvement in the community or their relations with their families or their use of services and the like.

Yet, at the same time, staff readily vouched for the success of the new placements, affirmed the movers were happy in them and agreed they would not want to go back. In other words, there appears to be a gap between the harder evidence obtained from staff and their more subjective impressions based on a close personal understanding of the individuals involved. Certainly, staff gave more weight in their assessments to what they saw as improvements in people's inner resources – such as self-esteem, personal confidence and social maturity – than was reflected in our choice of indicators. Let us explore this avenue further by first listening to what the movers themselves have to say before turning to the views of their families.

7

Learning to listen

For too long the voice of people with learning difficulties has been almost entirely absent from the debate about services. While 'consumer research' is well on its way to becoming an established tradition in many areas of the personal social services, for a long while this was not the case with residential services in general (Booth 1983b) and residential services for people with learning difficulties in particular. Thus, writing five years ago, Richards (1984) could only identify five British studies with this client group spanning the previous 20 years.

The picture is now slowly changing. The last few years have seen widespread development of the self-advocacy movement (Crawley 1988), and increasing emphasis on the involvement of people with learning difficulties in the formation of individual service plans (e.g. see Blunden et al. 1987). This shift is reflected in the considerable number of user studies we were now able to find in the field, including over 20 British and many American research projects. Perhaps the greatest significance of these developments is the acceptance, implicitly at least, that the views of people with learning difficulties constitute as equally valid a perspective as that of professionals, practitioners, relatives or researchers.

This chapter opens with a detailed review of the literature. We do this for two reasons. First, our own research makes more sense when seen in the context of earlier work. Second, there has been a dearth of comprehensive reviews on this topic. The findings from this body of material should be more widely known as they have important implications for policy and practice.

There is little agreement on how to tap the views of people with learning difficulties, but what is striking about this diverse range of research is the remarkably consistent picture produced. The subjects of these studies value what independence they have achieved, and when given the chance to express a choice between the environments they have experienced, they invariably opt for the more normal and the least restrictive.

Some researchers bemoan the diversity of the methods we will review here: they lament the lack of a simple, established 'quality of life' measure that would allow direct comparisons between studies. On the whole, we regard this methodological eclecticism as a strength rather than a weakness. Many of the researchers were trying to answer quite different questions: a case of methodological horses for courses. The fact that the resulting picture is so consistent is all the more remarkable for that. In the review which follows we have grouped studies by method, ranging from structured surveys to ethnographic work.

Structured surveys

Some authors have tried to produce a standardized 'quality of life' outcome measure, complete with statistical estimates of reliability and validity. For example, Heal and Chadsey-Rusch (1985) found volunteers to develop the Lifestyle Satisfaction Scale (consisting of 29 yes/no questions), using statistical methods to control for response biases. Their sample included people living relatively independently in their own apartments as well as some from a 58-bed 'intermediate care facility'. They concluded that the former group were significantly more satisfied with their environment and their general life-style than the latter:

> The higher . . . scores by the apartment dwellers are consistent with the hypothesis that satisfaction is correlated with less restrictive settings.

Similarly, Seltzer (1981) assessed the 'satisfaction' of 153 people released from a 'state school for mentally retarded persons'. He reports a positive relationship between feelings about the placement and several aspects of the community residential environment. For example, satisfaction with in-house responsibilities was higher when in-house training was provided. Satisfaction with relationships was the only factor he found to be unrelated to the residential environment. Seltzer concludes:

> The results suggest that when residential environments are more normalized, along the lines of increased training opportunity, increased opportunity to assume responsibility for in-house tasks, more autonomy, clearer expectations on the part of staff members, and increased access to resources, residents are more likely to perform mastering skills and be satisfied with the residential settings.

However, none of these structured measures has attracted any support, and their use is largely restricted to their originating authors. There are two possible explanations. First, the constraints of producing an instrument that is, in technical terms, reliable tends to result in rather inflexible questions. Amongst a population who have trouble answering direct questions, this factor will limit the scope of the measure. Second, the measures tend to be concerned with absolute issues of what constitutes happiness, satisfaction or quality of life. They attempt to identify generalized dimensions that relate to quality of life (for example, good health, enjoyable work, affection, etc.) and design questions to tap these dimensions.

Unfortunately there is little consensus about how to define 'quality of life'. Moreover, the dimensions chosen are externally imposed; they do not necessarily relate to what the respondents in the study actually feel or consider important about their lives. At best they provide information about what service users think about issues chosen by the researchers. There is also the problem of making absolute judgements. Perceptions of satisfaction and happiness are simply not absolute in nature, but are inextricably bound up with expectations, experiences, and knowledge of alternatives. Most of the more successful studies have attempted to include an element of *relative* judgement ('Is X better or worse than Y?').

Semi-structured surveys

In the absence of any recognized instrument there has been a strong tendency for researchers to opt for a semi-structured format, each study developing a schedule geared to its particular purposes. A classic of this kind is *Coming Back* (Gollay *et al.* 1978). A sample of 440 people discharged from various hospitals was followed up. At the time of interview 87 per cent were still in their community residence (all with fewer than 25 beds). The vast majority liked where they were living, and only 5 per cent would have preferred to return to the original institution. On the basis of their answers the authors concluded that overall 75 per cent of the study group had adjusted 'very well' to the new environment, with 21 per cent falling into the 'all right' category (leaving just 4 per cent as 'not very well' adjusted). Interestingly, when the views of the families (here the authors rather oddly lump together natural and foster parents, along with direct care staff) were assessed in the same way, the aggregated results were strikingly similar (77 per cent 'very well', 20 per cent 'all right', 3 per cent 'not very well').

In one of the earliest British studies, Campbell (1968) interviewed 304 of the 314 people living in local authority hostels in Lancashire, the bulk of whom (88 per cent) preferred the hostel to their previous hospital placement. Scheerenberger and Felsenthal (1977) talked to 75 former residents of a hospital who were now in either foster homes, group homes or intermediate care facilities: here 88 per cent liked the placement and 83 per cent did not want to return to hospital.

The NIMROD scheme in South Glamorgan, intended as a pilot for a comprehensive community based service, has been extensively evaluated. A client study was carried out when the NIMROD services had been well established (Lowe *et al.* 1986). Those interviewed lived either at home (28), in the NIMROD 'ordinary housing' (18), or in non-NIMROD residential placements (16, almost all in hospital). Most people (87 per cent overall) in all three settings could describe things they liked about their current placement. A much lower proportion of people also identified a negative feature of where they lived, and this varied by setting. It was lowest (25 per cent) for those at home and highest for those in hospital (75 per cent); the group in NIMROD housing fell in-between. Friction with the other residents was the most frequently cited negative feature of all three types of placement.

Of the 18 people in NIMROD housing, 12 had previously lived in hospital or hostel. The comments on their experiences in these more institutional settings are by far the most negative. All 12 people included a strongly critical element: 'It was rotten', 'I used to get down in the dumps', or 'It was boring.' Only 4 of the 12 also mentioned something positive.

On a rather smaller scale, Passfield (1983) found that out of 20 former hospital residents now living in Priory Court (warden-controlled independent living accommodation), only 4 thought their new home was 'worse' than the hospital, and N. Booth (1981) comments that the 12 people in group homes he interviewed all agreed that their lives were now better than they had been in hospital.

Unstructured interviews

Malin (1983), in his work with residents of group homes, concluded that less structured interviews may help people who have difficulty in answering direct questions to talk more freely. Indeed some of the most successful and illuminating work has been done by researchers who have opted for what are traditionally described as qualitative methods. Of particular interest is Margaret Flynn's (1986a) work with people living independently in unstaffed accommodation in the North West of England. Most of the 88 people in her study had moved to their current houses from institutions. The core of her study consisted of unstructured tape-recorded interviews.

Some of the people she spoke to were in 'hard to let' accommodation, and she estimates that at least a quarter of her sample had experienced victimization of various kinds by people from the surrounding communities. Nevertheless, all but 3 of the 88 people interviewed said they preferred their current houses to their previous, more institutional placements:

> Despite adverse circumstances in which a number of people live, they do not express high levels of dissatisfaction with their lives. This indicates that independence matters a great deal to them. Further, it indicates that in the main this population do [*sic*] not complain excessively or sufficiently.

Sugg (1987) also opted for informal unstructured interviews in his study of 33 former residents of St Lawrence's Hospital. These people had moved mainly into local authority and voluntary sector hostels, with some going to private establishments. He reports that the majority were glad to have left hospital, although many still had positive feelings about it. Most people were said to be 'definitely happy' in the new placement (only 4 of the 33 being 'definitely not happy'), although there was rather more criticism of the day placements.

Ethnographic studies

The last group of studies examined falls into what might loosely be called the ethnographic tradition. Of these only Robert Edgerton's major study, *The Cloak of Competence* (Edgerton 1967) is widely known in this country. Edgerton followed up 48 people who had previously left hospital for 'vocational placements' and who were no longer under the supervision of an agency or relatives.

Although Edgerton does mention a 'loosely structured schedule', no interview would commence until a relationship had been established between the respondent and the researchers. Tape-recorded interviews were augmented by extensive participant observation. The researchers would visit people in their homes, go shopping with them, and generally interact with them during their ordinary day-to-day lives. Data about experiences – what they talked about, what they did, who they met – were subsequently recorded in the form of extensive field notes. Such methods of data collection are intended to be both unobtrusive and systematic. The researchers reported extensive contacts with the ex-patients, averaging 17 hours but ranging from 5 to 90.

Unlike the previous studies Edgerton did not take a comparison of the institution and community environments as his starting point; he was concerned with the *process* of coping with non-institutional life. However, it is not difficult to infer how these ex-patients felt about the institution.

For most of them the central concern in their lives was avoiding any of the stigma attached to institutionalization. They did this by adopting a number of strategies for 'passing' as normal people. At the same time many 'denied' the reality of their handicap by, for example, attributing their relative lack of competence to the depriving experience of being insti-tutionalized in the past. Although no longer part of the service network, Edgerton concludes few had achieved full independence, the majority relying on 'benefactors' who ranged from past social workers and landlords to employers and neighbours. Their influence was not always benign.

Edgerton attempted to follow up the original sample 10 years later (Edgerton and Bercovici 1976) and again after two decades (Edgerton *et al.* 1984). Twenty years on, the authors concluded that, for those people they could trace (15 of the original 48), not only had their dependence on benefactors decreased, but so had their concern about their institutional past, which most now reported rarely thinking about.

Few researchers in this country have used such methods, with the notable exception of a Scottish study (Cattermole *et al.* 1987). Their longitudinal study used participant observation and unstructured interviewing to explore the transition of people with learning difficulties from both hospital and home into more independent settings. Before the move people in the institution graphically described their restricted lives. They complained about the lack of privacy and the inflexibility of rules and routines. They were very aware of their segregation from the outside world and expressed resentment about it. Most were highly conscious of their position in the institution: at the bottom of the hierarchy and subject to discriminatory rules, being called derogatory terms like 'low-grades', and being treated like children by staff. All the people interviewed wanted to leave the hospital. After the move they reported that they liked living in the community, although their social lives remained relatively restricted.

Atkinson (1985) used participant observation as part of a study of the life-styles of 50 people discharged from hospital to ordinary housing in Somerset. The method was only partly successful; visits to people in their own homes produced detailed descriptions of their activities and routines, but attempts to accompany a group of residents on excursions into the community proved much more difficult. Some of the residents would go to great lengths to avoid being seen in public with the student acting as the observer.

Atkinson also persuaded some of her respondents to keep diaries over one week describing their activities. The amount of information provided varied enormously between individuals; some wrote detailed accounts of their lives, others managed little. The result is a series of detailed illustrative case studies which, amongst other things, emphasizes the importance of social relationships in determining quality of life (Atkinson 1987; Atkinson and Ward 1987).

Discussion

Some care needs to be taken in interpreting the results of all these studies. The terminology is potentially confusing and inconsistent. As Booth *et al.* (1987) show, even within Britain, let alone abroad, terms like group home can cover a wide range of provision. Furthermore, the 'community placement' in some studies turns up as the more institutional placement in others (e.g. local authority hostels). The point is not that any particular class of placement is better than others in terms of the results of user studies; we lack the evidence to make that judgement. Rather, a general pattern emerges. Given the choice, the vast majority of people opt for the least institutional environment in their experience. These judgements are, however, relative. So, for example, while Halpern *et al.* (1986) found that 87 per cent of people in semi-independent living schemes liked where they were living, 44 per cent would still have preferred to move to even more independent situations. Brandon and Ridley (1983) report a similar desire for greater independence after their discussions with a group of hostel residents.

For further insight it is worth examining the situation of the small minority of people who do not fit the general pattern. In an unusual study Dunn (1984) talked to people in hospital who had no immediate prospect of moving. She found that over one-third of the residents were worried about life out of the hospital. Compared to those who were positive about the idea of living in the community, this group were likely both to know less about the community and to have less direct experience of the world beyond the hospital.

Experience prior to placement can have quite a specific effect. We have already noted that most people in Campbell's (1968) study preferred their hostel to their previous placement, but this varied from between 88 per cent for ex-hospital residents to just 40 per cent amongst those who had been living at home.

Finally, there are a number of reminders that a 'community placement' is not always less restrictive than the hospital that preceded it. Gollay *et al.* (1978) talked to the 13 per cent of their sample who returned to an institutional placement, and they found them less satisfied with life in the community than those remaining there. Over half claimed they preferred the institution; some were quite bitter about their experiences outside it. On a different scale Passfield (1983) mentions one man who returned to the hospital every day to feed his pet birds; the housing association managing his new home did not permit pets.

These observations suggest that the minority who apparently do not want greater freedom are not making arbitrary choices or demonstrating an inherent preference for institutional life. Rather, they are reacting to negative experiences in the community or are simply treating the unknown with an understandable caution.

Interviewing techniques

One limiting factor in all the work discussed so far is the extent to which researchers have relied on verbal methods with a population among whom a significant proportion do not have good speech skills. Indeed, some studies explicitly screened out less verbally able potential respondents (e.g. Scheerenberger and Felsenthal 1977). Some researchers acknowledged that communication can extend beyond just speech – for instance, Campbell (1968) writes of using tones of voice, facial expressions, gestures, etc. as pointers to attitudes and opinions – but they do not tell us how they collect this information.

A small number of studies have used imaginative and innovative means to get round the problem. One good example is Conroy and Bradley's (1985) evaluation of the closure of the Pennhurst State School and Hospital in the USA. They used a variety of question styles in their interviews before and after the residents were relocated. These included seven items based on a visual Likert scale, comprising five simple, stylized facial drawings (big smile, small smile, neutral, small frown, big frown). The questions took the form of 'Which face is most like how you feel about. . . ?' A big frown was assigned a score of one, while a big smile scored five.

A sample of 56 people who were expected to move participated in the baseline interviews. Although by the end of the user study 26 of the original group had yet to move, both 'stayers' and 'movers' were inter- viewed a second time. The authors stress that the stayers should not be seen as a control or comparison group since the allocation process was uncon- trolled. Rather, the results from this group should be seen as a separate study of the effects of the hospital run-down on its inhabitants.

All the different question formats used by Conroy and Bradley showed that the movers were more satisfied with the various aspects of life outside the hospital. They scored significantly higher on the smiling/frowning face scales in three areas: how they felt about where they lived, what they thought staff felt about them, and how they felt about other residents. For three of the four remaining areas (how other residents felt about them, how they felt about staff, and how they felt about themselves), the movers' scores in the community placements were higher than in hospital, but the differences were not statistically significant. In the last area (day activities) there were no differences.

The results of the two interviews with the 26 stayers present a marked contrast. There were no significant differences between first and second interview scores on any of the seven items. But it is of interest to note that responses to the question about how residents felt about life at Pennhurst produced lower scores at the second interview.

In this country Richards (1985) studied a group who had left Lea Court Hospital for various types of hostel accommodation. He used photographs of different aspects of the physical environment (living room, grounds, bathroom) and asked the group whether they preferred the arrangements in the hospital or where they were now living. In general he found people consistently chose the latter, although some did show approval of the hospital grounds and living and dining rooms. Richards suggests that some of the hostels were 'very cramped' in comparison. The significance of the study is not so much that people preferred the life outside but, as Richards points out, the fact that: 'It was possible, through the use of a method of enquiry inspired by the desire to communicate, to demonstrate the consistency with which even very poor communicators were able to indicate their preferences.'

Howie *et al.* (1984) describe an attempt to develop a tool to involve residents directly in a review of residential provision in New Zealand. They used both a structured questionnaire and what they describe as a 'forced choice non-verbal measure', both comprising material taken from a quality of care checklist formerly administered to staff. In the forced choice scheme, residents were asked to put cards with statements such as, 'This is a place where people come into your bedroom all the time without knocking', into one of three boxes. One box was labelled with a drawing of the residents' own home, and the other two were designated a 'good residence' and a 'bad residence'. If the statement applied to the residents' home, then they were told to put it in the appropriate box. If it did not, they were asked to assign it to one of the other boxes. A similar process was used for statements about staff. Analysis of the results showed that both questionnaire and forced choice measures could discriminate between the residents' accommodation.

Studies with other client groups have faced similar problems. Baker and Intagliata (1982) used the same kind of smiling/frowning faces as Conroy and Bradley (1985) in their evaluation of a community facility for the mentally ill, while Willcocks (1984) devised a visual game for sounding residents' views in a consumer study of elderly people's homes. Residents were asked to sort cards depicting 'key features' of the residential setting into four categories: 'important', 'don't know', 'don't mind', and 'unimportant':

> results appear to show that, with the exception of the 'safeguard against fire' card, residents chose aspects of the environment that were normal, unexceptional and non-institutional.

Reliability, responsiveness and validity

One common concern among researchers, particularly those using more structured interview schedules, has been the reliability of the instruments. Indeed, most authors have stressed the technical difficulties of interviewing people with learning difficulties. A number of studies have investigated the effectiveness of different question formats for this population. For example, Wyngaarden (1981) reports that asking scaled questions ('Is X a big problem, somewhat of a problem, or not a problem?') proved singularly unsuccessful. As a result he opted for extensive use of the yes/no format. However, Sigelman and Budd (1986) conclude that yes/no questions represent a 'poor technique'.

In a series of papers Sigelman and colleagues systematically evaluate the impact of question format on response bias. They use three criteria: responsiveness, validity and reliability.

Taking responsiveness first, they argue that it is pointless asking questions in a way people find difficult to answer (Sigelman *et al.* 1982). In their three studies they found that pictorial multiple choice questions got the highest levels of response. Response levels progressively decreased from verbal yes/no (relating to activities), yes/no (subjective judgements), verbal either/or, verbal multiple choice, to open-ended questions at the bottom (Sigelman *et al.* 1981a).

Reliability was investigated a number of ways including extensive comparisons based on asking the same question in reverse format. For example, their respondents were asked both 'Are you usually happy?' and 'Are you usually sad?' at different points in the same interview. Sigelman *et al.* (1981b) report that between 40 and 50 per cent of the subjects in each of three studies answered yes (acquiescence) to both questions. They conclude that acquiescence is a greater problem when the question is not understood or, possibly, when the correct answer is not known.

Both verbal either/or and verbal multiple choice questions were vulnerable to 'recency': the tendency to choose the last option presented. For example, in response to the question 'Are you sad or happy?', 85 per cent said they were happy; for the reverse form – 'Are you happy or sad?' – only 67 per cent chose happy. The use of pictures reduced the effect of recency.

The researchers found relatively low levels of agreement with the answers given by significant others for all question formats. For example, when staff were asked to judge how much the resident liked living in their particular institution, fewer than one-third of the assessments coincided with a judgement made by the resident regardless of whether or not pictures were used (Sigelman and Budd 1986). While we see the value of this exercise with more factual questions, it is not clear why disagreement with others on such a subjective rating is necessarily indicative of response bias.

Conroy and Bradley (1985) also attempted to evaluate the extent of acquiescence in their sample. They included a reverse yes/no question set, and were also able to compare the answers to questions in different formats. They report a much lower rate of acquiescence in the first phase of interviewing (14 per cent), which fell even further (to 5 per cent) in the second phase. Their measures of recency also suggest a lower rate than that found by Sigelman and colleagues.

Although we recognize that these potential response biases are an issue, we also have some reservations about Sigelman's important work. We suspect the very high levels of acquiescence she found might well be a function of the kind of interviews she conducted. If acquiescence is a problem when the respondent is not sure of the appropriate answer, then being asked questions to which the researcher obviously knows the answer

('Is it raining outside now?'), which are patently absurd ('Are you Chinese?'), or which they have already asked (albeit in a different format) seems likely to induce uncertainty and doubt – a positive incitement to acquiesce. Such question formats would not seem to be conducive to talking freely, and may well have reduced the effectiveness of the more open-ended questions.

Some of the individual questions also seem to contain potentially confusing elements, underlining the difficulty of designing yes/no question pairs that represent genuine alternatives. For example, half the instances of acquiescence reported by Conroy and Bradley were in response to one particular pair of questions: 'Do you want to keep on living here?' and 'If you could, would you like to leave here and live somewhere else?' The inclusion of the 'If you could' appears to us to substantially change the meaning; it introduces an element of the ideal which is missing from the alternative. Perhaps the worst example is given by Heal and Chadsey-Rusch (1985). They coupled 'Would you like to move back to [previous placement]?' with 'Do you like living here?' and counted a yes to both questions as an example of acquiescence, yet it is quite plausible that their interviewees liked where they were living but would still have preferred to return to their original placement.

There is an implicit assumption that response biases represent a barrier preventing researchers from getting at how this population 'really feels'. At some stage, or so the reasoning goes, someone may ultimately develop a reliable and valid questioning strategy, but in the meantime we must test for, and discard, invalid answers. It would be wrong to overstate the issue since there is considerable ambiguity in much of this writing, but the assumption seems bound up with the idea that acquiescence and related response biases are a function of the disability itself:

> Due to deficient cognitive, verbal and social skills, mentally retarded persons might be especially susceptible to response effects.
>
> (Sigelman *et al.* 1981a)

A more plausible hypothesis is that response biases are not simply attributable to people's intellectual difficulties *per se*, but to the impact of their experiences. Thus acquiescence is part of the way people relate to their environment and is therefore itself of interest. Similarly, while consistent answers may be desirable in most circumstances, inconsistency can reflect ambiguous or mixed feelings and should not simply be interpreted as a technical problem.

However, the practical implications of the work on response bias are important. Answers should not be treated uncritically, and a variety of question formats should be used. In particular, pictorial multiple choice and either/or questions offer great potential. Flynn's advice (1986b) that any interviews should be as relaxed and unthreatening as possible, and that questions which people may find difficult to answer (e.g. about time and frequency) should be avoided, seems sound (see also Atkinson 1988).

However, there are two serious problems with most of the studies cited: many lack a longitudinal element and involve retrospective assessments of the original placement, and, further, most are limited to the more able residents. As Fisher (1983) points out, studies in social work have tended to report high levels of satisfaction irrespective of the outcome for clients. Commenting on a study of elderly people in residential homes, Willcocks (1984) notes a similar phenomenon:

> They were very likely to express complete satisfaction with services they were actually receiving. . . . Furthermore, residents' expressed attitudes tended to be strongly influenced by the present environmental experiences and they generally accepted the familiar and feared the unknown.

It is conceivable that the positive picture of the less institutional settings that has emerged from the studies described earlier is a function of a similar kind of process: a tendency to be positive about where you are at the time of rating. Would the same set of preferences have emerged if the choices had been offered prior to the move out of the institution? The few studies that do include a longitudinal element (e.g. Cattermole *et al.* 1987; Conroy and Bradley 1985) suggest this is likely to be the case, but the value of a pre-post move comparison is clear.

The tendency to include only more able people is, of course, partly a consequence of the predominantly verbal methods used. However, even in studies that have used visual elements, a similar kind of preselection occurred. For example, Conroy and Bradley note that through a combination of screening and rigorous consent procedures, only 13 per cent of their achieved sample were regarded as 'profoundly retarded', compared with 62 per cent of the total population of Pennhurst.

In our study we have taken the opportunity to explore some of these issues. We set out to discover if the people involved wanted to move in the first place, and then examined how the *process* of moving changed the way the different environments were perceived. The methods we used (see Chapter 2) are unusual and innovative, designed to maximize participation in the study through the inclusion of simple visual questions.

Mover preferences before relocation

The weight of evidence shows that most people wanted to move. At the first interview 33 of the 37 respondents chose the photograph of the new placement in preference to their current residence when asked where they would most like to live. Three of the remaining four were hospital movers.

Interestingly, however, the majority put a happy face on the photographs of *both* placements (see Table 9). There are two (possibly inter-

Table 9 Feelings about placements before the move by hospital and hostel respondents

	All movers		Hospital movers		Hostel movers	
	Current placement	New placement	Current placement	New placement	Current placement	New placement
Happy	23	29	10	7	13	22
In-between	5	4	0	2	5	2
Sad	8	3	2	3	6	0
N	36*		12*		24	

* One respondent refused to make a choice.

linked) explanations for this response. It may indicate that people were happy to move, but not out of any deep-seated dissatisfaction with their current placement. Possibly their desire to leave where they lived was more a matter of pull than push: of wanting to grasp the new opportunities they sensed might await them rather than of wanting to escape from their current way of life. Equally, it might be that the movers were simply indicating a willingness to fit in with the plans made for them, expressing a degree of passive resignation to decisions they saw as being beyond their control. On balance, the evidence of the 'visual game' exercise suggests that before relocation both sets of movers were relatively uncritical of their current placement, although at the same time expressing a clear choice in favour of moving on.

However, as Table 9 shows, there were some differences between the views of the two groups of movers. The only people who said they felt sad about moving were hospital patients, and they also put more happy faces on the photograph of the hospital than on the photographs of their new placements. In fact, only just over half of the hospital respondents actually declared themselves happy at the prospect of moving. By contrast, the hostel movers were much less positive towards the homes they were about to leave. A quarter of them actually put a sad face on the photograph of their hostel, and almost as many again affixed a neutral face. The great majority were looking forward to moving into their new placements.

Several factors may account for these differences. For those involved, the move from hospital to hostel may have seemed like a bigger step than that from the hostel into supported housing, involving many more unknown factors. Most of the hostel movers would have been used to participating in activities outside the unit, were likely to be moving with someone they knew, would probably be attending the same day activities as before, and living in the same area. For the hospital movers, things would be substantially different – new activities with new people in a new town.

Moreover, the hostel movers generally received more intensive preparation and more personal support than their counterparts in hospital (see Chapter 4), while the business of moving into the community placements seemed to offer more opportunities for participation (for example, in choosing furniture and crockery). In view of the greater degree of uncertainty involved for the hospital residents, it is perhaps not surprising they were more inclined to hedge their bets.

On balance, the evidence from the 'visual game' shows that, before relocation, both sets of movers were relatively uncritical of their current placement, although the great majority wanted to move when presented with a straight choice between staying put or making the break.

Mover preferences soon after relocation

Shortly after the move we still found the movers were positive about their new homes. Of the 40 participating in this phase of the study, 36 chose the photograph of their new home as the place where they preferred to live, and all but one (who refused to make a choice) put a happy face on it. Of the four people who expressed a preference for their old placement, two had already returned there by the time they were interviewed. The firm conclusion is that once they had moved, people did not want to move back.

Table 10 shows how the hospital and hostel movers felt about their old and new placements during the settling-in period following relocation, as revealed by the 'happy/sad faces' exercise. A number of significant shifts in opinion had taken place by comparison with the position before the move. Taking all the movers together, there appeared to have been a major re-evaluation of the old (pre-move) placements. This was evidenced by a very substantial drop (from 23 to 13) in the number of people attaching a happy face to the photograph of where they had lived before the move, matched by a corresponding increase (8 to 21) in the number choosing a sad face to represent their feelings about their former homes.

Among the hostel movers, the number putting a sad face on the

Table 10 Feelings about placements after the move by hospital and hostel respondents

	All movers		Hospital movers		Hostel movers	
	Old placement	New placement	Old placement	New placement	Old placement	New placement
Happy	13	35	5	13	8	22
In-between	5	3	1	1	4	2
Sad	21	1	9	1	12	0
N	39*		15*		24	

*One respondent refused to indicate a choice.

photograph of their old placement doubled after the move. People who had said they were happy in the hostels while still living there now looked back and put a different interpretation on their feelings. At the same time, there was no change in the numbers saying they were happy with their new placements, and no signs of disillusionment. For the overwhelming majority the move appeared to have lived up to their expectations.

Among the hospital movers, three simultaneous and interrelated changes in attitude occurred following relocation: the number saying they had been happy in hospital halved; the number putting a sad face on the photograph of the hospital increased commensurately; and the number seeing themselves as happy in their new homes almost doubled.

Mover preferences a year after relocation

A year after the move the broad pattern established during the second phase of interviews still applied: 30 out of the 35 people successfully interviewed chose the photograph of the new placement when asked where they preferred to live. The remaining five were all hospital movers. Interestingly, only three of them expressed a preference for their old placement. The other two were in fact involved in definite plans to move out of their hostels into more independent accommodation, and they were looking forward to this happening.

Indeed, there were some signs that the hospital movers were becoming more critical of the hostels (see Chapter 10). In addition to the two people already mentioned, another two also indicated that they would like to move on at some stage. However, the 'happy/sad faces' data for this group must be interpreted cautiously. Almost all the attrition within our sample occurred among the hospital movers. On top of the five people who from the beginning were unable to act as respondents, six others did not take part in the exercise during the follow-up stage of the study (because they declined, were too ill or had returned to hospital). Thus the seven people who put a happy face on the photograph of their new placement (see Table 11) actually constitute a minority of our original group of 21 hospital movers, although they form a majority of those who were able and willing to participate in the exercise.

No similar qualifications need to be made in the case of the hostel movers. They remained as strong adherents as ever to their new way of life; the one man who put a sad face on his community placement had in fact just been moved back to the hostel.

It is sometimes claimed that the novelty of a new placement is a big element in its attraction and soon wears off when life settles down. We can find no evidence for the existence of such a short-term, so-called 'honeymoon' effect. On the contrary, over the three sets of interviews the consistency with which all but a tiny minority of our respondents have

Table 11 Feelings about placements a year after the move by hospital and hostel respondents

	All movers		Hospital movers		Hostel movers	
	Old placement	New placement	Old placement	New placement	Old placement	New placement
Happy	11	28	4	7	7	21
In-between	5	2	2	1	3	1
Sad	17	3	4	2	13	1
N	33*		10*		23	

*Two respondents refused to make a choice.

expressed preferences for the new placements is really most striking. It is impossible to avoid the conclusion that our respondents thought the new homes were better than the old. Furthermore, the act of moving seems to have opened new horizons and forced a substantial reassessment of their earlier experiences.

Overall, then, comparing the results from the three stages of the study it seems that, despite being quite positive about their original circumstances prior to relocation, most people were looking forward to moving. Some months later, settled in their new placements, they liked where they were living and had become more critical of their previous homes. A year after the move people were still saying they were happy in the new placements, although there were signs that some of the hospital movers were beginning to express a wish for more independence than their hostels could offer and to look forward to branching out on their own. The lesson seems to be that it is the experience of alternatives which allows people to evaluate their situation, frame their preferences and make clear choices. Certainly the experience of an alternative life-style enabled our movers to reappraise their former living situation and to state a clear preference for life in the less restrictive setting.

The question remains as to why precisely our respondents' attitudes developed and changed as they did. The next chapter deals with some of these issues by examining what they actually told us about their lives. This further analysis both confirms and augments the pattern we have already established, allowing us to add some colour and detail to the picture derived from the 'visual game'.

8

Speaking for ourselves

She had a good life here, guaranteed a holiday twice a year, rigged out with clothes . . .
(*Hostel keyworker*)

No, I shouldn't want to go back there. I know they used to look after us and take us for holidays and buy us new clothes and that, but no, I wouldn't want to go back there no more.
(*Hostel mover*)

Although the keyworker never quite finished her sentence, implicitly she was asking, if people are well cared for in the hostel, why move? The answer from a former resident suggests there is more to life than simply being looked after. Having established in the previous chapter that people wanted to move and, after making the break, preferred the new placements to the old, we now explore what influenced these choices and helped to shape these preferences, paying particular attention to the movers' own opinions about the services they received.

Before the move

Movers' feelings about their original placements

The most striking feature about the comments recorded in the pre-move interviews was that virtually *everybody* could say *something* good about where they were living. Involvement in domestic tasks was the aspect of life most liked (23 out of the 33 movers with speech). People referred to the pleasure and satisfaction they derived from a range of normal household duties: cooking, shopping, 'doing your jobs', and even 'cleaning the toilets'. To some these tasks gave the sense of being valued, to others the means of asserting their competence:

> I like helping them – not them doing it all. I like going up to night school, setting the tables, and I like putting the sheets, putting the towels away, sorting the tights out and helping . . . making beds.

Despite some staff scepticism about residents' enthusiasm for chores, involvement in the day-to-day maintenance of a unit was important to the movers. Other features of the original placement which attracted positive comments from residents included leisure activities ('watch telly or we might go to the Gateway Club'), the physical environment ('your own bedroom') and relationships with staff ('nice staff on').

Most respondents were notably uncritical of their old homes even though they wanted to leave. When asked directly, 19 out of the 33 said there were 'no bad things' about where they lived. Only 3 of the hospital movers expressed any complaints about the daily routines and caring practices in their units, and none of the hostel movers voiced any discontent with either the behaviour of staff or the way their hostel was run. Where movers did have a grievance, it was mostly directed against other residents, underlining the interpersonal stresses that characterize institutional living: 'He follows staff up and down. I can't stand him following. You've seen him, haven't you?'

Movers' expectations about their new placements

Most people were enthusiastic about their coming move. Everybody made some positive statement about their new home, although many had difficulty in answering questions about how it would be *different* from the old. Consequently, the things they thought would be 'good' about the new placement were often very similar to those they liked about where they were.

Top of the list again were domestic tasks (mentioned by 19 out of the 33 movers with speech):

> I'm looking forward to it, yes I am. I think it'll be . . . it's a good idea. I'm going to enjoy it. Oh yes, shopping and that, and cooking and cleaning.

Undoubtedly, the link between doing for oneself and autonomy lends a strong symbolic meaning to domestic work. Doing household chores was tantamount to having more personal independence. But moving had its other attractions: for example, 18 movers mentioned the prospect of forming new relationships or strengthening old ones: 'Well, I mean they're nice, right homely, and they're nice company. I mean it's near my mother's, it's near my brother as well.' Eleven people were impressed by aspects of the physical environment of their new placement: 'It has different lights to what they have. The bedroom I have picked is number six. It has a gas fire in and a chair and some wardrobes. It's very good, that bedroom I picked.' Another 10 talked about the opportunities for new leisure pursuits ('Gardening', 'Going hiking – never been hiking before'), while eight movers mentioned the prospect of fewer rules and restrictions ('I'll be my own boss'). They also discussed having their own possessions around them, the food, the chance of going to a Social Education Centre (SEC), and the area to which they were moving. Two of the hospital movers laid particular stress on the fact they were returning to an area from which they had originated:

> Well, Dewsbury was where I was born, and my auntie told me that before she died she wanted to see me in a local, so I'm trying to fulfil that wish if I can, you see.

Overall, the movers saw more good features in their new placements than in their current ones, although those coming out of hospital had slightly more reservations than those leaving the hostels. For example, one woman indicated that although she liked the hostel flat into which she was about to move, she had been bored when there on her introductory visits. Another woman was anxious about whether she would be able to cope in the new environment:

> You have to watch where you're going, there's buses, there's cars. Everything on the road. That's what it is like . . . I'm not used to crossing the road, because of my fits. I wouldn't know whether I was coming or going.

The majority of the hostel movers (17 out of 24) were unable to think of any drawbacks and faced the move with unbridled optimism: 'It'll be all right. I've never lived outside before, but I'll like it.' Some acknowledged that to begin with they might be a bit lonely and that things might be a bit strange: 'We shall have to wait and see, won't we? It's a big place though, isn't it? It's going to take some cleaning but I suppose I'll get used to it.'

But mostly the uncertainties boiled down to nothing more specific than an understandable apprehension about the new and unfamiliar world they were about to enter: 'I mean it's a big change. It's a big change from here. I shall miss them down here, going out.'

Mover preferences after relocation

At the first set of interviews after the move, we found that people were still very positive about their new homes. It would seem that having moved out they did not want to go back. At the same time there was evidence that some movers had become much more critical of their previous placements. The further analysis of what people said during the Phase II interviews clearly confirms this assessment.

Looking back on the old placements

Of the 36 movers making some kind of comment, only seven now claimed there had been 'no bad things' about their former homes compared with 19 before the move. The number of people complaining about the atmosphere rose (from 14 to 19), with more recalling violence against themselves: 'Once I went up there and he got hold of me and he banged my head on the wall, and that's why I wanted to get out of that place.' Similarly, the number of movers criticizing the regimes doubled (from 9 in Phase I to 18 in Phase II), and grievances were aired that we had not heard before.

Three of the hostel movers, quite independently, expressed resentment at having had to queue for their personal allowances:

> This is what annoyed me of all things. You'd queue up for it a lot and you're there waiting and waiting, taking it into the office to sign your name down, and they say come in, and you're waiting up to eight o'clock for your money. That's what annoys me most of all.

Others complained about the lack of privacy, inflexible routines and block treatment:

> I didn't like, you know, when staff come up steps, just come up. I'd have liked a bell on that door downstairs.

> They made me get up, and if you didn't get up they pulled the bedclothes off you.

> They used to get them [new clothes] from the [store] room. . . . Everything got small for you.

Looking back, the movers remembered few redeeming features of these original placements. In Phase II only 17 people made any positive statements about the old placement, compared with 35 in Phase I, and these most commonly concerned old friends (both staff and residents), the satisfaction derived from domestic tasks, and leisure activities. Listening to the interview tapes, these praises come over as very low key at best.

Settling-in to the new placements

Most movers, particularly those now living in ordinary houses, were enthusiastic about their new homes. Jack spoke for the majority when he said, 'Smashing. I'd choose here, yes I would.'

When it came to describing what they liked about them, the importance of 'doing for yourself' was stressed time and again: 'I can do my own washing and things like that. I do . . . my own ironing, baking a lot.' Almost half of the movers specifically said they enjoyed greater freedom and had fewer rules and restrictions placed on them than before. Such comments were as likely to come from someone who had moved from hospital into a hostel as from someone who had moved out of a hostel into a community placement.

Better relationships with relatives, carers or other residents were important reasons for preferring the new placement (cited by 24 of the movers). Clare summed up what many people felt when she said simply, 'There's friends, isn't there, here.' Just over a third of those who had moved from hostels into community living schemes noted there was now less stress and tension caused by arguments among the residents.

It would be wrong to give the impression that all was sweetness and light. By the time the Phase II interviews were underway, two of the hostel movers had already left the staffed house they were sharing with four others, partly because of difficulties in relationships. As one of the occupants said bluntly, 'They got on my nerves here.' The supposed trouble-makers acknowledged the strains but put a different slant on them. As one of them explained:

> If I went for food anytime of day, Bill used to follow me in and say, 'Oh, you can't have that.' I'd say I'm paying same board as you, I've got it just same. I told [keyworker] that many a time when I were down there. She just said ignore them. Well, you don't want people hanging about when you're preparing your stuff.

However, a large number of people did experience a qualitative improvement in their relationships with others after the move. Moreover, their network had begun to reach beyond the narrow circle with whom they lived. Half of the hostel movers referred positively to people (mostly neighbours) from the local community: 'Nice people [neighbours] . . . sometimes they bring us clothes in when it's raining.'

These wider contacts mostly consisted of passing the time of day; few involved home visits although there were exceptions. Jim, for instance, had moved from hospital into a hostel in his home town. Many of the staff at the hostel could remember him from his childhood; his keyworker had gone to school with him; the escort on the SEC bus knew him well; old friends from the local Irish National Club now visited him and he visited them. As Jim said:

> I should have been back at Dewsbury before . . . if they'd brought me here at first as they should have it'd been better. . . . I said look, I want to get back where I belong, where I were born, back t'lads.

Living in the community also had its downside. One house had been the unwelcome focus of trouble from local children, and this had caused problems for the occupants: 'They are little devils at times. . . . They ring doorbells, bang on windows, they do all sorts of tricks.' Similarly, a man with a pronounced hump on his back was subjected to frequent abuse by children and adults, although he made it clear this had happened most of his life, and not just since moving out:

> Little kids even say what's that and how did you get that. . . . I'm used to that like. I don't like it but I'm used to it. Just one of them things. Even grown-ups, even men's said to me, grown-up men. Even in cars, when cars pass you by.

However, there were fewer such examples of harassment and victimization than might have been expected given their vulnerability, and, for the most part, the movers themselves seemed to shrug them off: 'You know them big boys that lives down there? They keep laughing at us when we're going past. I don't take any notice of them.' Perhaps one reason·for such composure is that public unpleasantness was something they were used to and had encountered throughout their lives.

After one year

As shown in the previous chapter by the happy/sad faces exercise, the pattern established soon after the moves was still apparent after a full year: people opted for the new placement when asked where they preferred to live and generally said they were happy with their new way of life.

Remembering old times

Most of the movers with at least some speech remained critical of their old placements: 'I've lost interest in up there now'; 'Oh no, don't want to go back there. They drive me round the twist.' The number of people claiming there had been 'nothing bad' about their pre-move homes stayed much lower than before the move (10 as against 19), and complaints about the stressful atmosphere in the more institutional settings were undiminished (14 in Phase I, 19 in Phase II, 20 in Phase III): 'Noise and falling out, you know it were terrible, had to get away, get away altogether. I'm happier now.'

There was a slight drop from Phase II in the number of people making negative comments about the regimes in the old placements (from 18 to 15), but this was still substantially higher than Phase I (9), and many were even more forceful. For the first time some people were prepared to criticize individual staff: 'I weren't struck on. . . . Soon as I speak to her she'd say I'm busy, and I'd wonder why.' As earlier, control over their money was an issue for some people: 'He made me go into town without money, on Saturday, into town with no brass.' There was clear resentment at the arbitrary, childish punishments that had sometimes been imposed on them: 'They used to make us go up to us bedroom. . . . They used to say go upstairs and stop there.'

Certainly many movers also made positive comments about their previous home – in fact more than during the settling-in period (22 compared to 17). Perhaps the length of time since the move had allowed them to get things a little more in perspective. Possibly some felt a little more secure and had less need to distance themselves from their former homes. In any case, all these comments were muted, most people simply recalling a single feature of their earlier lives that they had valued. Some mentioned old friends ('I liked talking to people, didn't I'), others leisure activities ('Going for walk'), or helping run the unit ('Washing the pots').

Life in the new placements

The great majority of people continued to prefer their new homes, although there were hints of some disaffection from a few of the hospital movers seeking greater independence (see Chapter 10). The hostel movers, in particular, were as enthusiastic as ever: 'Oh it's lovely, you can do what you like you know. I like it, I wouldn't go back no more.'

As always the issue of involvement in running the homes dominated the discussion: 'I like living here. . . . Making coffee, sometimes taking it in turns with the tea, cooking. Taking it in turns washing up.' The extraordinary consistency with which the movers emphasized independence through domestic activities is one of the more striking features of their comments. When asked which they would prefer, cooking their own meals or having their meals cooked for them as in the hostel or hospital, all but three (all hospital movers) wanted to cook for themselves. A similar question about washing clothes brought the same pattern of responses. Regardless of how some of the movers might react when actually presented with a frying pan or a packet of washing powder, the symbolic importance of 'doing' for themselves is unquestionable.

There were some subtle changes in the thrust of people's comments in comparison to the settling-in period. For example, there was a distinct shift of emphasis away from relationships towards the pleasure to be gained from leisure activities (although at times the two could be difficult to disentangle). Gary, a hostel mover, told us, 'I like getting out and meeting more people, that's what I've done. I've been to Leeds and I've joined a cricket club since you last came.' William, who came from hospital, said, 'We go across there . . . to the pub once a week with staff, so I've nothing to grumble about.' Gary's social life is very much under his control. He has taken the initiative and now has the opportunity to mix with more people. William's social activities are determined by staff, and although he does use facilities in the community, his contacts do not extend much beyond staff and fellow residents. The former has pushed a bridgehead into the local community; the latter may be physically in the community but is not part of it. It would be wrong to suggest that many people had achieved such a degree of integration as Gary; for most of the hostel movers contact with people apart from staff and family remained largely at the level of nodding acquaintance: 'Next door neighbour, she's nice. . . . She once gave me cigarettes, that were good of her.'

The number (5) of people complaining about harassment from the local community stayed about the same as during the settling-in period ('Spit on Larry's coat. . . . I went like this to them, I says you dare'). However, it was difficult to tell whether this was a continuing problem – some seemed to be recalling incidents already described earlier.

The importance of leisure activities was confirmed when people were asked if there was anything to which they looked forward. By far the most common response (13 people) was to talk about holidays and trips ('Yes, going to Majorca'; 'Oh, I'm looking forward to going to Rhyl, when it comes'). People's lives are largely uneventful, and their holidays represent a high point of change and variety. Indeed, their aspirations were on the whole remarkably limited ('Television at night in armchair and a cup of tea'). Only one man had ambitions that might involve some struggle; despite anticipated opposition from her parents, he hoped one day to move in with his girlfriend.

Another interesting change since Phase II was the drop in the number of people who compared the new placement favourably with the old in terms of freedom from restrictions. During the settling-in phase of interviewing, nearly half the movers commented on the greater personal independence they enjoyed; by the follow-up phase just nine people still felt the difference keenly enough to mention it again (and only two of these were hospital movers). Perhaps they had got used to their increased freedom and now took it for granted. However, the number of complaints about the rules and regulations in the new placements also appeared to be on the increase. A number of the hostel movers complained about staff intrusiveness and were irritated by the seeming inability of some staff to resist interfering in even the smallest details of their lives. For instance, John voiced just this frustration over an incident the previous day: 'That annoyed me, yesterday, that new lady. I had a drink out of the bottle and she played heck with me. I were thirsty you know when I came home.' Having surmounted the important step from a hostel into their own house or flat, such governessy attitudes were seen as demeaning their new status and an affront to their self-image. Although hospital movers too confessed to sometimes being upset by the way staff treated them ('I can't get to sleep at night because they've been like that with me'), they were more inclined to direct their complaints against other residents (see Chapter 10).

These discontents have to be seen in context. Over half of the hostel movers still considered there was 'nothing bad' about their new homes. While there was some evidence of resentment against the perpetuation of old institutional practices, their comments also suggest that many people had begun to develop a greater degree of assertiveness. Even though things were not perfect, it was clear that most of the hostel movers had gained enough satisfaction and fulfilment from the changes to make the thought of any return to their former lives unacceptable. The hospital movers, on the other hand, had started to come up against the limitations of what essentially were still relatively institutional placements (see Chapter 5). It must be acknowledged that our data here are less conclusive than we should have liked. As we have mentioned before, all the attrition in our sample occurred among the hospital movers, leaving us with just 11 respondents in the follow-up phase from the 21 people in this group. Nevertheless, one point comes through clearly. Whereas none of the people who moved into their own house or flat expressed any desire for change when we interviewed them a year later, those who moved into the hostels were much less settled and content. Only two said there was 'nothing bad' about the hostels. Over half of our respondents talked about moving on. Two were enthusiastically involved in plans to move to a more independent setting and already champing at the hostel bit; two others were contemplating the possibility; and two more expressed a wish to return to their previous placements, largely we suspect out of dissatisfaction with the hostel and a lack of knowledge about other alternatives. Only four people indicated that they were happy to remain where they were. Given the choice and enough support, it seemed likely that many of the hospital movers might now prefer some form of accommodation based on ordinary housing.

Self-perceptions and mental handicap

Significantly, *none* of the movers in our study ever spontaneously used the term 'mental handicap' in any of the interviews, even when asked why they had first left home or gone into an institution. In all the extensive informal contact we had with them, there was only one instance where the subject was ever mentioned. One woman was overheard bitterly complaining to a friend that someone at her day centre had referred to her as mentally handicapped.

Choosing how to pursue this topic with our respondents raised delicate and sensitive issues. We had no wish to offend people or challenge their sense of identity. In the end, we were only able to explore this subject with 25 of the movers. We began by commenting that their original placement was often described as a hospital (or hostel) for people with a mental handicap. We then asked each mover what they thought the term 'mental handicap' meant.

The most frequently proffered definition involved some reference to physical disability or illness (9 out of the 25 people involved). As Jack said:

> Oh, they're different. It's a shame when they're different, isn't it? They can't walk, they can't talk some of them, no arms – have they? Some of them, no legs and some can't see a thing.

Similarly, Heather told us, 'A lot of cripples. . . . Mental's an illness and handicap's what they get with it.' A further six movers emphasized the inability to look after oneself as a distinguishing feature of a mental handicap ('It means they can't help themselves'; 'I think it's them that can't do for themselves'). Three others saw it in terms of problem behaviour ('It means if there's anybody misbehaving and that').

Each of these definitions was phrased in the third person, deliberately excluding the respondent. Those who mentioned physical disability were all hale and hearty. Those who referred to lack of competence in self-care had already stressed their independence. This implicit rejection of such a status for themselves was sometimes reinforced by direct disavowal. As John asserted, 'Well, I'm not handicapped because I can work.' Others made the same point by naming people they knew who were said to be 'mentally handicapped'.

Another five respondents declared bluntly they did not know what mental handicap meant. This left just 2 people out of the 25 we interviewed who accepted the label as applying to themselves ('I'm mental handicapped. . . . It means you go to a handicapped party and enjoy it there'; 'I don't know . . . unless it's to do with my brain damage').

We also asked if people with a mental handicap were similar or different to other people. Of the 18 movers who had directly or implicitly denied being 'mentally handicapped', 13 insisted there was a difference. However, of the remaining seven, all but two opted for 'similar'. At the same time, our respondents were not unaware of their own limitations, even those who rejected the mental handicap label. 'I can read a bit,' Bob said, 'but I can't reckon money up.' Frank didn't try shaving: 'If I did it myself I might do something, get cut.' Sandra acknowledged that she wasn't ready to live on her own: 'No, I can't do that. I might do something. I might get burnt.' These admissions rarely came in response to direct questions. When asked if they found anything difficult, people usually said no. Their first inclination was to identify with the crowd and assert their ordinariness. They preferred to talk about their difficulties on their own terms and in the right context. Perhaps this is why they distanced themselves from the term 'mental handicap'. It has the same effect as always introducing Steve Cram as the man who failed to win an Olympic gold.

The same desire to identify themselves with the commonplace showed in other ways. Many of our respondents associated more closely with staff than other residents. Over two-thirds of the movers named at least one member of staff as a friend. One in every six people listed staff to the exclusion of residents, and nearly a third claimed more staff than residents as friends.

Equally, a lot were at pains to shake off the stigma of institutional living. Both the hospital and the hostel movers saw relocation as a step in the right direction: towards a less restrictive way of life. After the move, as we have seen, both groups looked back critically on their previous placements. These criticisms were more than just a commentary on their past experience. It was also a way of saying that, as individuals, they did not belong in such an environment. Similar preferences also showed in attitudes towards day activities. The few with jobs were proud of them, and many others aspired to one as an ideal. Greg confided, 'It's a shame I can't get a building job. I'd be singing, "That's Living All Right".' A job means entry into a world no longer exclusively for handicapped people; it confers status, and it gives a measure of independence by providing more money than the benefit system.

Adult education classes were also popular and attracted few criticisms. Some provided opportunities for mixing with a wider circle of people and used integrated facilities like the local technical college. By contrast, the Social Education Centres were judged less favourably. Most people attending them could point to some positive features, and just about everyone said they would rather go to the centre than stay at home. Nevertheless, they were also the target for a lot of complaints. Emma, for instance, told us, 'The fighting's not nice at the centre. They start hitting and doing all sorts they shouldn't.' Interestingly, some of the fiercest critics were those who had left the SECs, as with the movers looking back on their former placements. George was uncompromising: 'I call it the doghouse, and they're always falling out and fighting there at the centre. No, I don't like the centre at all.'

Once again, we can see the same pattern behind the replies: people consistently expressed their preference for services and activities that are less institutional, unexceptional and more suggestive of an ordinary life. One way by which they tried to reinforce their sense of personal identity was by emphasizing their differences from their peers. In this light, it is unsurprising that the majority of our respondents should not apply the label 'mental handicap' to themselves.

The local People First group in our study area captured the feelings to which our research bears witness in a letter to Kirklees Social Services Department. 'We are pleased', they wrote, 'that councillors are changing their use of words and not using the word "mental" when they speak about people with learning difficulties. . . . We want to be treated like ordinary people. "Mental" makes people think we are stupid, silly and dumb.'

Summary and conclusions

The evidence from this study of the impact of community care policies on users is unambiguous. Taking our cue from people who have made the break from hospitals and hostels, it is quite clear that most wanted to move in the first place, and once established in their new placements they did not want to return.

Why they wanted to move is less clear. On the whole they looked forward to ordinary, everyday activities like being with people they liked, simple leisure pursuits (watching television, listening to records) and being involved in domestic activities like cooking and cleaning. For most people these were not new things. Indeed, some had difficulty in articulating how the new placement would be *different* from their old one. Admittedly, many hoped to escape the more antisocial behaviour of their fellow residents, but there was little sense of hostility, resentment or rejection in their attitudes towards the institutional environment. Nevertheless, they found their limited, introductory experience of the new placements to their liking, and were able to make a reasonably informed and consistent choice in their favour.

After the move the pattern changed considerably. People were more articulate in saying what they liked about their new placement and, perhaps more significantly, they were much more critical of the old. They commented negatively on the rules and restrictions they had experienced in the past, and complained about the friction with former peers. Most were adamant they did not want to return to the original institution.

We can only speculate on the nature of the processes underlying this change. But part of the answer seems likely to lie in the social context in which the movers lived. Most people had very low expectations of what they might get from life. To many of them the nature of the institution was given; their adaptation to it was largely unquestioning. Things happened the way they did because that's the way they happen; if staff say it's good then it must be good.

The change in attitude reported after the move is probably due partly to the fact that the movers had a yardstick against which to measure previous experiences; they discovered that things could be different. For many the process of moving may have helped them become more assertive. Considerable energy was put into reviewing how new placements were progressing; people were probably asked for their opinions far more than before.

There is a danger here of portraying the movers as entirely passive. Mest (1988) argues that most of the literature on this subject fails to acknowledge the extent to which people with learning difficulties actively develop a positive sense of self. Like Cattermole *et al.* (1987) we found that, although aware of their limitations, most of the movers fiercely rejected the view of themselves as 'mentally handicapped'. They tended to see themselves as essentially similar to people in the community, many identifying themselves with staff rather than other residents.

These attitudes are reflected throughout the interviews. It is no accident that the respondents put so much emphasis on the importance of domestic tasks and 'doing your jobs'. Through their comparative abilities in these activities, many movers had articulated a strong sense of worth and competence. Where day activities reinforced people's self-esteem, either through employment or participation in adult education classes, they appeared to be popular. Where the day provision cut across these feelings, being in large, regimented, segregated settings, there was far more criticism.

The respondents' comments also underline the importance of relationships. This manifested itself both positively in the way they looked forward to meeting new people and making new friends after the move, and negatively in the extent to which relationships with fellow residents were often a major source of stress. However, with a few exceptions, relocation did not produce any radical transformations in our respondents' friendships. Such developments may well require much time and effort before they mature. For many there was a desire to keep in contact with old friends, although some movers wanted to distance themselves from the institution. As Atkinson (1987) argues, in the absence of compensating friendships in the community, maintaining relationships through the transition of a move is an important ideal. Rehabilitation work may well be as much about the conservation of existing links and friendships as about starting afresh.

Fortunately our movers did not experience the level of victimization described by Flynn (1984, 1986a, 1987). This is not surprising since none of the people in our study was in the kind of hard-to-let accommodation she describes. Some problems did emerge where people were living on the edge of fairly tough estates. The outcomes were not entirely predictable. The greatest problems occurred in a stable, well-maintained council estate that just simply had a lot of bored children. Nevertheless, Flynn's advice to avoid problem housing areas and to minimize the extent to which people are conspicuous seems sensible. However, the issue calls for one rider. It is true that those who go and live in the community risk some degree of harassment, but secure environments like hostels and hospitals are no guarantee of protection from similar problems. Many of our respondents reported distressing instances of assault and harassment by other residents and, in a few cases, by staff and outsiders.

Overall, the picture that emerges is positive. As far as the movers were concerned, almost all clearly felt that they had gained from the changes. Whatever the limitations of the new services in Kirklees, few wanted to return to their former lives.

9

Relatively speaking

This chapter tells of the families caught up in the relocation process and how the moves affected them. We wanted to know how families reacted to the relocation of their relatives, their hopes and fears and how those feelings changed over time.

To understand fully the attitudes of parents towards the changes, it is first of all necessary to consider something of their own past. Placing a child in a long-stay institution is a heartbreaking decision. In our study, parents had experienced intense sadness and guilt, often mixed with anxiety and some relief at the separation. For many these conflicting emotions persisted for a long time and never entirely disappeared. Elderly parents in particular, who had only made the break with their son or daughter when they themselves had lost the ability to cope, felt their absence acutely. One mother in her 70s, now living alone, said, 'I cried every day for two years. I didn't want him to go, but the doctor and my elder son said he must or I would have a nervous breakdown.' Her feelings were echoed by another mother: 'I was very upset when he went. I hadn't had time to make friends, he was my life.'

Remembering the difficulties parents suffered at this time, it should be anticipated that having their decision reversed by policy changes might bring about a return of the emotional havoc that those earlier times provoked. As Stedman (1977a) suggests, it forces the family to wonder whether institutionalization is, or ever was, appropriate. Indeed many families had only conceded because of strong professional recommendation to 'let them go'. Stedman warns that resistance to the re-entry process is understandable and should be expected.

Of the 28 families (14 hospital/14 hostel) we interviewed in our study, 19 were parents and 6 were brothers or sisters. The remaining 3 respondents were made up of an uncle, a trustee and a surrogate 'auntie'. Among the 19 parents there were 12 mothers and fathers over 60 years of age who were living on their own and having to come to terms by themselves with the new ideas behind community care.

Before the move

Nearly all the families had been aware that people were moving out of the hospitals and hostels long before they themselves were caught up in the process. Initially, some parents had not linked the moves with their son or daughter. As Mrs McCann said, 'I didn't connect it with Stuart at all because I thought, well Stuart's all right where he is.'

Nevertheless, half of all the relatives reported that their initial reaction to the rumours and media reports of the impending changes had been unfavourable, with only four people having felt positively about them. At this stage most of the anxieties of families were based on inadequate information and scare stories in the press and on television about the shortcomings of community care services. Frohboese and Sales (1980) reported similar reasons for parental opposition to deinstitutionalization in the USA, where 'several particularly shocking examples of perceived inadequacies in the community-based system were repeatedly relied upon and used to generalize about the efficacy of the whole system.'

By the time people were due to move, some of this initial opposition had abated. In fact, more than two-thirds of our respondents thought that moving people out of hospitals and into hostels was a good course of action, although nobody went along with the opinion that it was fitting for people to move straight from hospital into ordinary housing. Most families agreed with the view that 'they need a half-way house after having been used to a lot of people and organized activity.'

Apart from two relatives of hostel movers, however, everyone declared that no matter how good the facilities were in the community, there would always be a role for hospitals in providing care and accommodation for people with severe learning difficulties. Among the sorts of people mentioned as needing hospital care were those with 'multiple and severe handicaps' and others who require constant supervision. People, in short, who need a lot of individual attention. Ironically, personal attention is something families had found intrinsically lacking in the long-stay hospitals they had known. This raises the question of why they continued to see a place for them when their own experience shows that hospitals do not deliver the goods.

There are many reasons that may help to explain this apparent contradiction. In some cases it may be necessary to go back to the parents' earlier decision to institutionalize and to the feelings of guilt and relief that this generated. As part of the legacy of these emotions, perhaps they are unable to turn on the hospital without turning on themselves. In other cases families, especially those of hostel movers, may only be convinced of the merits of care in the community when viewing it in terms of their own relative. They are hard pressed to perceive how others with more pronounced difficulties could be accommodated in the same residential settings.

Four out of five families in our study had been visiting the hospital and hostels for more than ten years, and most had a clear idea of their good and bad points. In the main, the majority of families had not found their visits particularly pleasant, although the hostels fared better than the hospital. In the former, families had usually been offered something to drink when they called and given an opportunity for privacy in a quiet room. Conversely, many hospital families spoke of the deterioration in standards and facilities since the start of the relocation programme. Some people were given a cup of tea, but much depended on the member of staff on duty. Others took their own flasks and food. Privacy inside the hospital buildings was also scarce, leaving families little alternative but to walk round the hospital grounds if they wanted a few quiet moments with their relative. As one mother commented, 'Visitors were definitely an afterthought.'

On the whole, the majority of families had been quite content with their reception in the units, although there were a few who had experienced problems, been upset on occasions, or felt unwelcome as a result of the attitudes of staff: 'I think the staff didn't really care if you went or you didn't.' All but three families were satisfied with the care and support the hospital and hostels gave their relative: 'I'm very grateful for her being looked after, I know I couldn't cope with her.' Nevertheless, a third of our respondents, mainly the hospital movers' families, said there was room for improvement and cited the need for more staff ('They're left very much on their own'), more personal attention ('He was very untidy, unshaved and with shoelaces undone'), more care with diet and clothes, and more privacy for residents.

These last comments indicate a measure of dissatisfaction with the underlying limitations of the hospitals' and the hostels' regimes. The importance of these issues for families becomes more evident after people have moved into their new homes.

First impressions

During the settling-in period all but three families said they had spoken to the care staff when visiting the new placements. Three-quarters of the hospital movers' families agreed that members of staff were welcoming, helpful and pleasant when they visited, and that they had been informed how their relative was settling down and adapting to the changes. The families of people who had moved into the community homes were mostly unable to express an opinion as they said they rarely saw support staff.

The features that families liked most about the new homes were many

and varied. Most commented on the improvement in the physical environment ('It's much more comfortable, like a hotel, with pictures and ornaments, lovely bedcovers, fitted wardrobes and her own sink' – *hospital
mover's family*). They praised the individual attention their relative was
now receiving from staff ('More personal attention, there's someone with
them all the time and they can see no one's hurting them' – *hospital mover's
family*). Some families mentioned the fact that the placements were more
home-like ('They all seem to mix together like a family' – *hostel mover's
family*), and others had seen evidence of a new found independence.
Families had greeted with enthusiasm even small changes, such as being
able to have a bath every day. One mother summed up what the move
from hospital had meant for her son:

> There is no restriction on Clive, he can go to his bedroom and outside.
> There's so many looking after them [at the hostel] he gets a lot of
> attention. He can go into the kitchen and let them know what he wants
> to eat. He helps out, sets tables, butters the bread. He keeps his bedroom
> tidy and is particular about his room. In fact it takes more people to
> supervise him doing things than for them to do it themselves.

Although families were not prepared to criticize the hospitals openly, and
even though they saw them as having a role for other people, the sum total
of all these small, domestic improvements they had noticed amounted to
an implicit criticism of the hospital environment and its regime. The
responses from parents clearly demonstrated that the hospital had never
been the right place for their sons and daughters, even if the truth was too
painful for them to admit openly.

There were also aspects of the new placements about which families had
reservations. Although nearly all the hospital movers' families felt the
hostels were an improvement on the hospital, only half the hostel movers'
families expressed similar satisfaction with the changes. Those who had
doubts worried about the lack of supervision ('At the hostel they were
supervised 24 hours a day, now we're not sure when staff is there') and the
possibility of loneliness and isolation ('No neighbours, no garden, just four
closed doors face him when he comes out of his flat'). They also had
misgivings about the neighbourhoods in which the homes were situated
('We don't like the area the house is in, it's a right rough area') and the
houses' proximity to busy roads ('It's a corporation house facing on to the
main road, and I'm still apprehensive because of the traffic'). Indeed,
the single most frequently cited worry among families related to the
location of the new placements. These findings are confirmed by Meyer
(1980), Latib *et al.* (1984) and Atkinson and Ward (1987), who also found
that many families have real fears about staff supervision, support and the
quality of life and are worried that protection in community homes will not
be adequate.

For both groups of movers the changes were considerable, and in the early stages of settling down and establishing new routines it was only to be expected that there would be problems. Fully two-thirds of hospital movers' families indicated that difficulties had arisen during this period, whereas only a quarter of hostel movers were said to have experienced some trouble. The problems that occurred included pilfering, breaking equipment, exploitation by other residents, overspending, health problems, disturbed behaviour and fighting. (For further analysis of this subject, see the section in Chapter 3 on transition shock.)

Even in the face of these problems, just over half of the families said they had not thought about what might happen if the new placement did not work out or their relatives did not settle. Most assumed that people would be moved back to the original placement or moved on elsewhere. The remaining families had no idea what the plans might be. Only one mother said she would bring her son home. Two out of three families had not asked anyone what would happen, nor had they been told. Just five families were given definite indications that their relative would return to the original placement, and another four were given vague reassurances ('before this move [staff] said they had contingencies for this kind of thing, but they never said what'). In keeping with the air of uncertainty that surrounded the new homes, two mothers of hospital movers had been informed at the hostel that their relatives were being assessed over a 12-month trial period.

Visiting and access

In many ways the agenda was also being rewritten for the families. Over the years some of the parents had formed longstanding friendships with each other, in particular the older mothers and fathers who had regularly made the journey to the hospital. There was a group of ten parents, eight of whom were in our study, who would habitually meet on Saturdays. They would often sit together on the bus and then have a drink in the teabar while they visited their sons and daughters. Some had been friends since before the hospital was built, in the days when their children had first left home to live in Meanwood Park Hospital in Leeds. These friendships were a great source of strength. Parents kept one another company and they shared each other's problems. As Robinson (1978) points out, 'they can take for granted with each other what would need much explanation to outsiders'.

After their adult children moved out of the hospital, only five parents had the chance to maintain that friendship: the other five, all widowed mothers, have since gone their separate ways:

I suppose I'm on my own now. I telephone Mrs Evans but I've lost contact with the others. We used to talk about them when we travelled. We've known each other a long time.

As far as our evidence shows, no similar friendships had developed among the families of people living in the hostels and no mutual support networks had formed out of visiting routines.

The implementation of the relocation programme brought positive benefits in terms of access and ease of visiting for 11 families in our study, and 9 of these were elderly parents who had been travelling to the hospital. For some, visiting had involved using as many as 6 buses. They had left their homes at 10.00 a.m. and arrived back at 5.00 p.m. or 6.00 p.m. in order to spend little more than an hour with their relative at the hospital. As one family complained, 'It's worse since deregulation. The buses don't connect and sometimes there's an hour to wait between them.' Being that much closer since the move created other spin-offs for these families. Mrs Williams said, 'With being nearer I can go up for an hour in the light nights and during the week.' Likewise Mrs Garstang added, 'I'll be able to see him more often and my family who live around here will go more often too.'

On the other hand, four families of hostel movers now lived further away from their relatives, and because community placements were more likely to be off the beaten track, the houses were less accessible. Distance was also a problem for other reasons, as Mrs Schofield explained: 'I don't like the thought of him being at [the new house] in winter because he insists on walking home and it's three miles now.' In another example, the mover was living in a first floor flat which proved impracticable for his disabled father to visit.

In terms of access, however, the changes made little difference to nearly half the families, although this fact should not lead us to underrate the importance of the access issue. It is something which planners and managers should take into consideration when placements are being discussed. Problems of access impact differently on different groups, and those who are most likely to be adversely affected are old and disabled people and the poor.

Keeping in touch

Family relationships are an important source of support to people in institutions, and visits by parents have been associated with more confidence and less wariness of adults (Hill *et al.* 1984). Halliday (1987) too confirms that for people in long-stay hospitals and hostels the family is 'an important emotional and strategic link to the community'. Our study shows that visiting also brings rewards for the family. As one mother with severe arthritis said, 'Louise keeps me going. I don't think I'd go out much if it wasn't for going to see Louise every week.'

Apart from visiting, families had kept in touch in other ways: through phone calls, cards, presents, holiday postcards, calendars, letters and photos. Significantly, in the case of hospital movers, this traffic was no longer mostly one way. As one 81-year-old Auntie said wistfully, 'I have had a letter from her, the first time she's ever written to me.' In fact nearly half our respondents (mostly families of hospital movers) said that this kind of contact had never happened before. Hostel staff also helped in other ways to keep lines of communication open. Mrs Wallace remarked, 'I can't phone her and speak because she's frightened of phones, but staff always bring her to the phone and I can hear her breathing.'

Even so there was still a strong tendency for staff to keep families at arm's length. Before the move 18 families had attended various social activities such as Christmas and birthday parties, cheese and wine parties, sales of work, coffee mornings, summer galas and barbecues. During the first year following the move there was some evidence that families had begun to join in organized activities at the new placements. However, the number of families receiving invitations had dropped to 12, and events were restricted in some cases to a single occasion such as a housewarming party. The one exception was a new hostel that held regular 'theme' parties in the middle of the week, and families had appreciated the efforts made by staff. A mother commented, 'I like to go, especially to the parties, shoe, laundry and linen, cheese and wine, cosmetics and perfume. It's nice to be able to relax there with staff and residents.'

All the same, nobody at any time had been asked to go on holiday with their relative, and just two families had been invited on a day trip. In fact, participation by families in social events had dropped off since the moves, and there had been significantly more happening at the hospital to include families than was now on offer at the hostels.

Twelve months later

Phase III of the study enabled us to look back at the changes that had taken place since relocation. It gives a clear picture of how the families themselves assessed and interpreted those changes. It also shows that some things remained pretty much the same. The areas examined are relationships with staff, visual and social change, problems and other points of concern.

Relationships with staff

What has become evident through the literature is the importance of relationships between families and staff. These relationships shape attitudes to institutionalization and can sometimes make it difficult for families to adjust to new philosophies. In our study poor communication between staff and families was a recurring feature, both before and after the moves:

When they see me they always say hello, how are you? But I sometimes get the impression that they're waiting for me to stop talking so they can get on with their work. Nobody says sit down and talk, or come to see you out of the door.

For the most part, families are reluctant to criticize careworkers, and more often than not their dissatisfaction lies festering beneath the surface. The reasons for people's unwillingness to speak their mind are complex. Some families, for instance, lack confidence in discussions with professionals (Robinson 1978), while others believe they have no right to be critical of services: 'I wouldn't ever complain unless it was something really serious. We don't have to pay for their keep or anything, we should be grateful they have such marvellous people looking after them.' Sometimes families are fearful that professionals might take any complaints out on them or their relative (Robinson 1978). Equally it is often easier to explain away bad professional conduct in terms such as overwork, staff shortages or lack of resources rather than find fault with the staff: 'They didn't really have much time for us, perhaps that's because we went in the evening.' Even those who do express their concerns often find there is a lack of sympathy: 'Mr Young always makes me feel uncomfortable, as if we shouldn't be there.'

These subtle pressures can undermine parents' confidence and keep them from voicing their opinions: 'I've been a bit upset really. I feel they want to get rid of me. I've been disappointed because I would like to talk about her and hear what they have to say.' Likewise, according to Gliedman and Roth (1981), case reviews are usually structured in such a way as 'to intimidate, to silence and to push the parent toward compliance'. In this situation, families often remain cautious about giving too strong an opinion, or frustrated by the insignificance attached to their feelings.

During the settling-in stage of our study, three-quarters of hospital movers' families indicated that staff had kept them informed about how their relatives were adapting to their new way of life. (As we have noted already, families had very little contact with the support workers attached to the unstaffed homes in the community.) By the third stage of interviews, however, the number of families who felt they were being told enough by staff had fallen still lower. It seemed as if staff were slipping back into their customary role of keeping quiet unless approached by families. As Mrs Halford said, 'I always have to do the asking before I learn anything. I usually find I'm telling them how I find Clifford rather than the other way round.' Even when further plans were in the air for someone to move again, the way it was handled showed that few lessons had been learnt the first time round:

> I kept asking when he was moving and nobody would tell me, even up to a fortnight before he moved. It was my son who told me in the end and then I checked with staff and they confirmed it.

Perhaps the surest sign that families' feelings were not always given sufficient consideration by staff was in their reported omission to inform parents in a number of cases about possibly serious or distressing matters affecting their son or daughter:

> Staff haven't said anything but Jenny [who has epilepsy] told me that she's had a blood test and her eyes have to be checked again at the Infirmary. She's also to be fitted with some false teeth that screw in and she's to have a brain scan at Pinderfields.

Whatever choice Jenny had in the decisions, her mother should have been regarded as someone with a right to know what was happening.

Before the move just nine families felt their point of view was listened to by staff. After one year in the new placements, this number had increased to a modest 11 families. Relocation did not appear to have brought about much improvement in this important aspect of the relationship between staff and the families. Robinson (1978) cites several studies in the fields of social care and education which report similar findings and show 'between 40 per cent and 60 per cent of clients dissatisfied about the amount of information received, about the opportunities for finding things out or the difficulty of discovering what they want to know.'

The failure of professionals to recognize the role of families is a recurrent theme running through the interviews. Only six families had been invited to a case review during the first year; five had subsequently received a written report. One mother who had not received an invitation said, 'They had a review of Clifford and I got to know from someone else. I challenged them because I hadn't been invited. I told them it was my right.' A further eight families had been contacted at some time, usually by telephone, to discuss a particular aspect of the settling-in process. The rest had been ignored or excluded. Astonishingly, two families said that the only information they had *ever* received about the move was from the Kirklees Relocation Project newsletters produced by the research team.

Visual and social change

A good proportion of families had been concerned by the poor physical appearance of their relative in hospital, and many had tried over the years to make minor improvements to a few of the shortcomings. Some mothers, for example, had taken their child's better clothes home to wash, had cut their nails and sewn on buttons. Others had prompted staff about hair that needed a trim, regular shaving, missing shoelaces and minor medical conditions that had gone untreated:

> When he was living at the hospital David used to look so shabby I felt ashamed to take him out. His clothes didn't fit properly, they were like old men's clothes, and he had a thick crust of scurf on his scalp.

Many families voiced similar feelings to this mother's and, as a result, had spent most of their visiting time within the confines of the hospital rather than face any possible embarrassment in public places.

After relocation, changes in the personal appearance of people who had moved from hospital happened over a very short period. Four areas of improvement were observed by families: general hygiene, dress, appliances, and chronic ailments (Booth, W. 1988). Families commented that relatives were now having their hair individually styled, new teeth provided and glasses prescribed. Most mentioned changes in dress where new clothes not only fitted and were fashionable, but were seen to be appropriate for their relative's age and the time of year. A few longstanding ailments such as excessive salivating and chronic catarrh had started to receive treatment, and cosmetic irregularities also were being sorted out.

In general, the majority of families spoke of their relatives being tidier and cleaner, having regular baths and showers, and most had noticed changes for the better in their relative's appearance. One mother summed up the difference the move had made for her young adult daughter:

> She always had a certain smell about her. I think it was because she was invariably stuck up with food. It was in her hair and all down her clothes. Now she's much cleaner and at last they're doing something about her teeth which really stick out at the front. Staff have said that she'll be having a brace fitted to pull them straight. It will make her look so much better. She has all her own clothes too. Before we stopped taking good clothes because they used to ruin them. Now she has all modern clothes suitable for her age, like a denim suit, track suit and boots.

Improving the way people looked had also increased their confidence in themselves and given them a surer sense of their own identity. One year after the move almost all the families could see positive changes in the movers' social adjustment and general manner.

The hospital movers' families felt their relatives were 'more settled and content', 'more aware', 'more responsive', 'improved in their speech', 'more mature', 'more confident' and 'less frustrated'. One mother reflected:

> When I used to leave him at the hospital, he would always want to know when I was coming again. Now he just waves me goodbye. He's not clinging, he's coming out more, he's letting me go.

The hostel movers' families spoke of their relatives being 'more self-reliant', 'more talkative with more to talk about', 'easier to get on with', 'more responsible', 'having wider interests', 'calmer and more sensible' and 'much more confident'. One father noted:

> He's becoming a leader among his own kind instead of being led. At the hostel he had the reputation of being a heavy drinker, but now he doesn't drink at all except for an odd shandy. He doesn't need to make himself noticed like that.

For one or two families though the changes had been quite profound:

> At the hospital I had to haul her out of the chair and put her back. Now she gets in and out of a chair unaided. There she had to wear incontinence pads, but now she's taken to the toilet every one and a half hours. She even sings on the toilet and has much more confidence when she walks. At one time it always seemed as if she looked through you, now she's aware of everything that's going on. The expression on her face is different and her eyes fair sparkle. She's so much happier and she loves to have a cuddle. Before she just looked like a little lost soul, and she was tensed up as if she'd been pushed down or dropped. Now she's more relaxed in every way. She's lost that fear.

In conjunction with the visual and behavioural changes, just over three-quarters of families felt their relative had also become more independent. The definition of independence, however, fell into two distinct categories. For some, independence had a more worldly, adventurous meaning: it meant more money; being able to choose what, when and how things are done; going out to tea or for a drink; joining clubs and taking the bus for a shopping trip or a day out. For others, and especially the men and women who had moved from hospital, independence centred on the small steps achieved. People were beginning to learn to eat and drink on their own; use a fork and spoon; drink from a cup instead of through a spout; dress and undress themselves; make a hot drink; get out of a chair; go to the toilet by themselves; change a sanitary pad; speak into a telephone; shave and clean their own teeth; and bath unattended. No great matter for most people but for some of the hospital movers the difference to their lives was monumental.

Problems and areas of concern

In the year after relocation, the number of families who were concerned about aspects of the new placement remained more or less the same as during the settling-in period. Their worries, however, had broadened into areas other than the issue of location that had bothered them before the move, although four families were still anxious over the siting of the houses: 'The type of property Social Services put them in are isolated and therefore the success of the place depends on those they live amongst.'

Busy roads were a cause of concern as was the lack of night-time supervision. The fact that hostel doors remained unlocked until late at night worried a few families, and others felt that an unfenced hostel garden restricted the freedom of people who might wander as they were not allowed out on their own. Some parents suspected that people were being taken advantage of, although this was largely a matter of hearsay: '[Staff] feel that some of the local shopkeepers rip them off, like going in with a pound coin for a Mars bar and coming out with three pence.'

Other worries had crept in such as anxiety about what might occur when only two people are sharing a flat: 'We just worry what will happen if one or other of them should fall ill or die and the other is left on their own.' Most of these examples are what Frohboese and Sales (1980) call 'ongoing concerns': things that might or might not happen sometime in the future and as such create uncertainties and worries which can never be entirely dispelled.

Problems, on the other hand, are the solid evidence that occasionally things do go wrong. In our study, only four families mentioned problems that had occurred since the settling-in period. It should be emphasized, however, that families are only usually informed by staff when the problems are of a serious nature and not always then. Anything less than serious rarely gets passed on. Even when families are notified, as the following remarks from parents illustrate, their role is still often construed as that of a passive spectator. Mrs Wallace, who normally took her daughter home every weekend and who had lost one child already as a result of severe epilepsy, said:

> She had a series of fits from Tuesday until Saturday and then she was taken into the Infirmary for three weeks. They did what they could although they didn't let me know until the Friday when I went for her [to bring her home] that she was so poorly. We should have been told earlier.

Another mother, Mrs Ellis, whose daughter had previously been sexually assaulted by a member of the public after walking out of Meanwood Park Hospital, explained the circumstances surrounding a second incident that had happened to her daughter since moving into the hostel:

> She went out one evening in a temper and was picked up by a man in a car. He interfered with her and took her glasses. The police brought her back. The officer-in-charge [at the hostel] rang me on Sunday afternoon and I went up straightaway. It happened Saturday night. They should have told me she was missing and what had occurred then. Jenny was very quiet when I saw her, in shock I think. She blamed herself for what happened because she knew she shouldn't have been out.

Underlying these two examples is a 'staff knows best' attitude of a kind which we have shown elsewhere mediates the wider relationship between staff and families. Not surprisingly, parents see their role as givers of emotional and practical support being continually undermined and devalued by professionals.

Frohboese and Sales (1980) highlight the importance of alleviating family fears and explain why these concerns need to be addressed directly. They argue that professionals should not only listen to what families have to say, but also discriminate between their founded and unfounded concerns. Founded concerns need to be taken seriously and acted upon immediately. For example, parents may need a guarantee that their son or daughter will have the necessary support when they are no longer around, or the family may be concerned about deficiencies in a community-based home. But 'unfounded concerns' need to be addressed also; otherwise, Frohboese and Sales argue, the public perception of care in the community is damaged and can cause a barrier to development. Parental opposition could also threaten the viability of the whole deinstitutionalization movement. If parents support the ethos of institutions and prefer to have their sons and daughters segregated in such places, then public attitudes regarding people with learning difficulties, and the belief that these men and women are somehow deviant, will help crush successful integration into society.

Predictions and outcomes

Our interviews with the families included a 'predictions and outcomes' exercise through which we sought to compare their pre-move expectations with their evaluation of the move 12 months after it had taken place. In the first (pre-move) stage of the study our respondents were asked to forecast how they thought their relative would get on in their new placement. They were presented with a series of four 'option cards' each referring to a different area of functioning: personal skills, behaviour, physical problems and friendships. Each card comprised a list of statements ranging from the optimistic to the pessimistic, and respondents were invited to choose the one which accorded most closely to how they imagined things would turn out. Some 12 months later in the follow-up stage of the study, the families were presented once again with a similar set of options and choices, and asked to select the statements best describing how their relative had actually coped in the new placement. Using these predictions and outcome assessments, we were able to judge what changes families had seen in these areas of their relative's experience and, to some extent also, what changes had taken place in the families' perceptions of their relatives as a consequence of the move.

Skills

Among the hostel movers few families doubted that they had the skills to manage in their new placement and, a year later, most felt this confidence had been borne out by experience. Even those who had harboured some doubts before the move reported afterwards that their relatives were learning to cope. There were no families in this group who said that lack of skills was causing a problem in the new placement.

The families of hospital movers were a little more wary though still optimistic in their predictions: wary because most thought their relative currently lacked important coping skills, optimistic because most were sure of their potential for developing them in the new placement. Twelve months later almost all of them reported that their relative either had acquired the necessary skills or was on the way towards doing so. Only one family considered that lack of skills was still a problem.

Behaviour

For the most part the families anticipated that relocation was unlikely to have much effect one way or another on the occurrence of problem behaviour, and their later assessments confirmed this judgement. Only a small minority of hostel movers were said to present any problems of challenging behaviour either before or after the move. Interestingly, though, there were a few families who only saw there had been problems with hindsight, after the move, when their relative's behaviour had changed. Invariably, these problems concerned rebelling against staff and quarrelling with other residents. As one brother said, 'She used to be very stubborn at the hostel, but now she doesn't get goaded by the other residents and drawn into arguments.'

The incidence of problem behaviour reported by families was noticeably higher among the hospital movers. Most of them did not expect to see any improvement as a result of the move, and their post-relocation assessments vindicate their pessimism in this respect. No one who presented problems before the move was reported as not doing so afterwards.

Physical problems

None of the hostel movers' families thought their relative would have any physical difficulties in coping in their new accommodation, and none were said to have encountered any in the follow-up interviews.

The situation of the hospital movers was more problematic. They were going from single storey accommodation into hostels with three or four floors. Families might have expected some problems of mobility, access or safety. In fact, only one mother expressed concern for her daughter who, she felt, might find the stairs troublesome. The remainder were about equally divided between those who anticipated little change and those who expected to see an improvement. In the event, all but one family said their relative had experienced no obvious physical problems in their new placement. The Worthingtons, for instance, were relieved to find that the hostel presented their severely disabled daughter with none of the problems they had been led to expect: 'She can even get up the three steps which the staff at the hospital said she'd never manage.' Even the mother who had foreseen her daughter having difficulties found something to be positive about: 'She needs someone to walk upstairs with her, but she's improving because she used to need two people.'

Friendships

Relocation threatens to separate friends and break up friendships. For the hostel movers in our study genuine efforts were made to ensure such ties were not broken. Where friends were separated it was still possible for them to keep in contact – by visiting, at the SEC, the Gateway Club, evening classes and so on.

So far as the families were concerned, the move turned out better than they expected. Some had feared it would disrupt important relationships in the lives of their relatives that would be hard to replace. These fears proved groundless. The great majority of people were said to have moved with their friends. Most of the others were reported as having made new ones, often where they had none before. No one was felt to have lost any irreplaceable friendships.

The position was more complicated with the hospital movers. The decision to relocate people on the basis of where they came from cut across friendships formed in the hospital. Afterwards they no longer moved in the same circles. Distance made it harder for them to remain in touch. Before the move, just under half our respondents said their relative had formed no significant friendships in hospital ('She's always kept herself to herself'; 'He likes his own company'), and only one family anticipated that relocation would leave their daughter worse off for friends. A year later, almost half the movers were said to have struck up new friendships and, excepting the case just mentioned, no one reportedly missed old friends. At the same time, nearly as many people as before the move were felt to lack friends and seemed unlikely to develop any close relationships in the new placement.

Overview

Looking at the results of this 'predictions and outcomes' exercise across all four areas of competence and experience shows that in the main the families held high expectations of the move and, 12 months later, were broadly satisfied that there had been net gains in the movers' personal development. The families' predictions were consistently weighted towards successful rather than unsuccessful outcomes, and their post-move evaluations put a similar stress on the positive benefits that relocation had brought for their relatives. By and large the hostel movers' families were more upbeat in their predictions and their assessment of the outcome than hospital movers' families, but overall, on these measures at least, the moves have to be judged a success in the eyes of both these groups.

Happiness, success and choice of placement

Before the move, families were equally divided between those who felt their relatives would be happier in their new homes and those who thought they would feel about the same. Only four families considered that their relatives would be less happy. A year after the move, family impressions had changed quite dramatically. The people moving had settled, and the families could see the gains made by the changes. At the follow-up stage just one mother felt her daughter was less happy than before ('though not unhappy'), while fully 20 families (9 hospital/11 hostel) now considered their relatives were happier in the new homes ('He has a place of his own now, it's what he's always wanted'). Indeed it had started to dawn on some families that perhaps their relative had not been as happy in the original placement as they had presumed:

> Looking back I think that perhaps she wasn't very happy at the hospital. She never made a noise or showed any emotion at all. She spent much of her day asleep out of boredom. Now she smiles and laughs and is brighter altogether.

A similar change took place in family judgements about the success of the new placements. Before relocation under half the families felt the new homes would be better than the old. In fact, one in four of those making a prediction believed the move was likely to be unsuccessful. Twelve months later there had been a marked shift in the families' evaluation of the hostels and community homes. Altogether 21 families, including *all* the families of hospital movers, said that things were better now than they had been before ('She's changed so much I just wish her mother was alive to see her'). Only two families still maintained that the hostels were better suited to their relative's needs than the more independent houses in the community. As one brother said, 'The accommodation and facilities are more than adequate, but in an emergency they can't wait until staff come on duty.'

In simple terms, family expectations for both sets of movers had been well exceeded. Over twice as many families felt their relative was happier in the new homes than had predicted so before the move.

Correspondingly, almost twice as many families were pleased with the outcome as had been pleased at the prospect of the move 12 months before.
In addition, nearly three-quarters of families were satisfied that the
new homes represented the best possible placement for their relative.

Fisher (1983) has rightly warned against reading too much into such
expressions of satisfaction, pointing out that it is difficult to know exactly
what they mean. There is a well-documented tendency for people to
register a high degree of satisfaction with just about everything (Gutek
1978). Simply asking them to rate something usually produces a favourable response. One reason for this may be that unless respondents can,
there and then, think of an alternative, they express themselves content
with the status quo (Taylor 1977). Another reason for the high levels of
satisfaction recorded by user studies may be that people know very little
about the range of other services they might have received. Certainly users
are very hesitant about seeing themselves as qualified to comment on the
adequacy or quality of services (Craig 1981) and, in the absence of
comparative information, might feel safest in sticking with what they have
got.

In an attempt to get around some of these problems, we presented the
families with a list of alternative types of accommodation and asked them
to select the one they regarded as closest to what they saw as ideal for their
relative. Five main points emerged:

1 No one chose a hospital. (Although, interestingly, the third most popular
   choice was for a village community where, as one elderly mother said,
   'They could have made friends among themselves, communicated with
   each other and made their own life together.' It could be said that
   village communities present some of the same features as a hospital
   environment, at least in their self-sufficiency and segregation.)
2 None of the families of people who had left hospital now wished them to
   return.
3 Only just over half the families of people who had moved from hospital
   into hostels actually chose the hostel as their ideal placement.
4 The great majority of the families of those who had moved out of the
   hostels into community placements selected as their ideal the type of
   accommodation in which their relative was now living.
5 The most popular option overall among the families of both hospital and
   hostel movers was a staffed house or flat (although some qualified their
   choice with conditions such as 'as long as she's with someone else' or 'he
   needs to be on the ground floor' or 'as long as staff go shopping with
   them and check their diet'). Most of the families who picked this option
   as their ideal, including all the families of hospital movers, felt that 24
   hour supervision would be essential. Interestingly, however, while
   stressing the importance of supervision, they did not necessarily regard

trained staff as a must. An ability 'to care' and 'to be dedicated and capable' was seen as a much more desirable attribute in staff than being well trained.

Conclusions

Almost half the people in our study had moved from the care of one service agency to another, and yet, remarkably, not one of the families interviewed received formal notification when their relative was transferred from hospital. People were discharged on a date decided by the authorities, and the families found out through other channels. Administratively there were yawning gaps in the arrangements for keeping families informed about relocation plans and decisions, and this slackness led a few of our respondents to think that the new placements were perhaps only a temporary measure. As it turned out, some parents had good cause to be wary of these plans and decisions, as one year after the move stability for some people had still not been achieved. All the same, nearly two-thirds of families had become firm believers in the policy of moving people into less restrictive settings. As one mother said, 'I was very much against it at first but now I see the benefit of it.' After a year, though, there were still over a third of families who had criticisms of the way the move had been handled, and many referred to their continuing grievances about the lack of communication on the part of professional decision-makers.

Families appreciated the advances their relatives were making in the new homes and welcomed the opportunity to see them more frequently in pleasant surroundings. Against this, most of them still harboured some reservations and uncertainties. The main concern for the hospital movers' families was the adequacy of the community-based services and the shortage of daytime activities. Many were not convinced either that a hostel environment was the right one for their relative or that the particular hostel in which they were living met their needs. For hostel movers' families the problems focused on the risks of independent living and their continuing doubts and worries about their relatives' capacity to manage with limited supervision.

In the relocation of adults from long-stay hospitals and hostels, service providers would do well to remember that families are and will remain an essential part of the plan and as such need involvement and reassurance every step of the way. If anything is learnt from this chapter, it should be that families continue to be a stable and necessary link in the lives of most people with learning difficulties.

10

From all sides now: the changes in perspective

So far we have looked at the outcomes of relocation from the separate perspectives of the men and women who have moved, their families and the staff who support them. In this chapter we bring them all together. The first section explores the experiences of 16 people who left hospital to live in local authority hostels. We have excluded from the analysis five people about whom we only had information from staff. The second section concentrates on eight people who moved out of the hostels into more independent living accommodation and for whom there was a complete set of interviews covering all respondents at each stage of the study. In both sections we assess the impact of relocation and compare the most and the least successful aspects of the new placements from the standpoint of all those involved.

From hospital to hostel

For Jenny the journey back had taken 32 years to fulfil. Louise had entered hospital as a small child and spent most of her time on a locked ward. Now she was coming back to her home town as a young woman. Raymond was returning after having lived a good part of his life in one institution after another. He said, 'I weren't used to it at first. Everything was changed you see and I've adapted myself to it. It's near where I was born. . . . I'm in my own county now.' For all these people the journey home was more than just a change of address. It was a reshaping of their lives.

Most successful aspects of the move

Staff, with one exception, had no knowledge beforehand of the people who had moved from hospital, and their impressions were based solely on the changes that had occurred during the first year since relocation. Many of the successful outcomes mentioned by staff were of a general nature, such as increased confidence, independence and maturity. Some had noticed an improvement in speech and that people had become more relaxed and better behaved: 'She's not needing to use the sort of behaviour she used to produce in the past to make life interesting.' Other spin-offs from living in a hostel, according to staff, were that people now had more freedom, choice and involvement in making decisions. Living in smaller groups with people of mixed abilities also gave a few the chance to learn from their more competent companions:

> On the ward there were a lot of 'Sarahs' so she couldn't develop by watching others who were more capable. Here she can learn from us all.

Overall, staff felt the quality of life had improved greatly for the movers. The most successful aspects were summed up in the comments of one keyworker:

> The opportunities she has, getting out more and staff meeting her needs. She may never lead a normal life, but we're making it as normal as possible.

Families, on the other hand, were in a better position than staff to make before-and-after comparisons, and they saw the positive side of the move in richer detail. They remarked on the visual transformation that had taken place in their relative and made frequent references to parallel improvements in self-awareness and social skills (see also Halliday 1987): 'Her behaviour is better, she's brighter and more with it'; 'He's more grown up'; 'He's more sociable and not so frustrated.'

Changes had been perceived by families in both the dress and hygiene of their relative (Booth, W. 1988). Living in the hostels, people now wore only their own clothes, many of which were new and modern and appropriate for their age. Families also commented on how their relatives were being fitted with new appliances such as teeth and spectacles, having their hair styled, and how chronic medical problems were in the process of being treated. Such attention to detail was something that had delighted families. One mother spoke for all of them when she said, 'It shows they care about him.'

Families also remarked on the improvements in the physical environment: 'The rooms are lovely, like she'd have at home.' They approved of the smaller number of people living in the hostels compared with the hospital villas. One mother commented, 'There are just enough people at the hostel for her to get to know.' Living closer to each other also meant that visiting was easier and family members could see one another more frequently.

Fully two-thirds of families considered their relatives were receiving more personal attention than at the hospital. Having more staff around had given one mother greater peace of mind:

> There's someone with them all the time and they can see no one's hurting them. [At the hospital] one woman used to bite Lucy's fingernails right down until they bled and went septic. I used to be so worried who would be at her because she couldn't get out of the way.

Other features noticed by families were that the hostels offered more opportunities and were less restrictive in their day-to-day management. Staff had more time to involve the residents in new responsibilities such as looking after their own rooms and possessions, and most people now had money in their pockets. Some people were learning new skills such as using a knife and fork, shaving, dressing, and taking themselves to the toilet. Others were clearer in their speech and more able to converse. Two people were noticeably less docile, one as a result of a more stimulating environment and the other as a result of a reduction in medication. All but two families confirmed that their relative was becoming more independent and assertive:

> He starts doing things now like washing up. He sits with us more at home. He's more sure of himself. He's not so shy, he's quiet and he always will be, but he's more ready to come forward.

For the movers themselves the most successful aspects of relocation matched in some measure the views of staff and families. Knowing the area was important for many of the more able people, along with being close to their relatives and friends. The positive features of the hostels as seen by the movers can be classified under seven main headings: increased domestic occupation, more privacy, more personal possessions, more choice, positive community relationships, greater opportunities, and a better environment.

The majority of people enjoyed going out and about and helping with the everyday tasks of running a home: 'We go to shops, go for walks, watch telly. I do dusting, do carpets, make my own bed, tidy my own bedroom out. Washing up, drying up, I help to bake.' One man who was living a more independent life outlined the domestic side of his day:

> Living here you've to wash up and you've to do your own washing and your own cooking. Shopping this morning with Sally, butcher's first, then we went to Co-op. Then we called at greengrocers on way back. And then we walked slowly down. Put kettle on, had a warm cup of tea.

Many people mentioned that they liked having their own bedrooms, which offered them privacy and protection for their possessions ('got my own lamp, pictures, new bin, new clothes'). Others spoke of being free to bath and shower when they chose ('Anytime I like. One morning, one after dinner, one night.') and to lock the door, whereas before they were more than likely to find themselves sharing the bathroom.

To some movers it was a novelty to have money in their pockets and a bank book for savings. Most people agreed that going out to choose new clothes and shoes was a great deal more pleasurable than having a selection brought into the unit. One woman who had worn a helmet at the hospital to protect her head during epileptic attacks had been allowed to choose whether or not to wear it at the hostel. She kept it in her wardrobe: 'I like my hair being nice and curly and set and cut, and it's like that when I haven't got helmet on. I look very nice.'

For others there was the luxury of being able to 'go out when you want', to visit family and look up old friends. Just a few people spoke of making new friends at the hostel, of liking their keyworker, of friendly neighbours and of a welcoming local social club where some of the members bought them drinks. One or two people had begun to learn to swim. Ordinary, everyday activities like going to the pub, the park and the club, or pottering in the garden and watering the plants, were valued alongside events such as watching a wedding at the local church. Instead of attending Occupational Therapy, many of the movers now had places at a Social Education Centre and were enjoying learning, among other things, pottery, sewing, painting and how to keep fit. Even the warmth and contact of the hostel cat was a new and welcome experience. In broad terms most people commented on the improvement in their personal milieu. The food was better, the houses were cleaner and more homely and, in particular, they liked the comfort of carpets on the floor.

Unsuccessful aspects of the move

Many of the hostel staff had no previous experience of working in a residential setting for people with learning difficulties. Some had started out with enthusiasm and high ideals, and it might be expected that these careworkers would be protective of their own role and defensive when asked about any unsatisfactory outcomes for the movers. Yet surprisingly, out of the three groups of respondents, individual keyworkers were the most critical of the support services:

> There's a limit to how much staff can actually do. I think they get a bit sick of seeing us every day. They need a structured day and more stimulation from outside.

Staff were also willing to acknowledge the inherent limitations of the hostels:

> The more you try and put things right, it just throws up another problem, usually to do with size and fairness and not doing too much for one against the other.

Eleven of the 16 people who had left the hospital were said to be bored for significant periods of the day, and the lack of daytime activities meant that a few people had very restricted opportunities for escaping the confines of the hostels. Even with a high staff/resident ratio, individual attention from keyworkers was still infrequent: 'I only work four hours a day and that's split between Daphne and the other residents, getting meals ready, etc.' One young man who was a keen swimmer was often unable to use the local pool because there was no male member of staff to help him in the changing room. Ten people were considered by staff to have unfulfilled needs for more outings, and 'more confidence building'.

Another group of movers was felt to lack friendships and the emotional satisfaction that comes from a one-to-one relationship. People's needs in this area were linked to their life-style: 'She needs to go out with people other than staff and mix with people who don't go to the Gateway Club.' Having to compete for attention left many people bereft of close physical contact: 'He cannot relate to anybody here other than staff. It's more of a problem for him because there are times when no one has time to sit down with him.' These opinions are a comment on the serious deficiency in what the services are able to offer in the way of social intercourse to anybody living in a care setting. Staff suggested that the gap could be filled by volunteers. Making friends with people, however, calls for commitment and regular contact over a long period of time, and it would seem that not many volunteers are prepared to do that. As a consequence attempts to involve hostel residents in relationships beyond their immediate acquaintances all too often result in gestures rather than any sustained achievements. Thirteen of the 16 people were also considered by staff to lack essential supports. Some were said to require further remedial services such as speech therapy, physiotherapy or attendance at a Special Care Unit. Others, it was felt, would benefit from educational services including adult literacy, tuition in creative art and gardening, and places at the Social Education Centre.

The least successful aspects of the hostels, according to staff, derived from communal living and the problems of getting on with a group of people not of one's own choosing. The high turnover of staff and staff shortages only added to these difficulties. They were also aware of the restrictions imposed on their ability to give a comprehensive service to people with severe emotional and physical needs:

> I don't think any of her needs are being met, we only do basic care. Looking to the future, if we cannot offer her anymore than she has here, then all we've got is a mini-institution. If we don't keep going forward she will start to regress. Already the residents are in fixed routines; they all need more than we can give them.

The families, by contrast, offered very little in the way of criticism of the hostels. In this context it should be remembered that, unlike staff, they were making a comparison between the hospital and hostel environments. Family concerns about the hostels were mainly to do with the physical setting ('the busy roads', 'unfenced garden', and 'doors not locked until after it's dark') and the reticence of staff to confide in parents. Indeed two-thirds of families could find no fault at all in the new regimes, and only a few thought that perhaps more daytime activities were needed, 'something like O/T during the day' or 'some sort of job'.

Service shortfalls, however, are difficult to monitor when families are often only visiting for a brief hour at a time, or calling to take their son or daughter home for the weekend. In comparing the hostels with the hospital, visual improvements in both the personal appearance of their relative and the state of the living environment are, for the most part, the main indicators by which families measure change.

In the interviews with the movers, there was evidence of just how much the compatibility of those they lived amongst affected the success of a placement. At the settling-in phase of our study, only five people could think of something they disliked about their new home. Four of these men and women mentioned missing old friends and staff from the hospital ('I don't see them no more'). Other worries at this early stage were problems with local children who had knocked down a bird-box, thrown stones, broken a window and pinched equipment. Just two people spoke of minor disagreements with staff, and one woman had experienced difficulties with another resident: 'Sometimes Dorothy comes up and hits me, causing bother and screams.' Only one man among the people we interviewed wished to return to the hospital; the rest were happy in the hostels. But one year after moving, cracks were beginning to appear in the hostels' veneer. Poor relationships within the homes were becoming more than trifling irritations. Other residents were 'not pulling their weight', 'noisy and fighting', 'causing problems', 'a bit of a nuisance', 'keeping me awake', 'hitting me and pushing me downstairs', 'shouting'. Trouble from children living close by had continued to be a source of aggravation and, as might be expected, there were a few grumbles about staff. Eight movers in all mentioned aspects of hostel life they disliked, and six of these people indicated that they wished to move on, five because they were not happy in their present placement. The different reasons why people wanted to leave show the complexity of the issues involved, and it is worth taking each individual separately to illustrate what lay behind their aspirations.

Three people with limited experience of the wider options available to them tended to compare their present accommodation with the only alternatives they had known and wanted to move back to hospital. All these three movers came from the same hostel.

Henry, for instance, was having a tough time with one of two women with whom he was sharing, 'I'd like to get away. . . . Sheila goes slamming doors and then she bangs on the table. No need for all that. She's showing her temper all time.' Given a choice, Henry would prefer to move back to his semi-independent flat in one of the hospital villas, 'Because it's nice there.'

Dora shares a bedroom with a fairly disruptive resident. 'She keeps me awake all night because she's got a lot of tablets off of doctor.' Dora mentioned that she would like her own room, which unfortunately was not possible in her particular hostel. She spoke of being, 'Fed up, I don't like it here.' Dora indicated that she would like to move back to the hospital although, having a close friendship at the hostel with another young woman of similar age and ability, she added that she would like her friend to come with her.

Janet, at the time of interview, was going through a particularly stressful phase for both herself and staff. As a person who suffered a great number of epileptic fits, she was also prone to faking them for attention. As a result of this behaviour, Janet had recently spoiled a holiday for herself and a number of residents. On her return, she had been 'confined to barracks' for three weeks and denied special attention from her keyworker. When asked where she would most like to live, Janet chose a hospital where she had once stayed for a short while: 'I'd like to live with Mrs Braddock because she were all right with me. I used to have fun with her.' Enquiring how she felt at present, Janet said simply, 'I think it's nice when you can be cared about and looked after, but I don't think it's nice when they're not caring about you and you've got no keywoman. . . . I have a right hurting inside but hurting inside that I cannot hold. You see when they hurt me, it hurts me but very nasty.'

Two men who had been given the chance of moving into homes in the community were eager to get out of the hostels, even though neither of them had seen where they were going to live:

Dave had originally moved from the hospital with his girlfriend but now he was ready for more independence. 'It's right noisy up here, they've been fighting, carrying on, hitting me . . . shouting.' Without doubt, living in a small house in the community with two more young men from the hostel was an experience Dave was looking forward to trying out as an escape from the tumultuous nature of hostel life.

Wesley had a more practical reason for showing his dissatisfaction with the hostel. 'It's all right . . . I mean some things all right but some things, I mean they're very good but when it's your day off you do every job, I mean I don't like that. I don't like it when you have a sink of pots to wash up, leave them for me to do on my days off. . . . I mean I have to help them when we haven't got a cleaner, I have to do toilets, do bathroom, I do everything with clothes. . . . Moving to a bungalow, won't be as much work . . . it's too much here.'

The common factor linking the motivations of the five people who were disillusioned with the hostels was that they thought the cause of their complaint lay beyond their control: bossy or disruptive roommates, isolation as staff closed ranks, noise and aggression from other residents, feeling exploited by staff. All of them felt powerless to do anything about their situation. It seemed that only by removing themselves would these headaches disappear.

One woman, who indicated that she was happy in the hostel, still had a personal ambition to move into a flat.

> *Elizabeth* had, for 22 years, only known a hospital environment until she moved to a hostel. Recently, however, a male friend of hers had left the hospital to live in a single, independent flat in what had once been nurses' accommodation. Elizabeth had visited him a few times and felt that, given the opportunity, a flat was what she would like too, 'Cook my own dinners, do my own shopping . . . live by myself, bit frightened, get used to it.'

In addition it is by no means clear that all the remaining men and women were happy in hostel accommodation. For example, one man with limited communication skills was regarded by staff as having 'mixed feelings' about the hostel. Overall, however, so far as the movers themselves were concerned, most felt they had gained more than they had lost from the change of environment. This showed up clearly in the settling-in phase of interviews when most respondents were hard pressed to think of any criticisms they had of their new placements. Undoubtedly this reflects the real improvements that leaving hospital brought about in people's lives. At the same time, too much should not be made of them. A close examination of the reasons people gave for preferring the hostels reveals, more than anything else, the low expectations and aspirations on which their judgements were based. Against these yardsticks, improvements were not hard to achieve. Indeed, the increase in the number of people voicing criticisms after 12 months or so in the new placements may perhaps be seen less as a symptom of disillusionment than a sign that the movers' horizons had widened and their expectations had risen accordingly.

The three views compared

For the most part, all three groups of respondents involved in this study were agreed that living in a hostel had given movers a greater degree of freedom, more privacy and wider involvement in decision-making. Better opportunities and increased independence were also cited as evidence that the new placements were an improvement on the old.

Families, on the whole, were more perceptive of the visual and cosmetic changes brought about by the move. They emphasized the improvements in the physical appearance of their relative and the more homely decor of the hostels. For the families, practices in the hostels were much more free and easy than in the hospitals, and staff were more visible and accessible. A good number of families also commented on the greater attention their relative was now receiving. Visiting was easier and parents had noted how their sons and daughters were becoming assertive and learning the skills necessary for greater independence. Richardson and Ritchie (1986) report a similar reaction to hostel living on the part of parents in their study.

Hostel staff, while not knowing the movers' history, had nevertheless watched them make advances in self-awareness, confidence, maturity and speech during the first year in their new placements. This reinforced their view that the hostel routines allowed a greater opportunity for self-development than was possible in a hospital setting. In one or two of the hostels the teaching element was foremost, even though some of the new skills people had begun to learn were found to be just old ones rekindled.

All the families agreed that the new placements were an improvement on the old, and most believed their relatives were happier now than before. Only two parents had reservations after the first year about whether the hostel was the best place. All the same, as was shown in Chapter 9, when given a list of types of accommodation available in the area for people with learning difficulties, only just over half chose a hostel as their first preference for their relative. A good third of respondents opted for a staffed house with 24-hour supervision. The implication would seem to be that although most families regarded the hostels as an improvement on the hospitals, they did not all recognize the former as the only option or an ideal placement.

By comparison with the families, staff were more conversant with the hostels' failings. Restrictions and pressures for conformity were seen by most as major drawbacks to hostel life. In addition, the deficit in important services and lack of opportunities outside the unit meant that many residents were closeted in the same four walls for a good part of every day. Staff were aware of the friction that resulted between residents and of the destructive quality of boredom, but were often impotent to do much about it. Some keyworkers found they were not only responsible for keeping residents stimulated and occupied, but were required to fulfil their emotional needs too. From the staff's point of view, however, 15 of the 16 movers were thought to be happy, and all the new placements were said to have been a success. Yet in a similar fashion to the families, only a quarter of the movers were regarded as living in the placement best suited to their needs. When staff were asked to select from a list the ideal type of accommodation for each individual, in three out of four cases they chose either a small house with staff support or a family placement in an adult fostering scheme. As one keyworker added, 'Paul needs love and closeness, not people doing things for him. He knows a family is the norm and he wants to be part of it.'

It is arguable that the real effects of relocation can only be understood and evaluated in the light of the responses from the movers themselves. In the case of both staff and families, their views are shaped to some extent by their own personal interests in the outcome. Only by listening to the movers can we learn the meaning and significance of the changes they have experienced. Without doubt, for the 16 men and women who made the return journey, the most successful aspect of the move was the shift to a less restrictive life after having lived for many years in an inward-looking environment that was locked into its own rules and customs. Living close to friends and family was an important aspect of the move that, for many people, contributed to a greater sense of belonging, irrespective of the frequency of contact they actually had with them. They enjoyed helping with the day-to-day running of the hostels, having their own bedrooms and money in their pockets, going out to choose clothes and calling into a pub or cafe for a drink and a bite of something to eat.

Others have observed that *how* people live is more important than *where* they live (West 1983). Evidence from our study endorses this simple dictum but goes further by suggesting that *who* people live with matters just as much (see also Lowe *et al.* 1986; Atkinson 1987). In other words, a precondition of successful relocation is the compatibility of the people who find themselves living under the same roof.

At the heart of the question of whether or not the hostels were considered a good place to live was the critical matter of relationships: relationships that adversely affected their privacy (sharing a bedroom), their choice (doing jobs they disliked), their environment (residents fighting and neighbourhood children being a nuisance), their opportunities (holidays and other activities spoilt by antipathy between residents). All these relationships had a profound effect on their subjective well-being. Broadly speaking, the least successful features of the hostel placements for the movers could usually be traced back to the problems of communal living, and the strains and frustrations these engendered in the personal relationships of people who must involuntarily share each other's lives. Aggression, domination and rejection all caused pain and upset for a few people and, for some, led them to look beyond their new homes for contentment elsewhere.

From hostel to independent living

Emily is one of the people who moved out of a local authority hostel. She enthused:

> Oh, it's great, lovely, better than the hostel, really it is, love. You can do your work on a morning and then go out when you like. You couldn't up there, love, you'd got to do as you were told. I was never out of that office up there. I was always in bother.

Getting a slant on what community care means, however, is not easy. We can see it represents different ideas and expectations when we look at how the three groups of actors in our study interpret the problems and rewards of life in the community.

Most successful aspects of the move

Care staff stressed the personal development achieved by the movers, mentioning, in particular, their greater confidence and self-esteem, their new found independence and the increase in control showed over their own lives. Staff also laid emphasis on the freedom the new placements afforded the movers. People no longer had to ask before they did something, nor had they to be back at a certain time or go to bed at a set hour. They had more money and were able to choose what they wanted to do. One staff member explained how personal skills had also been allowed to develop through a change in life-style:

> She goes on the bus, uses the telephone, communicates with the neighbours, goes to the shops on her own and does the cooking all by herself. She's just absolutely blossomed.

For one man, now living on his own in a flat with minimal support, his greatest achievement, according to staff, is that 'he can cope'. For him to be able to do that means he has gained what he most wanted – a chance to lead his own life.

Staff comments were almost always short and to the point, in contrast to those of the families who would relate at length the changes they had observed, especially the increase in their relative's social awareness:

> At one time we couldn't have a conversation with him, but now he's freer he chats all the time, and really sensible conversations.

The families agreed that their relatives had become 'much more talkative', 'more responsible and more interested in practical things like housework' and 'much easier to get on with'. They reported how the movers had begun to associate with a world beyond the hostel and were leading more stimulating and satisfying lives:

> As she is now there is only four of them, and it's better for Sally than living with lots of people. It's like a little family. At the hostel there were more restrictions. Now they can choose what they have for their meals, go out or watch TV. They please themselves.

All the families of the women movers commented on their attractive appearance, their modern dress and hairstyling:

> She puts a bit of make-up on now, and she's not interested in sweets like she used to be. Now she'd rather have a pair of nylons or even a packet of washing soda.

As Mrs Peabody said of her sister and flatmates, 'They're even smart when they're not going anywhere.' One brother felt his sister's flat was better for her because she used to resent being watched all the time at the hostel. He also added that, 'She's happier being further away so that the flat isn't interfered with by staff moving the furniture around.'

A key part of our research focused on the views of the movers themselves and what they had to say about their new life-styles. For nearly all of them, perhaps the most enjoyable aspect of the move was being able to assert a measure of independence by going about their daily domestic business as and when they pleased. Doing household jobs and shopping featured very largely in the things they liked most about having moved – being able to choose what programmes they watched on television, digging their own garden and going for walks. One man even had his own allotment. Life had begun to take on the shape that most of us take for granted:

> It's better because we've got keys and just go out and come back when you like and go to your sisters. I go to Wakefield and Leeds at weekends sometimes.

There is a shrewd understanding in one man's comment that, 'it's better cooking for ourselves because if we don't, we're not going to get anywhere, are we?' He knows that it is one more step up the ladder of independence, whether he likes cooking or not. Emily also showed a capacity for self-reflection and an insight into her position, 'I'm happy. I get a bit cranky at times but I get over it. I know I'm not all I should be, but I do my best.' For Jeremy living in his own house had meant an escape from some of the unwritten rules of hostel life:

> Well, he used to stop my money like, if you did anything. Well, I know it's natural . . . but I don't think that were fair. I know it's their job to do it, going to bed for a week, making you stop in your bedroom, just call you down for your meals.

During the course of these conversations there was evidence that the community outside of their small homes had begun to accept them. As Geoff said:

> I've met some friends at the pub. I'm not sure what jobs everybody does, but I know two of them's ambulance men. And I've met my neighbours. They call the lady Mary. I just sort of say hello, and sometimes if I say I'm going to the shop and Mary's going out at the same time I'll walk with her.

Gary too had begun to widen his social network: 'I like getting out and meeting more people, that's what I've done. I've been to Leeds and joined a cricket club.' Gary is also a founder member of the local People First group and has helped to arrange sponsored walks and outings for the group. For someone living on their own, making contact is not easy, but both Geoff and Gary have managed it without help.

Emily too had ideas on how she could improve her position: 'Tell you

what I'd like to do. Look after, you know, disabled all time. I'd like to help.'
What became obvious as we talked to these men and women was that they
recognized more keenly than before the move their own competence and
potential. They had begun to lead a much more *useful* life, however limited
their abilities or however small the tasks they performed. Believing in one's
own usefulness matters almost as much to them as being independent. It
had given them a feeling of self-worth and of belonging, as well as a sense of
purpose.

Least successful aspects of the move

On the whole, staff were positive and enthusiastic about the changes that
had occurred. They expressed very few reservations. In three cases care
staff were unable to identify any negative effects of the move f ɔr the people
concerned.

One area that did trouble staff centred on people's lack of friends outside
the home. For instance, one able woman was cited as having latched on to
staff for friendship because the other residents in the home could not fulfil
that role. The same concerns are echoed in the wider literature. Atkinson
and Ward (1987), in their study of people who were now living independently, found few who had moved beyond 'community acceptance' to
'community participation'. Another area of concern was the difficulty of
keeping an eye on people with minor but chronic ailments. Staff pointed by
way of example to a man in his 60s who had an ulcer and worried about his
own health, and whom they felt they were unable to monitor quite as well
as when he lived at the hostel.

Some anxieties were also voiced by staff about the location of one of the
houses and the neighbourhood where it was situated, although there was
little evidence that the occupants shared these fears:

> It's a bit isolated and on quite a tough estate. The neighbours have been
> good but they're likely to move. We would apply for a move but they've
> got used to the locality, shops, etc. People know them and ask about
> them.

The signs were that some staff become more flexible in their attitudes to
people after their move and were beginning to adjust the standards
previously applied in the hostels:

> Some would argue that his standards have dropped, for example his
> bedroom's not as clean as he was expected to have at the hostel, but I
> don't attach much importance to that compared with him being happy
> and confident.

We also noticed that whereas staff would refer to some hostel residents as
being stubborn, once they had moved out they were more often described

as being assertive and showing independence. At the same time it was clear that many found it difficult to come to terms with the implications of the movers' new status for their own role. One care assistant, for example, referred to changes in a mover's feelings towards staff in a downbeat way, rather than seeing them as a positive development indicating his growing self-reliance:

> His relationship with staff has changed. When [staff] first went to see him it was as a friend, but now he resents the fact that staff are calling so often and that he has to do certain things.

By comparison with staff, families, while still warm in their praises, were far more critical of aspects of the move. Their fears were broad-based and touched on some issues not recognized as problems by staff. Perhaps understandably, they preferred the idea of someone 'being around to keep an eye on them'. Three families mentioned the need for more supervision, and four families felt their relatives were isolated in the community. They had also taken stock of the type of areas in which the houses are situated and saw trouble ahead:

> It's outside influences that make me hesitate to say the house is better than the hostel, especially since someone took a shot through one of the windows.

> It's just night-times really, if there's any trouble.

> It only takes a particular age group of yobbo to see they're a soft touch and they'll have a go at them.

> Sally says she can hear people going past drunk some nights, singing and shouting out. It's a right rough area.

In some cases families found it harder to visit the new houses and flats than the hostels, which had mostly been situated in the centre of town. Wing (1985) reports similar problems in her study. Five families had no car and were limited to public transport and walking. For two families, visiting now involved four bus rides or a fare of £6.50 to send a taxi to fetch their relative for a visit to their home. Two sisters commented, 'We have to catch two buses and then there's a long walk from the main road past the cemetery, and we've both bad legs.' One father who has no sight and is confined to a wheelchair is unable to visit as his son has been given a first floor flat accessible only by a flight of stairs.

Without doubt, for some of the families the move into independent living accommodation was not seen as a progressive step. For them the ideal was a placement which offered both independence *and* security. Security from exploitation, from harassment, in emergencies, against carelessness: in short, security against risk. The new homes did not provide the same measure of protection, and left some families waiting for a crisis to happen. One brother sums up these doubts: 'The testing time is when something goes wrong really.' These views were not shared by either residents or staff, and perhaps they express the families' need for peace of mind more than their relatives' need for surveillance. Flynn (1986a), for instance, found that although a number of her respondents were suffering victimization from local people, they still valued their independence and did not wish to return to an institution.

Where the families were ambivalent, the movers themselves had few doubts about their new life-style. The one exception, Richard, was also named as the only person not to be seen to have gained from the move by both staff and his family. Although Richard said he liked working in the garden, doing some cooking, washing up and going for walks, he still remained uncertain about his position. This he found hard to articulate except to indicate that he had some worries, had difficulty doing the cleaning and sometimes felt fed up.

Two men who had moved into single flats were asked specifically if they liked living by themselves. Their reactions are probably typical of anyone who is living alone:

> I feel some days I do, some days I don't. But when it's holiday time I feel a bit bored.

> The only bad thing is it sometimes gets a bit lonely, but that doesn't bother me so much. I sometimes miss people, but I'd rather be on my own most times.

One woman had been worried by three accidental fires that had occurred in the house. One had been caused by a faulty toaster, and the other two had resulted from the grill on the cooker flaring up and catching fire: 'I'd like to see more safety in house, you know, house getting on fire and stuff like that.' In fact, one of the men in the house had handled the emergency very well, using a fire blanket to extinguish the flames before any serious damage was done. Some references were made to annoyance and aggravation caused by the thoughtless or spiteful behaviour of strangers and passers-by, and to occasional instances of harassment, but these were fewer than might have been expected and certainly less than the families feared.

The most common cause of upset among our group of movers was the behaviour of staff. Most of the people we talked to mentioned examples of professional bossiness. Perhaps this should not come as a surprise. After all, their relations with staff are still among the closest they enjoy, and as such are bound to have their ups and downs. At the same time, there is more than a suggestion here that some staff find it difficult to unlearn attitudes and practices acquired in the hostel and rooted in that environment. Geoff voiced some of these feelings:

Staff comes three days a week, too much for me. I prefer to have them come two days. A. comes tomorrow, B. comes Monday and C. comes Wednesday, and they come for two hours. But you know three's too much.

His complaint was not only about the three days staff were calling; he disliked the fact that it was a different member of staff each time. His role had changed and therefore his relationship with staff was altering also. But he felt less in control of his situation by not having a single keyworker to whom he could relate, and because the staff presence was too intrusive.

Other examples of what the movers saw as staff officiousness include shouting, over-protectiveness, being too strict or domineering and keeping too close an eye on them. Some complained of getting into trouble if they failed to carry out certain jobs. One woman had been forbidden from using buses on her own after once being reported for having an altercation with a fellow passenger in which she insisted she had been in the right. Another man had had his bank book withheld and his money strictly monitored after going on a spending spree with his savings. He was indignant about being warned by the police that if it happened again he would have to move back to the hostel, and rightly questioned their authority to do that.

The danger of independent living schemes being squeezed into a quasi-institutional mould and run in the style of mini-hostels is illustrated by the incident of the cooker blaze cited above. Despite the fact that the occupants had coped well, with little damage and no one hurt, they were prohibited from cooking without a member of staff in attendance, which meant farewell to toast and cooked breakfasts. As Felce *et al.* (1985) argue, providing high quality services depends more on staff procedures and practices than merely having small houses.

The three views compared

What stands out most clearly from our interviews is how staff, families and the movers see the problems of independent living in a different light. Families put most emphasis on the threat from outside, on the vulnerability of their relatives to exploitation and abuse. There was some basis for these worries. There had been some trouble from local children making a nuisance of themselves, and from youths laughing at them and calling them names. There had even been an air-rifle shot through a window. Significantly, however, the movers themselves gave little prominence to these incidents, and expressed no anxieties about their own safety.

Staff, on the other hand, were more concerned about the problems of group living and relationships among the residents. Some difficulties had been experienced on this score. In one house, a male resident became verbally and physically aggressive, particularly towards one of the women, and he was taken back to live in the hostel. In another house, one of the female residents dominated the other three, two men and a woman. She took money from them, impelled them to steal food from shops and was sexually rampant with one of the men. She too was moved back to the hostel.

For our eight men and women these setbacks reinforced their own concerns about their new status. The message seemed to be that unless they lived up to other people's expectations, then they too might be sent back to the hostel. The returnees demonstrated the continuing power that staff exert over all their lives. The hostel could still reach out and reclaim them at any time. In this context, their new found independence takes on a very fragile guise.

Four areas have often been identified as intrinsic to independent living – choice, privacy, control (over the daily routine), and integration into the wider community (see Chapter 5). All these features are very much in the forefront of what the movers see as the most satisfying and enjoyable aspects of living in the community. Of them all, perhaps choice remains the most problematic for the movers, as any decisions they make may depend on whether others judge the likely consquences to be acceptable.

The rules governing these people's lives are twofold. The standards are set both by society and by staff, and therefore discipline is much stricter than that regulating our everyday lives, although certainly not as rigid as in the hostels. Despite their achievements and the increase in their personal abilities, the hidden threat remains that if they falter or deviate on the way, as others have done, they will be returned to the hostels as failures.

Our study shows that these men and women have not changed fundamentally. They have simply begun to fulfil their potential and, to a certain degree, enjoy the kind of life they wish to lead with less interference than they encountered before. For most, moving into the community was not a move to a strange and hostile world; it was more like coming home.

Conclusions

The people who moved out of hospital and those who moved into the community placements had one thing in common: the experience of living in a hostel. This experience, however, assumed a very different meaning for these two groups. It would seem true to the views expressed in this chapter (and in Chapters 8 and 9) to say that whereas the former saw themselves as being better off in the hostels, the latter felt they were better off out of them. Whilst the hostel environment was welcomed by those who moved in for the greater freedom and opportunities it provided, those who had moved out looked back on it as restrictive and unfulfilling. Clearly these judgements reflect the different frames of reference of the movers: one group drawing their comparisons with their former life in hospital and the other with their new life in the community. Significantly, 12 months after relocation, many of the hospital movers were beginning to voice criticisms of the hostels that echoed those made by the people who had moved out, especially about the stress and upset caused by poor relationships among the residents.

These facts lend support to the view that while hostels may provide an environment for living that is preferable to a hospital, they are not the most preferable alternative. There seems little doubt that a number of the hospital movers would have been better served in the long run if they had been placed directly into some form of ordinary housing. Indeed, as Chapter 5 has shown, some of those people who left the two most resident-orientated hospital units might have found themselves in a more restrictive environment in the hostels.

The decision to rule out any direct placements from hospital into supported housing must be seen in this light as a deficiency in the planning assumptions underpinning the Kirklees Partnership in Community Care. However, it probably pre-empted a lot of opposition among movers' families. As is clear from this chapter, the aspirations of movers and their families diverge in important ways. Movers tend to stress the value of independence, an ordinary life-style and normal everyday activities. Families tend to give priority to security, supervision and the containment of risk. It is likely that a lot of anguish would have been caused if people had been relocated from hospital into community placements without more effort being put into involving the families than was ever demonstrated in practice.

11

Last words

In the first chapter of this book we spent some time discussing the background to the events in Kirklees. We attempted to show that the impetus for change came from national – and international – policies promoting deinstitutionalization and new thinking about appropriate patterns of services, as well as from a desire to resolve local dilemmas and concerns. At the end of that chapter we posed two questions. First, could this initiative in community care be considered a success within its own terms? Second, how does what was achieved measure up to broader notions of 'quality' in service provision? All the subsequent chapters set out to tackle those questions in a variety of different ways. The task now is to provide some kind of overview.

In response to the first question, the initiative launched by the Kirklees Partnership in Community Care did achieve some degree of success. There was a striking degree of consensus among all the groups we interviewed – movers, relatives and staff – that the new services represented an improvement over the old. There were, and still are, plenty of problems. However, they should not obscure the gains that have been made.

The second question is more difficult to answer. Certainly, the new services fell short of the ideals of normalization or 'social role valorization' (Wolfensberger 1984). They were not based on the needs of individuals. Most people still spent the majority of their time in segregated settings, and few were able to establish socially valued roles or occupations. Even in the ordinary housing there was a tendency for institutional practices on the part of staff to creep in. While some of the movers gained opportunities to learn (or relearn) a variety of skills and to exercise a greater control over their lives, this was not true for everyone. Where people might physically have lived in the community, few could be said to have been genuinely part of it. However, this would be true of most community care initiatives. For example, in an analysis of PASS evaluations (designed to examine the extent services conform to the maxims of normalization) carried out in this country, Williams (1986) reported that none of the 52 services evaluated reached the level defined by Wolfensberger as 'minimally acceptable' with the exception of two shared-life schemes. As a whole we have not yet learned to implement high quality services on anything other than the smallest scale. Implicitly, this was recognized in Kirklees. The new services we evaluated were seen as a base on which to build, rather than an end in themselves. Providing this point is grasped, then there is justification for a generally optimistic assessment. But people will have to be alert to the possibility that, after the initial effect of the changes wears off, things will settle back into the trough of routine.

Apart from the local issues, a number of general points emerge from the study. Perhaps the most significant of these relate to the users. Given a concrete choice, almost all opted for the less retrictive alternative. They criticized the petty limitations and the incessant frictions and tensions of living in large groups. They strongly rejected the label of mental handicap, and continually stressed the importance of opportunities to assert their independence and to lead meaningful, useful lives. We might be reluctant to generalize too widely on the basis of our study alone. However, these results add to a fast-growing body of evidence that all points in the same direction. There can be no doubt that, given the opportunity, the vast majority of people with learning difficulties would prefer not to live in large, segregated institutions.

Where our work differed from most of the earlier studies was in the emphasis we placed on enabling as many people as possible to take part. This is not just an issue for researchers. The chance to make choices and to participate in decision-making has usually been seen as the preserve of the more able. The challenge is to find ways of enabling people who have difficulty in speaking up to express themselves in their own terms. This is a task for anyone providing services for people with learning difficulties.

Another important point to emerge – with some force – is the tenuous position of the relatives and friends of the movers. As we noted earlier, families can be a source of continuity and support through the welter of relocation, and serve as an important link with the community. With a few notable exceptions, their role was not acknowledged in Kirklees. There was little evidence that staff saw the participation of families as a key part of the plans to relocate people into the community. The move presented a golden opportunity to overcome some of the historical divisions between staff and relatives, yet the chance was lost almost by default. By and large the services continued to keep relatives at arm's length; there was no sense of partnership. We are not saying families were ignored. But regardless of the extent to which they were or were not consulted about the changes, they did not *feel* involved.

There are complex dilemmas here for service providers. While both the movers and their families agreed that the new services were better than the old, there was also a genuine difference in perspective between them. Whereas the movers were generally seeking greater freedom and independence, the families continued to be wary about the risks of life in the community and to worry over the 'what if' fears that nagged them. As a consequence the families tended to view the ideal placement as something like a self-contained flat in the grounds of a hostel, a compromise between independence and security. In contrast, both the users who had moved out of the hostels into ordinary housing, and the staff who worked with them, regarded the prospect of a move back under the wing of the hostel as a thoroughly retrograde step. The issues behind these different perspectives often surface over the dangers of persecution or exploitation consequent on lack of supervision. We certainly came across instances where people did experience harassment by outsiders. However, these instances were not confined to people living in ordinary housing. Furthermore, the movers themselves placed just as much (if not more) emphasis on the hurt caused them by fellow residents in the institutional settings. From their standpoint, it did not seem to matter whether it was a stranger, staff or a peer who was victimizing them; it was all equally bad. It would be wrong to see the institution/community care division as a simple dichotomy between security and risk.

What the Kirklees system lacked was a set of structures that encouraged and supported service users in expressing their point of view. That burden was carried by the individual case conference (or IPP) system: a mechanism that was never up to the task. We did see examples of promising work, but the IPPs did not provide an effective conduit for getting the user's point of view into the planning process, and no more than casual attempts were made to consult residents about the day-to-day running of residential establishments.

There is no single solution. A serious approach to involving people in decisions affecting their lives requires a whole battery of measures, including support for self- and citizen advocacy, an open information system, and the inclusion of users and their families at all levels of planning. Above all, service providers must be prepared to be more accountable, to explain and justify their decisions. This works best when there is a clear vision of, and commitment to, what is being proposed. There was no sense in which the agencies in Kirklees set out positively to sell the proposals. Perhaps it is harder to sell a compromise.

Our discussions with all three groups of respondents raised two common areas of concern: the issue of integration into the community and the provision of meaningful daytime occupation. As we noted earlier in Chapter 6, study after study has found that a move into the community results in most people making greater use of community facilities, but few developing social networks that reach out into the wider society. Our research was no exception. Occasionally an individual could genuinely be said to have returned to the community from which they originated, but most movers had no direct connections with the locality in which they now lived. Where it is difficult for people to establish new relationships, then it would make sense to support them in maintaining old ones. Certainly, relationships are important in determining quality of life. Generally speaking, however, neither the development of new friendships nor the maintenance of old ones was seen as a priority by direct care staff. If the issue was tackled at all, it was through the tried and ultimately largely unsuccessful strategy of trying to recruit volunteers. There are no easy answers to this problem, and it may well be that it simply takes time for people to become established in a new place. However, there are a number of possible strategies that were not systematically pursued in Kirklees. For example, as Chapter 6 shows, there were relatively few attempts to help individuals become involved in local recreational and sporting organizations.

The difficulty of providing meaningful day activities crops up in many studies of community care. The developments in Kirklees were primarily about changes in residential settings, although there were some very promising developments in day services, such as the instigation of a small voluntary alternative to the SECs, an expanding work experience scheme, and increased use of adult education facilities by some of the people living in ordinary housing. However, for most people day provision continued to be about access (or lack of it) to a conventional SEC. These centres undoubtedly have many strengths. Certainly, in most cases they are better than sitting at home doing nothing. However, they share two important characteristics with the more institutional residential settings: they are large, and they are segregated. It is no accident that our respondents who attended produced the same kinds of criticisms of them as they did of hospitals and hostels. It is high time there was a radical rethink of day services in line with new directions in service provision as a whole (see, for example, King's Fund Centre, 1984).

There is another, wider lesson to be drawn here. What staff do (or fail to do) matters. There has to be a clear programme of staff development (Ward 1985): the days of *laissez-faire* management are numbered. In the traditional framework of hospitals and hostels, the staff were often just as institutionalized as the residents. What they could or could not do was largely determined by the constraints of the setting. New staff were soon inducted into 'the way of doing things here'. But in a service based on dispersed housing, this is no longer the case. Staff are more isolated. Even though the working conditions are usually preferable to those of a large hospital, the evidence is that turnover is higher in the community (de Kock *et al.* 1987). Expectations of staff have to be much clearer, and support and encouragement from all levels of management need to be built into the system.

As we showed in Chapter 5, many criticisms of hospitals are also relevant to hostels. It cannot be assumed that a hostel will automatically be a less restrictive environment than a hospital. Even in the most progressive of the hostels we examined, the residents still found themselves struggling against the demands and limitations imposed by communal living. Politically and financially, it was impossible not to use the hostels that were available in Kirklees. Yet the evidence of this study puts into question whether they should continue to feature in the long-term strategy.

Our evidence suggests that people with learning difficulties and their families either reject institutions when given an alternative or consider them only as a last resort. The Audit Commission (1989), however, estimates that nearly 60 per cent of the combined health and local authority budget is still locked up in this type of provision. Tying up these resources in the large institutions is a substantial barrier to the development of community care. What also emerges from the same Audit Commission report is that the mechanisms for developing community care are far from well established. As late as 1988, 60 per cent of the 50 local authorities assessed had yet to agree a joint strategy with their local health authorities for the resettlement of hospital residents. Indeed the majority had not even got to the stage of negotiating such an agreement. The Audit Commission refers to the 'web of problems' in the current funding and planning structures. The pragmatic, incrementalist approach in Kirklees may have had its shortcomings and blind spots, but it does seem to offer one model for dealing with the complexity of the planning environment.

More work needs to be done in sorting out the workings of the relocation process at the level of the individual mover. There are good grounds for believing that a person's experience of the way the move is handled is an important factor in determining how they react to the changes. Certainly for many people in our study it was a stressful period. By any standard, the changes which they experienced would count as 'major life events' of the sort known to precipitate physical and mental stress in the population at large. On top of this, the train of events was largely out of their control, their self-esteem was often low, and they lacked the extensive networks of social support which most of us take for granted. Even though in the main they wanted to move, inevitably they experienced doubt and uncertainty. It is a tribute to their resilience that there were not more problems. Clearly staff need to become more aware of, and responsive to, that stress. Many had little or no experience of the tasks involved and were casting around for possible approaches. Some showed great imagination and ingenuity, and we have drawn on these experiences in the suggestions we put forward in Chapter 4. It is not possible to impose empathy, but the chances of it developing can be increased. Even planners and senior management need to get involved with individuals; only then will they be able to see beyond the label and understand what the policies they are implementing will mean in reality.

One final point before we close. Ever since the Government launched its care in the community initiative in 1981, the institutional lobby has been fighting a determined rearguard action to slow the pace of change. In the mental health field, for example, the National Schizophrenia Fellowship (1988) has called for a halt to hospital closures (see also Riddet 1988). In the learning difficulties field, the British Society for the Study of Mental Subnormality has called for professionals, parents and relatives to join together in a united expression of views in favour of halting the relocation of people from hospital (BSSMS 1985). Already there is evidence to suggest that such pressure is having an influence on policy-makers and prompting second thoughts. In August 1988 a government circular declared that 'the closure of hospitals is not a priority aim'. A similar sequence of action and reaction has been seen in the United States (Payne 1976; Plum 1987). There is a real danger of a deinstitutionalization backlash. In this debate the voice of the users is conspicuous largely by its absence. Our study has taken a small step towards rectifying this omission. Whatever the limitations in service terms of the Kirklees Partnership in Community Care, there can be no doubt of the fact that the movers themselves would not wish the programme to be halted and would not call for a moratorium on hospital discharges. The last word is probably best left to one of our respondents:

No, I shouldn't want to go back there. I know they used to look after us and buy us new clothes and that, but no, I wouldn't want to go back there no more.

Bibliography

Atkinson, D. (1985). 'The use of participant observation and respondent diaries in a study of ordinary living', *British Journal of Mental Subnormality*, 3, 6, 33–40.

Atkinson, D. (1987). 'How easy is it to form friendships after leaving long-stay hospitals?', *Social Work Today*, 15 June, 12–13.

Atkinson, D. (1988). 'Research interviews with people with mental handicaps', *Mental Handicap Research*, 1, 1, 75–90.

Atkinson, D. and Ward, L. (1987). 'Friends and neighbours: relationships and opportunities in the community for people with a mental handicap', in N. Malin (ed.) *Reassessing Community Care*. London, Croom Helm.

Audit Commission. (1986). *Making a Reality of Community Care*. London, HMSO.

Audit Commission. (1989). *Developing Community Care for Adults with a Mental Handicap*. London, HMSO.

Avis, D. (1978). 'Deinstitutionalization jet lag', in A. Turnbull and H. Turnbull (eds) *Parents Speak Out*, Wooster, Ohio: Bell and Howell.

Baker, F. and Intagliata, J. (1982). 'Quality of life in the evaluation of community support systems', *Evaluation and Program Planning*, 5, 69–79.

Bercovici, S. (1981). 'Qualitative methods and cultural perspectives in the study of deinstitutionalization', in R. Bruininks, C. Meyers, B. Sigford and K. Lakin (eds) *Deinstitutionalization and Community Adjustment of Mentally Retarded People*. Monograph No. 4, American Association of Mental Deficiency, Washington, D.C.

Beswick, J. (1988). *Interim Report on the Aston Hall Project*. Aston Hall Hospital, Derbyshire.

Bjaanes, A. and Butler, E. W. (1974). 'Environmental variation in community care facilities for mentally retarded persons', *American Journal of Mental Deficiency*, 78, 4, 429–39.

Blunden, R. (1988). 'Quality of life in persons with disabilities: issues in the development of services', in R. Brown (ed.) *Quality of Life for Handicapped People*. London, Croom Helm.

Blunden, R., Evans, G. and Humphreys, S. (1987). *Planning with Individuals: An Outline Guide*. Cardiff, Mental Handicap in Wales – Applied Research Unit.

Booth, N. (1981). *Life in the Community: A Survey of the NHS Group Homes and Training*

Units in the Exeter District – The Residents' Opinions, Devon Area Health Authority, Royal Western Counties Hospitals.

Booth, T. (1981a). 'Collaboration between health and social services: Part I, a case study of joint care planning', *Policy and Politics*, 9, 1, 23–49.

Booth, T. (1981b). 'Collaboration between the health and social services: Part II, a case study of joint finance', *Policy and Politics*, 9, 2, 205–27.

Booth, T. (1983a). 'Collaboration and the social division of planning', in J. Lishman (ed.) *Collaboration and Conflict: Working with Others*. Research Highlights No. 7, University of Aberdeen.

Booth, T. (1983b). 'Residents' views, rights and institutional care', in M. Fisher (ed.) *Speaking of Clients*. Sheffield University, Joint Unit for Social Services Research.

Booth, T. (1985). *Home Truths: Old People's Homes and the Outcome of Care*. Aldershot, Gower.

Booth, T. (1986). 'Social research and policy relevance', *Research, Policy and Planning*, 4, 1–2, 15–18.

Booth, T. (1988). *Developing Policy Research*. Aldershot, Gower.

Booth, T., Bilson, A. and Fowell, I. (1990). 'Staff attitudes and caring practices in homes for the elderly', *British Journal of Social Work*, 20, 2, April.

Booth, T., Phillips, D., Berry, S., Jones, D., Matthews, J., Melotte, C. and Pritlove, J. (1988). 'Home from home: a survey of independent living schemes for people with a mental handicap', *Mental Handicap Research*, 2, 2, July, 152–66.

Booth, T., Phillips, D., Melotte, C., Matthews, J., Pritlove, J. and Jones, D. (1987). 'At home in the community', *Community Care*, 30 October, 20–2.

Booth, W. (1988). 'Look again', *Community Care*, 28 January, 28–9.

Braddock, D. and Heller, T. (eds) (1984). *The Closure of State Mental Retardation Institutions*. Alexandria, VA and Chicago IL, National Association of State Mental Retardation Directors and the Institute for the Study of Developmental Disabilities.

Braddock, D. and Heller, T. (1985). *The Closure of Mental Retardation Institutions: Trends and Implications*. Public Policy Monograph No. 4, Institute for the Study of Developmental Disabilities, University of Illinois at Chicago.

Braddock, D., Hemp, R. and Howes, R. (1986). 'Direct costs of institutional care in the United States', *Mental Retardation*, 24, 1, 9–17.

Brandon, D. and Ridley, J. (1983). *Beginning to Listen: A Study of the Views of Residents Living in a Hostel for Mentally Handicapped People*. London, MIND Publications.

Brost, M., Johnson, T., Wagner, L. and Deprey, R. (1982). *Getting to Know You*. Wisconsin Council on Developmental Disabilities, Madison, Wisconsin, USA.

Bruininks, R., Meyers, C., Sigford, B. and Lakin, K. 1981. *Deinstitutionalization and Community Adjustment of Mentally Retarded People*, Monograph No. 4, American Association of Mental Deficiency, Washington, D.C.

BSSMS. (1985). *British Society for the Study of Mental Subnormality Newsletter*, 11, 1 & 2, July and November, 1.

Campbell, A. (1968). 'Comparison of family and community contacts of mentally subnormal adults in hospital and in local authority hostels', *British Journal of Preventative and Social Medicine*, 22, 165–9.

Cattermole, M., Jahoda, A. and Markova, J. (1987). *Leaving Home: The Experience of People with a Mental Handicap*. Department of Psychology, University of Stirling.

Cawson, P. and Perry, J. (1977). 'Environmental correlates of attitude among residential staff', *British Journal of Criminology*, 17, 2, 141–56.

CMH. (1978). *Looking at Life in a Hospital, Hostel, Home or Unit.* Enquiry Paper No. 7, London, Campaign for the Mentally Handicapped.

Cohen, H., Conroy, J., Frazer, D., Snelbecker, G. and Spreat, S. (1977). 'Behavioral effects of interinstitutional relocation of mentally retarded residents', *American Journal of Mental Deficiency*, 82, 1, 12–18.

Commission on Accreditation of Rehabilitation Facilities. (1978). *Standards Manual for Rehabilitation Facilities*, Tucson, Arizona.

Conroy, J. (1985). 'Reactions to deinstitutionalization among parents of mentally retarded persons', in J. Conroy, R. Bruininks and C. Lakin (eds), *Living and Learning in the Least Restrictive Environment: Community and Family Perspectives on Integration.* Baltimore, Paul H. Brookes.

Conroy, J. and Bradley, V. (1985). *The Pennhurst Longitudinal Study: A Report of Five Years of Research and Analysis.* Philadelphia, Temple University Developmental Disabilities Center, Boston, Human Services Research Institute.

CPA. (1984). *Home Life: A Code of Practice for Residential Care.* London, Centre for Policy on Ageing.

Craig, G. (1981). *Review of Studies of the Public and Users' Attitudes, Opinions and Expressed Needs with Respect to Social Work and Social Workers.* London, NISW.

Crawley, B. (1988). *The Growing Voice: A Survey of Self-Advocacy Groups in Adult Training Centres and Hospitals in Great Britain*, London, CMH Publications.

Crine, A. (1986). *Better Lives: A Study of the Impacts of Relocation of People with Mental Handicaps from Hospital to Community Services.* MA thesis, Sheffield University.

Davies, B. and Knapp, M. (1981). *Old People's Homes and the Production of Welfare.* London, Routledge and Kegan Paul.

de Kock, U., Felce, D., Saxby, H. and Thomas, M. (1987). 'Staff turnover in a small home service: a study of facilities for adults with severe and profound mental handicaps', *Mental Handicap*, 15, 97–101.

DHSS. (1971). *Better Services for the Mentally Handicapped.* Cmnd 4683, London, HMSO.

DHSS. (1976). *Priorities for Health and Personal Social Services in England: A Consultative Document.* London, HMSO.

DHSS. (1980). *Mental Handicap: Progress, Problems and Priorities.* London, HMSO.

DHSS. (1981a). *Report of a Study on Community Care.* London, Department of Health and Social Security.

DHSS. (1981b). *Care in the Community: A Consultative Document on Moving Resources for Care in England.* London, Department of Health and Social Security.

DHSS. (1983). *Health Services Development: Care in the Community and Joint Finance.* HC(83)S/LAC(83)S, London, Department of Health and Social Security.

DHSS. (1984). *Health Services Management: Implementation of the NHS Management Inquiry Report.* HC(84)13, London, Department of Health and Social Security.

DHSS. (1987). *Homes and Hostels for Mentally Ill and Mentally Handicapped People at 31 March 1986.* (England), A/F86/11, London, Government Statistical Service.

Dokecki, P. R., Anderson, B. J. and Strain, P. S. (1977). 'Stigmatization and labelling', in J. Paul, D. Stedman and G. Neufeld (eds) *Deinstitutionalization: Program and Policy Development.* New York, Syracuse University Press.

Dunn, A. (1984). *Attitudes of People in a Mental Handicap Hospital Towards Living in the Community*, unpublished thesis, University of Glasgow.

Edgerton, R. (1967). *The Cloak of Competence: Stigma in the Lives of the Mentally Retarded*. Berkeley, University of California Press.

Edgerton, R. and Bercovici, S. (1976). 'The cloak of competence: years later', *American Journal of Mental Deficiency*, 80, 485–97.

Edgerton, R., Bollinger, M. and Hess, B. (1984). 'The cloak of competence after two decades', *American Journal of Mental Deficiency*, 80, 345–51.

Evans, G., Hughes, B., Wilkin, D. with Jolley, D. (1981). *The Management of Mental and Physical Impairment in Non-Specialist Residential Homes for the Elderly*. University of Manchester, Departments of Psychiatry and Community Medicine.

Fairbrother, P. (1983). 'Needs of parents of adults', in P. Mittler and H. McConachie (eds) *Parents, Professionals and Mentally Handicapped People*. London, Croom Helm.

Felce, D., de Kock, U. and Saxby, H. (1985). *Small Homes for Severely and Profoundly Mentally Handicapped Adults: Final Report*. University of Southampton, Health Care Evaluation Research Team.

Felce, D., de Kock, U., Mansell, J. and Jenkins, J. (1984a). 'Assessing mentally handicapped adults', *British Journal of Mental Subnormality*, 30, 65–74.

Felce, D., de Kock, U., Toogood, S. and Jenkins, J. (1984b). 'Housing for severely and profoundly mentally handicapped adults', *Hospital and Health Service Review*, 180, 170–4.

Felce, D., Kushlick, A. and Mansell, J. (1980). 'Evaluation of alternative residential facilities for the severely mentally handicapped in Wessex: client engagement', *Advanced Behavioural Research and Therapy*, 3, 19–23.

Felce, D., Saxby, H., de Kock, U., Repp, A., Ager, A. and Blunden, R. (1987). 'To what behaviours do attending adults respond? A replication', *American Journal of Mental Deficiency*, 91, 5, 496–504.

Firth, H. (1986). *A Move to the Community: Social Contacts and Behaviour*. Northumberland Health Authority.

Firth, H. and Rapley, M. (1989). *The Process of Friendship*. Kidderminster, BIMH Publications.

Firth Report. (1987). *Public Support for Residential Care: Report of a Joint Central and Local Government Working Party*. London, Department of Health and Social Security.

Fisher, M. (1983). 'The meaning of client satisfaction', in M. Fisher (ed.) *Speaking of Clients*. Sheffield University, Joint Unit for Social Services Research.

Flynn, M. (1984). 'Community backlash', *Parents Voice*, May, 16–17.

Flynn, M. (1986a). *A Study of Prediction in the Community Placements of Adults who are Mentally Handicapped*. Final report to ESRC, Hester Adrian Research Centre, University of Manchester.

Flynn, M. (1986b). 'Adults who are mentally handicapped as consumers: issues and guidelines for interviewing', *Journal of Mental Deficiency Research*, 30, 369–77.

Flynn, M. (1987). ' "The neighbours aren't nice with me": consumers' comments on independent living', *Community Living*, 1, 3, 16–17.

Frohboese, R. and Sales, B. (1980). 'Parental opposition to deinstitutionalization', *Law and Human Behavior*, 4, 1/2, 1–87.

Frost, D. and Taylor, K. (1986). 'This is my life', *Community Care*, 7 August, 28–9.

Gliedman, J. and Roth, W. (1981). 'Parents and professionals', in W. Swann (ed.) *The Practice of Special Education*, Oxford, Basil Blackwell in association with Open University Press.

Gollay, E., Freedman, R., Wyngaarden, M. and Kurtz, N. (1978). *Coming Back: The Community Experiences of Deinstitutionalized Mentally Retarded People*. Cambridge, Massachusetts, Abt Books.

Gutek, B. (1978). 'Strategies for studying client satisfaction', *Journal of Social Issues*, 34, 4, 44–56.

Halliday, S. (1987). 'Parental attitudes to the community care of their mentally handicapped children, before and after the move into the community', *British Journal of Mental Subnormality*, 33, 1, January, 43–9.

Halpern, A., Close, D. and Nelson, D. (1986). *On My Own: The Impact of Semi-Independent Living Programs for Adults with Mental Retardation*. Baltimore, Paul H. Brookes.

Halpern, J., Binner, P. R., Mohr, C. B. and Sackett, K. L. (1978). *The Illusion of Deinstitutionalization*. Denver Research Institute, Social Systems Research and Evaluation Division, University of Denver.

Hammer, P. and Howse, J. (1977). 'Legislation', in J. Paul, D. Stedman and G. Neufeld (eds) *Deinstitutionalization: Program and Policy Development*. New York, Syracuse University Press.

Heal, L. and Chadsey-Rusch, J. (1985). 'The lifestyle satisfaction scale (LSS): assessing individuals' satisfaction with residence, community setting, and associated services', *Applied Research in Mental Retardation*, 6, 475–90.

Heal, L., Sigelman, C. and Switzky, H. (1978). 'Research on community residential alternatives for the mentally retarded', *International Review of Research in Mental Retardation*, Vol. 9, New York, Academic Press.

Heller, T. (1982). 'Social disruption and residential relocation of mentally retarded children', *American Journal of Mental Deficiency*, 87, 1, 48–55.

Heller, T. and Braddock, D. (1985). *Institutional Closure: A Study of Resident Impact*. Public Policy Monograph No. 19, Institute for the Study of Developmental Disabilities, University of Illinois at Chicago.

Hemming, H., Lavender, T. and Pill, R. (1981). 'Quality of life of mentally retarded adults transferred from large institutions to new smaller units', *American Journal of Mental Deficiency*, 86 (2), 157–169.

Hemming, H. (1982). 'Mentally handicapped adults returning to large institutions after transfer to new small units', *British Journal of Mental Subnormality*, 28 (part 1), 13–28.

Hill, B. and Lakin, K. (1984). *Trends in Residential Services for Mentally Retarded People: 1977–1982*. Minneapolis, Center for Residential and Community Services, University of Minnesota, Department of Educational Psychology.

Hill, B., Rotegard, L. and Bruininks, R. (1984). 'The quality of life of mentally retarded people in residential care', *Social Work*, 29, 3, 275–80.

House of Commons Social Services Committee. (1985). *Second Report from the Social Services Committee: Community Care with Special Reference to Adult Mentally Ill and Mentally Handicapped People – Vol. I*. HC 13–1, London, HMSO.

Howie, D., Cuming, J. and Raynes, N. (1984). 'Development of tools to facilitate participation by moderately retarded persons in residential evaluation procedures', *British Journal of Mental Subnormality*, 30, 2, 59, 92–8.

Hulbert, C. and Atkinson, C. (1987). 'On the way out, and after', *British Journal of Mental Subnormality*, 33, 2, 65, 109–16.

Hunter, D. and Wistow, G. (1987). *Community Care in Britain: Variations on a Theme.* London, King's Fund Centre.

Intagliata, J. and Willer, B. (1982). 'Reinstitutionalization of mentally retarded persons successfully placed into family care and group homes', *American Journal of Mental Deficiency*, 87, 1, 34–9.

Jaehnig, W. (1979). *A Family Service for the Mentally Handicapped.* Fabian Tract 460, London, Fabian Society.

Jay Report. (1979). *Report of the Committee of Enquiry into Mental Handicap Nursing and Care.* Cmnd 7468, London, HMSO.

Jenkins, J., Felce, D., Toogood, S., Mansell, J. and de Kock, U. (1982). *Individual Programme Planning: Handbook on Chairing the Meeting.* University of Southampton: Health Care Evaluation Research Team.

Johnson, T. (1978). *Annotated Directory of Environmental Assessment Instruments.* University of California, Los Angeles – Neuropsychiatric Institute Research Group, Pacific State Hospital, Pomona, California.

Kelvin, P. (1973). 'A social-psychological examination of privacy', *British Journal of Social and Clinical Psychology*, 12, 248–61.

Kerr, G. (1982). 'The Aldingham Project', in A. Whittaker (ed.) *Mental Handicap: Care in the Community.* Durham, Association of Professions for the Mentally Handicapped, Report of the Ninth Annual Conference.

King's Fund Centre. (1980). *An Ordinary Life: Comprehensive Locally-based Residential Services for Mentally Handicapped People.* London, King's Fund Centre.

King's Fund Centre. (1984). *An Ordinary Working Life.* London, King's Fund Centre.

Kleinberg, J. and Galligan, B. (1983). 'Effects of deinstitutionalization on adaptive behavior of mentally retarded adults', *American Journal of Mental Deficiency*, 88, 1, 21–7.

Korman, N. and Glennerster, H. (1985). *Closing a Hospital – the Darenth Park Project.* London School of Economics and Political Science.

KPCC. (1985). *Kirklees Partnership in Community Care Position Statement and Proposals.* Kirklees Partnership in Community Care.

KPCC. (1987). *Services for People with a Mental Handicap: A Framework for Action.* Kirklees Partnership in Community Care, Mental Handicap Development Group.

KSSD. (1985). *Arrangement for the Kirklees Partnership in Community Care: Services for People with a Mental Handicap – A Corporate Discussion Document.* July, Kirklees Social Services Department.

KSSD. (1986a). *Kirklees Partnership in Community Care – A Framework for Services.* Kirklees Social Services Department.

KSSD. (1986b). *Kirklees Partnership in Community Care – The Present Position.* Kirklees Social Services Department, 4 June, Social Services Committee Item No. 12.

KSSD. (1986c). *Care in the Community: Progress in Mental Handicap Factsheet 1.* Papers for Seminar on 7 March, Kirklees Social Services Department.

Lakin, K., Hill, B. and Bruininks, R. (eds) (1985). *An Analysis of Medicaid's Intermediate Care Facility for the Mentally Retarded (ICF-MR) Program*, Report No. 20, University of Minnesota, Center for Residential and Community Services.

Latib, A., Conroy, J. and Hess, C. (1984). 'Family attitudes towards deinstitution-alization', in N. Ellis and N. Bray (eds) *International Review of Research in Mental Retardation, Vol. 12.* London, Academic Press.

Laws, M., Bolt, L. and Gibbs, V. (1988). 'Implementing change in a long stay hospital using an individual review system', *Mental Handicap*, 16, June, 74–6.

Lawton, M. (1970). 'Ecology and ageing', in L. Pastalan and D. Carson (eds) *The Spatial Behavior of Older People.* Ann Arbor, University of Michigan.

Lawton, M. and Nahemow, L. (1973). 'Ecology and the aging process', in C. Eisdorfer and M. Lawton (eds) *The Psychology of Adult Development and Aging.* Washington, D.C., American Psychological Association.

Lerman, P. (1985). 'Deinstitutionalization and welfare policies', *Annals of the American Academy*, AAPSS, 479.

Lowe, K., de Paiva, S. and Humphreys, S. (1986). *Long Term Evaluations of Services for People with a Mental Handicap in Cardiff: Clients' Views.* Cardiff, Mental Handicap in Wales – Applied Research Unit.

McHatton, M., Collins, G. and Brooks, E. (1988). 'Evaluation in practice: moving from a "problem" ward to a staffed flat', *Mental Handicap Research*, 1, 2, 141–51.

Macy, T. (1984). 'A resource manual on transitional adjustment of mentally retarded persons', in D. Braddock and T. Heller (eds) *The Closure of State Mental Retardation Institutions.* Alexandria, VA and Chicago IL, National Association of State Mental Retardation Directors and the Institute for the Study of Developmental Disabilities.

Malin, N. (1983). *Group Homes for Mentally Handicapped People.* London, HMSO.

Mansell, J. (1980). 'Susan: the successful resolution of a severe behaviour disorder with a mentally handicapped young woman in a community setting', in R. G. Walton and D. Elliott (eds) *Residential Care: A Reader in Current Theory and Practice.* Oxford, Pergamon Press.

Mansell, J., Felce, D., Jenkins, J., de Kock, U. and Toogood, S. (1987). *Developing Staffed Housing for People with Mental Handicaps.* Tunbridge Wells, Costello.

Mest, G. (1988). 'With a little help from their friends: use of social support systems by persons with retardation', *Journal of Social Issues*, 44, 1, 117–25.

Meyer, R. (1980). 'Attitudes of parents of institutionalized mentally retarded individuals toward deinstitutionalization', *American Journal of Mental Deficiency*, 85, 2, 184–7.

Morrisey, J. and Goldman, H. (1981). 'The enduring asylum: in search of an international perspective', *International Journal of Law and Psychiatry*, 4, 13–34.

National Schizophrenia Fellowship. (1988). *Mental Hospital Closures.* Surbiton, Surrey, NSF.

NDG. (1978). *Helping Mentally Handicapped People in Hospital.* London, National Development Group for the Mentally Handicapped.

Nihira, K., Foster, R., Shellhaas, M. and Leland, H. (1975). *AAMD Adaptive Behavior Scale: Manual.* Washington, D.C., American Association of Mental Deficiency.

Passfield, D. (1983). '"What do you think of it so far?" A survey of 20 Priory Court residents', *Mental Handicap*, 11, 3, 97–9.

Payne, J. (1976). 'The deinstitutional backlash', *Mental Retardation*, June, 43–5.

People First and the Self-Advocacy Project. (1985). *Speaking Up and Speaking Out: An International Self-Advocacy Movement.* Report on the International Self-Advocacy Leadership Conference, 23–9 July 1984, Washington, D.C.

Phillips, D. and Radford, J. (1985). *Any Fool Can Close a Long-Stay Hospital: Deinstitu-tionalisation and Community Care for the Mentally Handicapped.* Paper presented to a joint conference of the IBG/AAG on Medical Geography, July, University of Nottingham.

Plum, K. (1987). 'Moving forward with deinstitutionalization: lessons of an ethical policy analysis', *American Journal of Orthopsychiatry*, 57, 4, 508–14.

PSSC. (1975). *Living and Working in Residential Homes.* London, Personal Social Services Council.

PSSC. (1977). *Residential Care Reviewed.* London, Personal Social Services Council.

PSSRU. (1987). *Care in the Community Newsletter.* Spring, Canterbury, University of Kent.

Raynes, N. (1988). *Annotated Directory of Measures of Environmental Quality.* University of Manchester, Department of Social Policy and Social Work.

Richards, S. (1984). *Community Care of the Mentally Handicapped: Consumer Perspectives.* University of Birmingham.

Richards, S. (1985). 'A right to be heard', *Social Services Research*, 14, 4, 49–56.

Richardson, A. and Ritchie, J. (1986). *Making the Break: Parents' Views About Adults with a Mental Handicap Leaving the Parental Home.* London, King's Fund Centre.

Riddet, L. (1988). 'Dumped in a vacuum', *Community Care* (INSIDE supplement), 27 October, viii.

Robinson, T. (1978). *In Worlds Apart.* London, Bedford Square Press.

Romer, D. and Heller, T. (1983). 'Social adaptation of mentally retarded adults in community settings: a social-ecological approach', *Applied Research in Mental Retardation*, 4, 303–14.

Sarason, S. and Gladwin, T. (1958). 'Psychological and cultural problems in mental subnormality: a review of research', *Genetic Psychology Monographs*, 57, 3–290.

Schalock, R., Harper, R. and Genung, T. (1981). 'Community integration of mentally retarded adults: community placement and program success', *American Journal of Mental Deficiency*, 85, 5, 478–88.

Scheerenberger, R. and Felsenthal, D. (1977). 'Community settings for mentally retarded persons: satisfactions and activities', *Mental Retardation*, 15, 4, 3–7.

Schroeder, S. and Henes, C. (1978). 'Assessment of progress of institutionalized and deinstitutionalized retarded adults: a matched-control comparison', *Mental Retardation*, April, 147–8.

Scull, A. (1985). 'Deinstitutionalization and public policy', *Social Science and Medicine*, 20, 5, 545–52.

Seltzer, G. (1981). 'Community residential adjustment: the relationship among environment, performance and satisfaction', *American Journal of Mental Deficiency*, 85, 6, 624–30.

Shah, A. and Holmes, N. (1987). 'Locally-based residential services for mentally handicapped adults: a comparative study', *Psychological Medicine*, 17, 763–74.

Sigelman, C. and Budd, E. (1986). 'Pictures as an aid in questioning mentally retarded persons', *Rehabilitation Counselling Bulletin*, 29, 3, 173–81.

Sigelman, C., Budd, E., Winer, J., Schoenrock, C. and Martin, P. (1982). 'Evaluating alternative techniques of questioning mentally retarded persons', *American Journal of Mental Deficiency*, 86, 511–18.

Sigelman, C., Schoenrock, C., Winer, J., Spanhel, C., Hromas, S., Martin, P., Budd, E. and Bensberg, C. (1981a). 'Issues in interviewing mentally retarded persons: an empirical study', in R. Bruininks, C. Meyer, B. Sigford and K. Lakin (eds) *Deinstitutionalization and Community Adjustment of Mentally Retarded People.* Monograph No. 4, American Association of Mental Deficiency, Washington, D.C.

Sigelman, C., Budd, E., Spanhel, C. and Schoenrock, C. (1981b). 'When in doubt say yes: acquiescence in interviews with mentally retarded persons', *Mental Retardation*, April, 53–8.

Simons, K., Booth, T. and Booth, W. (1989). 'Speaking out: user studies and people with learning difficulties', *Research, Policy and Planning*, 7, 1, 9–17.

Sinclair, E. (1988). 'Guide to the evidence', in *Residential Care: A Positive Choice* (The Wagner Report), Appendix I, London, HMSO.

Sinclair, I. (1971). *Hostels for Probationers.* Home Office Research Studies No. 6, London, HMSO.

Sinclair, I. (1975). 'The influence of wardens and matrons in probation hostels', in J. Tizard, I. Sinclair and R. Clarke (eds) *Varieties of Residential Experience.* London, Routledge and Kegan Paul.

Staite, S. and Torpy, P. (1983). 'Who can live alone? The selection of mentally handicapped people for a supported independent living scheme', *Mental Handicap*, 11, 3, 94–5.

Stedman, D. (1977a). 'Introduction', in J. Paul, D. Stedman and G. Neufield (eds) *Deinstitutionalization: Program and Policy Development.* New York, Syracuse University Press.

Stedman, D. (1977b). 'Politics, political structures and advocacy activities', in J. Paul, D. Stedman and G. Neufeld (eds) *Deinstitutionalization: Program and Policy Development.* New York, Syracuse University Press.

Sugg, B. (1987). 'Community care: the consumer's point of view', *Community Care*, 22 January.

Sutter, P., Mayeda, T., Yee, S. and Yanagi, G. (1981). 'Community placement success based on client behaviour preferences of careproviders', *Mental Retardation*, 19, 3, 117–20.

Taylor, J. (1977). 'Job satisfaction and quality of working life: a reassessment', *Journal of Occupational Psychology*, 50(4), 243–52.

Thomas, D. and Webster, R. (1974). *The Application of the Adaptive Behaviour Scales in the United Kingdom.* An unpublished paper for the Workshop and Symposium on the AAMD Adaptive Behaviour Scales at the 98th Annual Meeting of the AAMD, Toronto.

Townsend, P. (1981). 'The structured dependency of the elderly: a creation of social policy in the twentieth century', *Ageing and Society*, 1, 1, 1–24.

US Comptroller General. (1977). *Returning the Mentally Disabled to the Community: Government Needs To Do More.* Report to the Congress HRD-76-152, 7 January, Washington, D.C., US General Accounting Office.

US Department of Health and Human Services. (1986). *Report to the Congress on Policies for Improving Services for Mentally Retarded and Other Developmentally Disabled Persons Served Under Title XIX of the Social Security Act.* January, Washington, D.C., Office of the Assistant Secretary for Planning and Evaluation.

Vitello, S. J. (1986). 'Deinstitutionalization progress in the United States', *Medicine and the Law*, 5, 4, 273–8.

Wagner, G. (1988). *Residential Care: A Positive Choice.* London, HMSO.

Ward, L. (1985). *Training for Change.* London, King's Fund Centre.

Ward, L. (1986). 'Changing services for changing need', *Community Care,* 22 May, 21–3.

Wertheimer, A. (1986). *Hospital Closures in the Eighties.* London, Campaign for People with Mental Handicaps.

West, H. (1983). 'Care in whose community?', *Parents Voice,* September, 22–3.

Willcocks, D. (1984). 'The "ideal home" visual game: a method of consumer research in old people's homes', *Research, Policy and Planning,* 2, 1, 13–18.

Willer, B. and Intagliata, J. (1984). 'An overview of the social policy of deinstitutionalization', in N. Ellis and N. Bray (eds) *International Review of Research in Mental Retardation, Vol. 12.* London, Academic Press.

Williams, P. (1986). 'Evaluating services from the consumer's point of view', in J. Beswick, T. Zadik and D. Felce (eds) *Evaluating Quality of Care.* Kidderminster, BIMH Conference Series.

Williams, P. and Shoultz, B. (1982). *We Can Speak for Ourselves.* London, Souvenir Press.

Wing, L. (1981). *Evaluation of New Services to be Provided for Residents of Darenth Park Hospital – First Annual Report.* London, MRC Social Psychiatry Unit, Institute of Psychiatry.

Wing, L. (1985). *Evaluation of New Services to be Provided for Residents of Darenth Park Hospital – Fifth Annual Report.* London, MRC Social Psychiatry Unit, Institute of Psychiatry.

Wolfensberger, W. (1984). 'A reconstruction of normalization as social role valorization', *Mental Retardation,* 21, 6, 234–9.

Wyngaarden, M. (1981). 'Interviewing mentally retarded persons: issues and strategies', in R. Bruininks, C. Meyer, B. Sigford and K. Lakin (eds) *Deinstitutionalization and Community Adjustment of Mentally Retarded People.* Monograph No. 4, American Association of Mental Deficiency, Washington, D.C.

Index